Learning Disability Nurse Survival Guide

Common questions and answers for learning disability nursing

Note

Healthcare practice and knowledge are constantly changing and developing as new research and treatments, changes in procedures, drugs and equipment become available.

The editors and publishers have, as far as is possible, taken care to confirm that the information complies with the latest standards of practice and legislation.

Learning Disability Nurse Survival Guide

Common questions and answers for learning disability nursing

edited by

Dave Dalby and Chris Knifton

QUAY
BOOKS

A division of MA Healthcare Ltd

Quay Books Division, MA Healthcare Ltd, St Jude's Church, Dulwich Road, London
SE24 0PB

British Library Cataloguing-in-Publication Data
A catalogue record is available for this book

© MA Healthcare Limited 2012

ISBN-10: 1-85642-434-0
ISBN-13: 978-1-85642-434-9

Edited by Jessica Anderson

Cover design by Louise Wood, Fonthill Creative

Publishing Manager: Andy Escott

Printed by Mimeo, Huntingdon, Cambridgeshire

iv

Contents

List of contributors

Nicola Brooks, PG Dip, BSc(Hons), Dip HE Nursing, RN, ENB998, ENB931
Senior Lecturer, Adult Nursing, School of Nursing and Midwifery, De
Montfort University, Leicester
Sharon Clay, RNLD
Deputy Ward Matron/Practice Development Nurse, Leicester
Dave Dalby, MA, Cert Ed(Adults), Dip Nursing, RNLD
Senior Lecturer and Academic Lead, Learning Disability Nursing, School of
Nursing and Midwifery, De Montfort University, Leicester
Karen Ford, MSc, PG Dip Ed, BSc (Hons), RNT, RGN, RHV
Senior lecturer and Prescribing Programme Leader, Adult Nursing, School
of Nursing and Midwifery, De Montfort University, Leicester
Martyn Geary, MA, PGCE(FAHE), BA(Hons), RGN
Senior lecturer, Palliative Care, School of Nursing and Midwifery, De
Montfort University, Leicester
Nicky Genders, MA, BA(Hons), Cert Ed, RNLD
Associate Head of School of Nursing and Midwifery/Principal Lecturer,
De Montfort University, Leicester; qualified Aromatherapist and Reiki
Practioner
Catherine Hart, DClinPsy, MSc, PGDip, BSc(Hons)
Clinical Psychologist, St Andrews Healthcare, Northampton
Jamie Hart, BSc (Hons) AAF Dip ITS MBCA
Specialist Biomechanics Coach, Physical Conditioning Coach and Sports
Masseur
Dorothy Hemel, Carer
Amelia Henry, RNLD
Learning Disability Health Facilitator, Leicestershire Partnership Trust
Julie Kew, RNLD
Learning Disability Health Facilitator, Leicestershire Partnership NHS Trust
Tina Kirk, BSc(Hons), Dip Social Learning Theory, RNLD, RMN, ENB936,
ENB998
Home Manager, Leicestershire Partnership Trust, Learning Disability
Division

Chris Knifton, SBStJ, MSc, MSc, MA, PGCertHE, LLB(Hons), BSc(Hons),
RNLD, Dip SW, Dip AROM, Dip Counselling & Psychotherapy, FAETC,
Advanced Dementia Care Mapper
Senior Lecturer, Dementia, Mental Health and Learning Disabilities, School
of Nursing and Midwifery, De Montfort University, Leicester;

Annie Law, MA, PGDAdEd, BA(Hons), DPNS, RGN, RNT, ENB100, N59,
ENB931, N14
Senior Lecturer and Education Lead Planned Care Division, University
Hospitals of Leicester NHS Trust, and De Montfort University, Leicester

Sue Lyons, MSc, Cert MRCSLT
Speech and Language Therapist, Leicestershire Partnership NHS Trust

Kathleen McNicholas, PGDip Advanced Healthcare Practice, PGCert HE, BA
(Hons), Dip HE(Child), RNLD
Senior Lecturer, Children's' Nursing, School of Nursing and Midwifery, De
Montfort University, Leicester

Cormac Norton, MSc, PGCert Practice Education, BSc(Hons), Dip N, RGN,
ENB199, ENB997/8, Independent nurse prescriber
Senior Lecturer, Emergency Care and Adult Nursing, School of Nursing and
Midwifery, De Montfort University, Leicester

David Parker, PGCE, Cert Ed, MiFL
Deputy Director St John Ambulance, Leicestershire and Rutland

Kevin Power, MA, BA(Hons), Dip N, Cert Ed, RSCN, RGN
Head of Quality, Faculty of Health and Life Sciences, De Montfort
University

Paul Rigby, MA, BA(Hons), Dip N, Dip AdEd, Dip PSI (THORN), RMN
Senior Lecturer, Mental Health Nursing, School of Nursing and Midwifery,
De Montfort University, Leicester

Sam Screaton, RNLD
Learning Disability Health Facilitator, Leicestershire Partnership Trust

Trish Sealy, MB ChB, MRCP
Consultant in Palliative Medicine, South Tees Hospitals NHS Foundation
Trust, Community Division (North)

Daniel Senior
Biomechanics Coach, Personal trainer and Nutritionist, Nutrafit,
Leicester

Laura Smith (Summers), MA, SPLD, RNLD
Change Manager (Learning Disabilities), Leicester, Leicestershire County

Judi Thorley MSC, RN, RNLD

Regional Lead Learning Disability Health and Adult Safeguarding, NHS East Midlands & East

Penny Tremayne, MSc, PGDE, BSc(Hons), Dip N, RGN

Senior lecturer, Adult Nursing, School of Nursing and Midwifery, De Montfort University, Leicester

Nikki Welyczko, MSc, PGCHE, BA(Hons), Dip N, RGN, C&G 7307,

Independent/Supplementary Nurse Prescriber; Academic Lead, Adult Nursing, School of Nursing and Midwifery, De Montfort University, Leicester

Russell Woolgar, MSc, BA(Hons), RNLD

Outreach Team Manager, The Agnes Unit, Leicester, Leicestershire Partnership NHS Trust

Introduction

Learning disability nursing has been defined as

...a person-centred profession with the primary aim of supporting the wellbeing and social inclusion of people with learning disabilities through improving or maintaining physical and mental health.

(Department of Health 2007:7)

Typically, learning disability nurses may find themselves working in a range of different settings to provide this type of support. The Department of Health (2007) indeed notes that whilst most learning disability nurses are now employed in community settings

...significant numbers do still work providing inpatient care, for example, in the assessment and treatment services, forensic services and working in mental health services where there are people with learning disabilities and mental health needs.

(Department of Health 2007: 16)

What, however, remains constant, is the focus on the people with learning disabilities and their families and carers. Nurses new to this area of practice can expect an exciting albeit challenging working environment. This book has been developed for newly qualified learning disability nurses, those returning to practice, and registered nurses from other fields of practice new to working with people with a learning disability. It is intended for everyday use, and as such, it is suggested a copy be left in your workplace, where it can be easily accessed. At the end of each chapter there is a blank page for you to add useful workplace information. Add notes on these pages, and make this book your own resource, to guide you through your introductory years to nursing people with learning disabilities.

Dave Dalby and Chris Knifton
De Montfort University Leicester 2012

Reference

Department of Health (2007) *Good practice in learning disability nursing*. London: Department of Health

Acknowledgements

We are grateful to our contributors who have shown willingness to share their knowledge and experience on the specific challenges faced by nurses new to working with people with learning disabilities.

We are also grateful to the student and newly qualified learning disability nurses from De Montfort University and to service users and carers who have taken time to comment on the text and give us important feedback based on their own experiences.

Chapter 1

Common syndromes and disorders in learning disability

Catherine Hart and Chris Knifton

- What is a learning disability?
- What terminology should I use?
- Do all forms of learning disability have a known cause/condition?
- What are some of the known common conditions associated with a learning disability?
- What are the known health risks in common conditions associated with a learning disability?
- What are autistic spectrum disorders, Asperger's and autism?

What is a learning disability?
Catherine Hart

Learning disabilities affect a person's ability to learn, communicate and carry out everyday tasks. The Department of Health (2001) has defined learning disability as:

- A significantly reduced ability to understand new or complex information and to learn new skills (impaired intelligence); along with
- A reduced ability to cope independently (impaired social functioning), and
- An onset of disability which started before adulthood, with a lasting effect on development.

Many services across the UK use both medical and psychologically-based criteria to define learning disabilities. Such definitions exist in classification systems such as ICD-10 (the International Classification of Mental and Behavioral Disorders; World Health Organisation 1992) and DSM-IV (Diagnostic Statistical Manual; American Psychiatric Association 1994). These definitions are mainly used when determining if a person is eligible to use specialist learning disability services. Recent thinking, however, has seen a shift towards access being based on need and not ability, although this has been slow.

Some people who experience other conditions, such as chronic psychosis or acquired brain injury in adulthood, may also meet the first two criteria of the clinical definitions of a learning disability, but they would not be considered to have a learning disability and may therefore not be eligible to use specialist learning disability services.

When working with people who have learning disabilities, you may come across references to the degree of disability – mild, moderate, severe or profound. These originate from a medical perspective. Policy makers are now encouraging services to focus on individual needs rather than previous groupings of people with learning disabilities. These terms are still however commonly used in practice, and are illustrated in *Table 1.1*.

Table 1.1. Definitions of learning disability categorisation		
Standard Score Range	*WAIS-IV* Descriptive Classification*	
130+	Very superior	
120–129	Superior	
110–119	High average	
90–109	Average	
80–89	Low average	
70–79	Borderline	
≤ 69	Extremely low	
50–69	*Mild*	Over three quarters of people with learning disabilities have a mild disability. The majority live independently; many have their own families, are in employment and have no need for extra support from services, except in times of crisis
35–50	*Moderate*	People in this category need a higher level of support. Many will need some support with everyday tasks and may have difficulty in communicating their needs. They are likely to be living with their parents, with day-to-day support, or in supported living schemes. They are also likely to use a number of support services such as day, outreach and supported living schemes

20–35	Severe	People with severe and profound learning disability may have significantly increased health needs, such as higher rates of epilepsy, sensory impairments and physical disabilities. They are
<20	Profound	likely to have more complex needs and greater difficulty in communicating their needs. Sometimes individuals engage in behaviour that others consider challenging, in an effort to communicate their need or as an expression of their frustration. Self-injury is particularly common in people with profound learning disability. In severe cases this can lead to additional disability, poor health and a significantly decreased quality of life
		WAIS-R: Wechsler Adult Intelligence Scale – Revised. *Adapted from Hardy et al. 2006*

What terminology should I use?
Catherine Hart and Chris Knifton

Some people with learning disabilities prefer the term 'learning difficulties'. This is the wording used by People First, an international advocacy organisation. However, this term also often refers to individuals who have a specific problem with learning, such as dyslexia. Particularly with children, a learning difficulty might arise as a result of medical problems, emotional problems, and/or language impairments. The term 'learning disabilities' however, indicates an overall impairment of intellect and function. In the past, terms such as 'mental handicap', 'mental subnormality', 'mental deficiency' and 'mental retardation' have also been used. These terms are to be avoided in contemporary practice. It is however worth noting that differing terminology may be used in other countries – America, for example, may still use the term mental retardation, and Ireland may use intellectual disability.

Do all forms of learning disability have a known cause/ condition?
Chris Knifton

No. It is suggested that in between 40 and 80% of cases the cause cannot be determined (Wymbrandt and Ludman 2000).

What are some of the known common conditions associated with a learning disability?

Chris Knifton

These are varied and include a range of genetic abnormalities (e.g. Down's syndrome, Edwards' syndrome, Patau syndrome, Cri-du-chat syndrome, Turner syndrome, Apert syndrome, tuberous sclerosis, galactosaemia, Sanfilippo syndrome, Tay-Sachs disease, phenylketonuria, fragile X syndrome, Coffin-Lowry syndrome, Prader-Willi syndrome, Hurler syndrome, Hunter syndrome, Cornelia de Lange syndrome, hydrocephalus); prenatal factors (e.g. rubella acquired, cytomegalovirus acquired), and maternal health (e.g. foetal alcohol syndrome, kernicterus). Other causes include hypoxia, infections, environmental risks, and trauma. Examples of conditions often associated with a learning disability are listed in *Table 1.2*, with the date of discovery/reporting of the condition.

What are the known health risks in common conditions associated with a learning disability?

Chris Knifton

Down's syndrome

This condition was first described by Dr Langdon Down in 1866. It is caused by an extra chromosome on autosome 21, commonly referred to as trisomy 21, and is the commonest chromosomal abnormality. There is an increased incidence as maternal age rises. Turner (2001) notes that, despite the risk of death due to respiratory infection reducing over the years, mortality rates still remain high. The biggest cause of death however is congenital heart disease.

Additional specific healthcare points you need to be aware of include:

- Alzheimer's disease, a form of dementia, is common as the person ages. This also brings the added risk of epilepsy in people with Down's syndrome.
- Atlanto-axial instability – strength in the neck joints/cervical spine are compromised. MacLachlan et al (1993) reported that 13% of adults with Down's syndrome were at risk, with additional risks of degenerative arthritis being common (Howells 1989).
- Cataracts (Pueschel 1987).
- Congenital heart defects – the biggest single cause of death (Turner 2001, McGrother and Marshall 1990).

Table 1.2. Conditions commonly associated with a learning disability				
Date	*Author/s*	*Condition*	*Also known as*	*Cause*
1853	Little	Cerebral palsy		Various *Note:* not all cases have a learning disability
1866	Langdon Down	Down's syndrome	Mongolism – term not to be used but may appear in old medical notes/ journals Trisomy 21	Extra chromosome at pair 21
1880		Tuberous sclerosis	Epilolia	Autosomal dominant gene
1881/ 1886	Tay and later Sachs	Tay-Sachs disease		Abnormal storage of fats (lipids) in tissue
1908	Reuss	Galactosaemia		Carbohydrate (galactose) disorder
1934	Fölling	Phenylketonuria	PKU	Raised levels of phenylalanine
1941	Gregg	Rubella syndrome		Infection with rubella virus while *in utero*
1942	Klinefelter et al	Klinefelter's syndrome		Extra X chromosome in males
1943	Kanner	Autism		Unknown
1960	Edwards et al	Edwards' Syndrome	Trisomy 18	Extra chromosome at pair 18
1960	Patau et al	Patau's syndrome	Trisomy 13	Extra chromosome at pair 13
1961	Sandberg et al	XYY syndrome		Extra Y chromosome
1963	Lejeune et al	Cri-du-chat Syndrome		Deletion of short arm of chromosome 5

- Gastrointestinal disorders – including duodenal stenosis, oesophageal atresia and Hirschsprung's disease (Levy 1992).
- Hepatitis B infections.
- Lack of the enzyme lysozyme (a natural antiseptic), which can lead to blepharitis and conjunctivitis.
- Leukaemia – there is a higher incidence of death from this than usually found in the general population (Turner 2001, Fong and Brodeur 1987).
- Poorly developed nose bridge, small mouth with a high palate and large tongue leading to mouth breathing and increasing risk of respiratory tract infection.
- Thyroid disorders.

Edwards' syndrome

This condition was first described by Edwards and colleagues in 1960. It is caused by an extra chromosome on pair 18, commonly referred to as trisomy 18. There are signs of hypertelorism, small low-set ears, and a short neck. Growth deficiency is common, and overlapping fingers are evident. Learning disability is often severe. Usually congenital abnormalities of the heart, abdominal organs, nervous system, kidneys and ears are apparent.

Turner syndrome

Turner syndrome was first described in 1938. Also known as X0 syndrome, it is caused by a lack of an X chromosome in females. Secondary sexual characteristics are under-developed. Notably, not all people with this condition have a learning disability. Nurses need to be aware of the risk of osteoporosis in Turner syndrome during later life.

Klinefelter's syndrome

This syndrome was first described in 1942. Also known as XXY syndrome, it is caused by an additional X chromosome in males. There are usually under-developed secondary sexual characteristics and longer lower limbs. Additional X chromosomes can occur (although these conditions are not referred to as Klinefelter's syndrome), and the greater the number of X chromosomes, the more severe the learning disability. Nurses need to be aware of the risks of gynaecomastia, leg ulcers, osteoporosis and breast carcinoma in this condition. Not all people with this condition have a learning disability.

Prader-Willi syndrome

This was first described in 1956. It is usually associated with chromosome 15 deletions. Features include growth deficiency, reduced muscle tone, small hands and feet, and an often insatiable appetite. Latterly this may lead to behavioural difficulties when appetite desires are not met. There is also an association with self-injurious behaviour. Nurses need to be aware of the insatiable appetite and both the mental and physical effects this has on the person, including risks of depression, obesity and diabetes mellitus.

Fragile X syndrome

This is the most common cause of inherited learning disability. It can occur in people of either sex. However, it is important to note that not all will develop a learning disability. Mortality for congenital heart abnormalities is higher in this group of people then in the general population (Turner 2001). Other health-related problems may include vision or hearing losses, and skeletal and connective tissue problems (Davids et al 1990).

Lesch-Nyhan syndrome

This condition was first described in 1964 by Lesch and Nyhan, and is caused by an X-linked recessive gene leading to deficiency of an enzyme responsible for purine metabolism. This leads to an accumulation of uric acid in the blood causing severe learning disability. An important healthcare implication is the increased risk of self-mutilation.

What are autistic spectrum disorders, Asperger's and autism?
Catherine Hart

The autism spectrum of disorders is a continuum of psychological conditions characterised by widespread abnormalities of social interactions and communication, as well as restricted interests and repetitive behaviour. Autism is a lifelong, pervasive developmental disorder. Approximately 25% of people with autism have learning disabilities (Chakrabarti and Fombonne 2001). The majority of people with autism who do not have accompanying learning disabilities are described as having either 'high functioning autism' or Asperger's syndrome.

Autism is referred to as a 'spectrum condition' because it varies considerably in how it affects each person. However, there are three core features of autism, known as the 'triad of impairments':

*   *Impairment of communication*: this affects both verbal and non-verbal communication. Some people may present with echolalia, repeating what they have heard. Difficulty in understanding certain types of words, such as abstract concepts and negatives, is common.
*   *Impairment of social interaction*: this can range from someone who seeks out social interaction, but lacks the social skills to develop and maintain relationships, to someone who is withdrawn and apparently indifferent or actively avoids other people.
*   *Impairment of imagination*: people with autism do not develop the same imaginative skills as other people; they tend to think in a very concrete way, for example, thinking in terms of actual objects, and have difficulty with abstract concepts, such as emotions.

People with autism are vulnerable to developing mental health problems, notably depression and anxiety disorders, and are particularly vulnerable around times of transition and change.

References

American Psychiatric Association (1994) *Diagnostic and statistical manual of mental disorders* (4th edn.) APA, Arlington, TX

Chakrabarti S, Fombonne E (2001) Pervasive developmental disorders in preschool children. *Journal of the American Medical Association* **285**(24): 3093–9

Davids J, Hagerman R, Eilbert R (1990) Orthopaedic aspects of Fragile X syndrome. *Journal of Bone Joint Surgery* **72**: 889–96

Department of Health (2001) *Valuing people: A new strategy for learning disability for the 21st century*. White Paper. Available from http://www.dh.gov.uk/en/Publicationsandstatistics/Publications/PublicationsPolicyAndGuidance/DH_4009153 [Accessed 16.1.2012]

Fong C, Brodeur G (1987) Down's syndrome and leukemia: Epidemiology, genetics, cytogenetics and mechanisms of leukemogenesis. *Cancer Genetics and Cytogenetics* **28**: 55–76

Hardy S, Kramer R, Holt G, Woodward P, Chaplin E (2006) *Supporting complex needs: A practical guide for support staff working with people with a learning disability who have mental health needs*. Turning Point, London

Howells G (1989) Down's syndrome and the general practitioner. *Journal Royal College of General Practitioners* **39**: 470–5

Levy J (1992) Gastrointestinal concerns, In Pueschel SM, Pueschel JK (eds) *Biomedical concerns in people with Down's syndrome* (pp.119-126). Paul H Brookes, Baltimore, MD

MacLachan RA, Fidler KE, Yehg H, Hodgetts PG, Pharand G, Chau M (1993) Cervical spine abnormalities in institutionalized adults with Down's syndrome. *Journal of Intellectual Disability Research* **37**: 277–85

McGrother C, Marshall, B (1990) Recent trends in incidence, morbidity and survival in Down's syndrome. *Journal of Mental Deficiency Research* **34**: 49–57

Peueschel S (1987) Health concerns in persons with Down's syndrome. In Peueschel S et al (eds) *New perspectives on Down's syndrome*. Paul H Brookes, Baltimore, MD

Turner S (2001) Health needs of people who have a learning disability. In Thompson J, Pickering S (eds) *Meeting the health needs of people who have a learning disability* (pp. 63–88). Ballière Tindall, London

World Health Organisation (1992) *ICD-10 classification of mental and behavioural disorders: Clinical descriptions and diagnostic guidelines*. WHO, Geneva

Wymbrandt J, Ludman MD (2000) *Genetic disorders and birth defects*. Facts on File: New York

NOTES

9

Chapter 2

Professional and legal responsibilities

Karen Ford, Martyn Geary, Nicky Genders, Catherine Hart, Chris Knifton, Annie Law, Kevin Power, Paul Rigby and Russell Woolgar

- What policy documents, reports or papers are specifically relevant to learning disability practice?
- What about specific legislation that may guide my practice?
- How is mental capacity assessed?
- What is meant by DoLS (Deprivation of Liberty Safeguards)?
- What do I need to know about vulnerability?
- Can I use complementary therapies with my clients?
- What happens when someone with a learning disability commits a criminal offence?
- What do I do if someone discloses an offence?
- What impact does the Mental Capacity Act 2005 have on mental health care?
- Which parts of the Mental Health Act 1983 might be of relevance to my work role?
- What legislation governs medications and are there other national documents that guide registered nurses in this area?
- What are the principles of safe practice for giving medication?
- Can a learning disability nurse become an independent prescriber?
- How do I contact relatives/carers following a death?
- What are my responsibilities in reporting malpractice?
- What are my rights and responsibilities regarding risk management?
- What do I do if someone presents an immediate risk to themselves or others?

What policy documents, reports or papers are specifically relevant to learning disability practice?
Chris Knifton

A range of documents is available to inform your practice. It is essential that, as a registered nurse, you ensure that you follow best practice and relevant national guidelines. Some examples published since 2000, are provided in *Box 2.1*. This list is not exhaustive, but may be pertinent to your role.

In addition to the documents detailed in *Box 2.1*, as a registered nurse, you also need to check the relevant National Institute for Health and Clinical Excellence (NICE) guidance on specific health-related conditions. Go to www. nice.org.uk for further details.

Box 2.1. Policy documents and papers published since 2000 pertinent to learning disability nursing

Department of Health and the Home Office (2000) *No secrets – Guidance on developing and implementing policies and procedures to protect vulnerable adults from abuse.* HMSO, London

Department of Health (2001) *Valuing people. A new strategy for learning disability for the 21st century.* TSO, London

Department of Health (2001) *Learning disability and ethnicity report to the Department of Health.* DH, London.

Department of Health (2001) *Making it happen: A guide to delivering mental health promotion.* DH, London

Department of Health (2002) *Action for health – Health Action Plans and health facilitation.* DH, London

Department of Health (2004) *Choosing health: Making healthier choice easy.* DH, London

Mencap (2004) *Treat me right! Better health care for people with a learning disability.* Mencap, London

National Patient Safety Agency (2004) *Understanding the patient safety issues for people with learning disabilities.* NPSA, London

Department of Health (2006) *Best Practice in Risk Management.* HMSO, London

Disability Rights Commission (2006) *Report of the DRC Formal Inquiry Panel to the DRC's Formal Investigation into the inequalities in physical health experienced by people with mental health problems and people with learning disabilities.* DRC, London

Mencap (2006) *Breaking Point. A report on caring without a break for children and adults with severe or profound learning disabilities.* Mencap, London

Royal College of Nursing (2006) *Meeting the mental health needs of people with learning disabilities: Guidance for staff.* RCN, London

Department of Health (2007) *Good practice in learning disability nursing.* DH, London

Department of Health (2007) *Valuing people now: From progress to transformation.* DH, London

---

Department of Health (2007) *Health action planning and health facilitation for people with learning disabilities.* Good Practice Guide. DH, London

Department of Health (2007) *Good Practice Guidance on Working with Parents with a Learning Disability.* DH, London

Healthcare Commission (2007) *A life like no other: A national audit of specialist inpatient healthcare services for people with learning difficulties in England.* Healthcare Commission, London

Mencap (2007) *Death by indifference. Following up the Treat me right! report.* Mencap, London

Royal College of Nursing (2007) *Mental health nursing of adults with learning disabilities. RCN Guidance.* RCN, London

Michael J (2008) *Healthcare for all: Report of the independent inquiry into access to healthcare for people with learning disabilities.* DH, London

Royal College of Nursing (2008) *Let's talk about restraint. Rights, risks and responsibilities.* RCN, London

British Psychological Society (2009) *Dementia and people with learning disabilities. Guidance on the assessment, diagnosis, treatment and support of people with learning disabilities who develop dementia.* British Psychological Society and the Royal College of Psychiatrists, Leicester

Department of Health (2009) *Valuing people now: A new three-year strategy for people with learning disabilities.* DH, London

Department of Health (2011) *No health without mental health. A cross-governmental mental health outcomes strategy for people of all ages.* DH, London

Royal College of Nursing (2011) *Meeting the health needs of people with learning disabilities. RCN guidance for nursing staff.* RCN, London

Mencap (2012) *Death by indifference: 74 deaths and counting. A progress report 5 years on.* Mencap, London

What about specific legislation that may guide my practice?

Chris Knifton

As a registered nurse you need to ensure your practice is guided by national legislation. In England and Wales, there are a number of Acts of Parliament that you need to be particularly aware of when working as a nurse for people with learning disabilities. Some of these are listed in *Box 2.2*. This list is not exhaustive.

Box 2.2. Some examples of legislation used in England and Wales of relevance to learning disability nursing

Medicines Act 1968

Misuse of Drugs Act 1971

Mental Health Act 1983 (amended 2007)

National Health Service and Community Care Act 1990

Medicinal Products: Prescriptions by Nurses etc Act 1992

Carers (Recognition and Services) Act 1995

Human Rights Act 1998

Public Interest Disclosure Act 1998

Carers and Disabled Children Act 2000

Sexual Offences Act 2003

Carers (Equal Opportunities) Act 2004

Mental Capacity Act 2005

Health and Social Care Act 2008

Autism Act 2009

Equality Act 2010

It is important that you are aware of the relevant 'Code of Practice' for each Act that affects your practice. A code of practice is published to accompany legislation to guide practitioners in its interpretation. Particular examples which you need to be familiar with include the code of practice for the:

- Mental Health Act 1983 (Department of Health 2008a).
- Mental Capacity Act 2005 (Department of Health 2008b).

It is advisable to have a hard copy of any relevant codes of practice accessible in your work area for guidance.

How is mental capacity assessed?

Catherine Hart

The legislation used for assessment of mental capacity can be found in the Mental Capacity Act (2005) (Department for Constitutional Affairs 2005). Assessment should be specific to making a particular decision, and should be made at the time that the decision needs to be made. Capacity can change over time and just because a person was previously unable to make a decision does not mean you should assume he or she still cannot. Some people may be able to make some decisions but have difficulty with others, so, again, it is important that you treat each decision independently.

The assessment of capacity should be based on whether the person can:

- Understand the information relevant to the decision and retain the information long enough to make the decision.
- Weigh and balance the information to make a choice.
- Communicate that choice through whatever means of communication the person uses (verbal, sign language, written).

Individuals can only be assessed as having or lacking capacity once they have been given the appropriate support and information to help them make the decision. People with learning disabilities might have difficulty understanding information, and should be supported as much as possible in the decision-making process. This involves providing them with all the relevant information in a format they will understand (such as pictures, symbols or audio) and giving them enough time to process and understand the information.

What is meant by DoLS (Deprivation of Liberty Safeguards)?
Catherine Hart

Over recent years, in England, there has been much legal discussion about the rights of those who lack the capacity to consent to, or refuse, admission to hospital for treatment or to stay in a residential care home. The Mental Health Act 1983/2007 provides safeguards for those who are detained in hospital.

A person who has capacity and agrees to go into a hospital or care home, and agrees to the restrictions on their liberty, can decide whether to stay or go. If they decide to leave, they can be detained if appropriate or allowed to leave. However, there was a gap in service provision for those who lacked capacity, were in care and were having their liberty deprived but were not detained under the Mental Health Act (1983). This commonly became known as the 'Bournewood Gap' after a landmark court case involving Bournewood Hospital.

The Mental Capacity Act (2005) (Department for Constitutional Affairs, 2005) has been amended to address this gap. The Act now includes the Deprivation of Liberty Safeguards (DoLS). For people who lack capacity and are not detained under the Mental Health Act, DoLS provides a process by which they are assessed to ascertain whether their liberty is being deprived, and provides a due legal process to safeguard their rights and ensure appropriate review. DoLS covers hospitals and residential care homes, but does not include people living in the family home or in supported living who have the capacity to and have signed a tenancy agreement themselves. For those who live in supported accommodation, where the local authority has signed the tenancy on the person's behalf, cases are currently going through the courts. The courts at present describe this type of service as 'imputable to the state', i.e. the State is responsible for the person's care, and has decided in the current cases that DoLS is applicable to these individuals if required.

People may be deprived of their liberty if all of the following are met:

- They have a mental disorder, *and*
- They are lacking capacity to consent to care in a hospital or care home, *and*
- It is in their best interests to protect them from harm and it is proportionate to the likelihood and seriousness of that harm, *and*
- Care can only be provided by depriving them of their liberty.

The DoLS Code of Practice (Ministry of Justice, 2008) provides some possible examples of restriction (which would be acceptable within a care plan and regular review) and deprivation (acceptable under the framework of a DoLS order). If a hospital or residential care home believes a person needs to be deprived of his or her liberty, it must apply to the local supervising authority (for hospitals the primary care trust, for care homes the local authority). An assessment will be undertaken by a number of trained professionals. If the assessment recommends that a deprivation of liberty is needed, the supervising authority can authorise an order. The order will state the duration of the order, any conditions attached (i.e. contact with family), name a representative for the person, and clearly lay out the terms for review. It is important to note that all deprivation of liberty orders are based on the best interests of the person with a learning disability.

The DoLS Code of Practice can be viewed at www.publicguardian.gov.uk.

What do I need to know about vulnerability?
Catherine Hart

People with learning disabilities are amongst the most vulnerable groups in society and are at a higher risk of suffering from abuse. This has been highlighted by a number of Healthcare Commission reports concerning abuse in NHS learning disability services (Healthcare Commission 2007a, b). They can be at risk of abuse and neglect by individuals as well as institutions. Unfortunately, abuse may often go unrecognised and unreported. People with learning disabilities are more likely to have communication needs that make it difficult for them to report abuse or they may not realise that what they have experienced constitutes abuse. From the Department of Health's *No secrets* guidance (2000a; and currently being revised) local authority and other services are required to work together to ensure there is a coherent policy for the prevention of abuse, and for the protection and safeguarding of adults. They also have to ensure all staff receive adequate training on safeguarding adults. The *No secrets* guidance provides a clear, comprehensive framework for how nurses, as well as other professionals, should respond if abuse is suspected.

Can I use complementary therapies with my clients?
Nicky Genders

There has, over recent years, been an increased interest in complementary therapies both within the health professions and amongst the general public. There are a number of considerations for nurses who wish to use complementary therapies with their clients.

Nurses must always work within the Nursing and Midwifery Council (NMC) Professional Code of Conduct (NMC 2008a). The code states:

> *You must ensure that the use of complementary or alternative therapies is safe and in the best interests of those in your care.*

Standard 23 of the Standards for Medicines Management (NMC 2010) states:

> *Registrants must have successfully undertaken training and be competent to practise the administration of complementary and alternative therapies.*

It is clear therefore that a nurse must be appropriately qualified within the complementary therapy they wish to practise. Most NHS trusts will have a protocol or policy around the use of complementary therapies which will identify that nurses must be appropriately qualified. Also, any external practitioners should be appropriately qualified and hold professional insurance.

A further consideration is that of consent. Does the individual have capacity to understand the therapy and engage appropriately?

Any treatment or therapy must be part of a care package and discussed with the multidisciplinary team.

What happens when someone with a learning disability commits a criminal offence?
Catherine Hart

Criminal offences by people who have learning disabilities, mental health problems and/or behavioural problems that require intervention from a specialist mental health team are subject to the same legislation and pathway through the criminal justice system as other mentally disordered offenders. This pathway is designed with safeguards to protect the rights of the individual. This is supported by initiatives such as the appropriate adult scheme, meaning that an appropriate adult is required by law to be present when vulnerable adults are identified at the police station. Appropriate adults represent people to guarantee their welfare. They should ensure that individuals are being treated appropriately by encouraging effective communication and making sure the process is fair. Other safeguards can be provided at a service level, such as local police liaison schemes that operate as a two-way process, with the eventual aim being that the person, whether a victim or perpetrator, is treated in a way that makes the whole process fair, accessible and controlled.

The assessment and treatment of this small group of people requires specialist knowledge as misinterpreting the way individuals present could ultimately affect their liberty, or could compromise public safety. There are some areas where you might observe differences in the way such people present. Examples of this include:

- *Suggestibility*: This is when an individual may be more responsive to suggestions and more like to answer in the affirmative. This could have serious consequences if being formally questioned.
- *Diagnostic overshadowing*: This is where the assumption is made that the way people present is due to their learning disability and therefore part of their normal presentation.
- *Acquiescence*: This makes individuals less likely to protest and to answer in the affirmative. This may mean they cover up limitations, to seek approval or praise.
- *Psychosocial masking*: This limits the expression of psychiatric symptoms often due to limited life experiences. Symptoms may appear to be childlike fantasies or have a less complex presentation, which may lead to severe symptoms being missed.

This is a diverse group and their offending patterns are mixed. Some people with learning disabilities are treated within mainstream forensic services, such as medium secure units and community placements for offenders. They are usually removed from the prison system if they are deemed to be vulnerable to other inmates or if the treatment programme cannot be tailored to meet their needs.

What do I do if someone discloses an offence?
Russell Woolgar

Issues to be considered ultimately relate to the nature of the offence disclosed. If offences have or are likely to pose immediate risk to the patient and/or others you will have a duty to alert the authorities. This relates particularly to incidents of abuse, under safeguarding of vulnerable adults and children. The NMC Code of Conduct (2008a) states that all nurses have a duty and personal responsibility to act in the best interests of a child or young person, and to inform and alert appropriate personnel if they suspect a child is at risk or has been abused. It is important to also remember that clients/patients have a right to confidentiality.

Police and Criminal Evidence Act (1984)

This Act allows nurses and midwives to pass on information to the police if they believe that someone may be seriously harmed or death may occur if the police are not informed. Before any disclosure is made, nurses and midwives should always discuss the matter fully with other professional colleagues. It is good practice to ensure a patient is aware of this as part of any contact and discussion around confidentiality within a therapeutic relationship. Informing a patient/client that, under highlighted circumstances, you have a duty to alert others is important. Gaining consent to pass on information is good practice.

The NMC (2008a) clearly states a duty of confidence arises when one person discloses information to another in circumstances where it is reasonable to expect that the information will be held in confidence. This duty of confidence is derived from common law – the decisions of the Courts and Statute Law passed by Parliament.

In relation to criminal law, as a nurse, you are only obliged to disclose information under the duty to inform the Police, when asked, of:

• The name and address of drivers who are allegedly guilty of an offence contrary to the Road Traffic Act 1998.

• The duty not to withhold information relating to the commission of acts of terrorism contrary to the Terrorism Act 2000.

Other information that may be disclosed includes that relating to notifiable infectious diseases.

What impact does the Mental Capacity Act 2005 have on mental health care?
Catherine Hart

The Mental Capacity Act's (MCA) (Department for Constitutional Affairs 2005), definition of incapacity also applies to decisions under the Mental Health Act (MHA) 1983. Where patients are detained under compulsion by the MHA, treatment other than that for mental disorder, such as physical health, for the person who lacks capacity, the MCA may be used. In this sense, the MCA continues to provide a mechanism for decision-making in a person's best interests for people lacking capacity to consent.

The MCA requires any 'advance decisions' made by the patient to be taken into account when considering what is in the person's best interests. Advance decisions can be used to state what treatment cannot be given and under what circumstances. This may have implications for patients who are detained under the MHA. However, under any section of the MHA to which Part 4 (consent to treatment) applies, an advance decision may be overridden. The exception to this is electroconvulsive therapy (ECT) for which additional safeguards are in place (section 58A of the MHA).

Which parts of the Mental Health Act 1983 might be of relevance to my work role?
Chris Knifton

This depends on the setting where you find yourself working, which may be community nursing, forensic services, mental health services or supporting people who exhibit challenging behaviour. These examples are not exhaustive, and settings as well as job role may be quite diverse. This will have a great bearing on which parts and/or sections of the MHA may be of particular relevance. As a registered nurse, it is your responsibility to ensure you have read and understood the necessary Code of Practice that accompanies specific legislation. The Code of Practice issued to accompany the MHA 1983, including the MHA 2007 reforms, is published by the Department of Health (2008a).

The main parts/sections of the MHA 1983 which may be of particular relevance are briefly outlined in *Table 2.1.*

Table 2.1. Sections of the Mental Health Act 1983 relevant to learning disability nursing		
Part 1: Definitions		
Section 1	Definitions of mental disorder	Includes reference to learning disability
Part 2: Compulsory admission to hospital and guardianship		
Section 2	Admission for assessment	28 days
Section 3	Compulsory admission for treatment	6 months, renewed for further 6 months, then renewable yearly
Section 4	Emergency admission	72 hours (a second doctor can change this to a section 2 if needed)
Section 5	Doctors and nurses holding power	Doctors – 72 hours Nurses – 6 hours
Section 7	Guardianship	6 months, renewed for further 6 months and then yearly
Section 13	Duties of approved mental health professionals	
Section 17	Leave of absence from hospital	Cannot be given if patient is on a section 35, 36, or interim hospital order s.38
Section 17A	Community treatment order (CTO)	6 months, renewed for further 6 months and then yearly
Section 26	Definitions of relative and nearest relative	
Part 3: Patients involved in criminal proceedings or under sentence		
Section 35	Remand to hospital for report on medical condition	28 days, renewable for further 28 days, up to a maximum of 12 weeks in total
Section 36	Remand to hospital for treatment	28 days, renewable for further 28 days, up to a maximum of 12 weeks in total

Section 37	Hospital order	6 months, renewed for further 6 months and then yearly
Section 47	Removal to hospital for patients serving prison sentences	6 months, renewed for further 6 months and then yearly
Part 4: Consent to treatment (applies to sections 2, 3, 17A and 19)		
Section 56	Patients where this applies	
Section 57	Treatment requiring consent and a second opinion	
Section 62	Urgent treatment	
Section 63	Treatment not requiring consent	
Part 5: Mental health review tribunals		
Section 65	Mental health review tribunals	
Section 72	Powers of tribunals	
Part 8		
Section 117	Duty to provide after-care to patients who have been detained under s.3. 37, 45A, 47 or 48	
Section 135	Warrant to search for and remove a patient	72 hours – not renewable
Section 136	Mentally disordered persons found in public places – Police power in public places	72 hours – not renewable

What legislation governs medications and are there other national documents that guide registered nurses in this practice?

Annie Law

Legal and professional frameworks

Two key pieces of legislation govern the use of drugs:

- The Medicines Act 1968.
- The Misuse of Drugs Act 1971.

These Acts are somewhat dated and there have been statutory instruments (secondary legislation) to supplement them as changes have occurred.

Medicines Act 1968

This act controls the manufacture and distribution of medicines, i.e. who can lawfully supply and be in possession of medicines, and how medicines are packaged and labelled. The Act classifies drugs into three categories:

- *Prescription Only Medicines (POM)*: Drugs that may be supplied and administered to a patient only on the instruction of an appropriate practitioner.
- *Pharmacy Only Medicines:* Drugs that can be purchased from a chemist shop only if the sale is supervised by a pharmacist.
- *General Sales List:* Drugs that do not need a prescription or supervision of a pharmacist – basically anything you can buy in a supermarket.

Misuse of Drugs Act 1971

This Act replaced the Dangerous Drugs Act, and controls the import, export, production, supply and possession of drugs. Changes in the legal status of some drugs have led to the Misuse of Drugs (Safe Custody) Regulations 1973 and the Misuse of Drugs Regulations 1985. These identify five separate schedules of controlled drugs, which you need to be familiar with as your responsibilities in terms of storage, checking and disposal relate to the different schedules.

Any discrepancies in the stock balance of controlled drugs may result in the police becoming involved. It is therefore vital that you familiarise yourself with local policies related to controlled drugs. You must know:

- The correct storage of these drugs.
- The scrupulous checking required when administering these drugs to a patient, and the stock balance each day.
- The disposal mechanisms.
- Record keeping.

Nurse Prescribing Act 1992

This piece of legislation reached the statute books directly as a result of the need for the law to catch up with the demands of the NHS (Shepherd 2002). This has been further developed by Nurse Independent Prescribing (Department of Health /National Practitioner Programme 2006).

NMC Standards for Medicines Management

The Nursing and Midwifery Council's (NMC) Standards for Medicines Management (2010) were produced by the professional regulatory body for nurses and midwives to set standards for safe practice in the management and administration of medicines.

European Union (EU) directive 92/27/EEC

This EU directive places a responsibility on all members of the EU to provide patients with information leaflets for each medicine dispensed. This became law in 1999. If you are teaching patients how to take medications before leaving hospital or in their own homes, patient information leaflets provide a useful information source for you and your patient. You should ensure that the patient or carer is aware of this information, which they can refer to if necessary when you are not there.

National Institute for Health and Clinical Excellence (NICE)

NICE was set up by the Government in 1999, and its role is to advise on best practice related to diagnostic techniques, medical devices and therapeutic interventions as well as drug prescribing practices. You should keep yourself up to date with any new guidelines that NICE produces related to the prescribing of drugs for particular conditions. These guidelines can be found on the website for NICE at www.nice.org.uk.

National Service Frameworks (NSF)

These frameworks have been produced by expert groups working with the Government to provide guidance to clinicians and health service managers on best practice in terms of service provision, e.g. for cancer, heart disease and older people. They contain guidance on specific drug therapy.

Maintaining your knowledge of any frameworks connected with your speciality will help you to understand not only any recommendations for particular drugs, but also why services may change and the impact that these changes may have on nursing. The National Service Frameworks can be viewed and downloaded from the Department of Health website: www.dh.gov.uk/Home/fs/en.

Other Government documents

The Department of Health published a report entitled *An organisation with a memory* (Department of Health, 2000b). This report made two recommendations specific to medicines:

- To decrease to zero the number of patients dying or being paralysed by maladministered spinal injections.
- To cut by 40% the number of serious errors in the use of prescribed drugs.

The Department of Health recently published guidance for extension of the list of medical conditions giving exemption from NHS prescription charges (Department of Health 2009). It is important that you know who can apply for exemption from prescription charges to enable you to advise your patients appropriately. People over the age of 60 are exempt on age grounds and this new guidance gives people with a diagnosis of cancer the right to apply for exemption. The same right for people with long-term conditions is being discussed.

The National Patient Safety Agency (NPSA) produces guidance on safe medicines practice which can be obtained from its website: www.npsa.nhs.uk. This Government body also produces alerts which are circulated to all healthcare institutions. These alerts are produced to warn institutions when a series of errors has been made or when potential dangers have been identified. One example is errors made in the administration of oral medicines into vascular access devices. This led to a directive to only use oral syringes to administer syrups/suspensions orally or via nasogastric tubes. These syringes have been designed to be incompatible with intravenous devices.

Keeping abreast of new reports from bodies such as the Audit Commission will help you to improve practice, maintain patient safety and avoid common errors. Audit Commission reports can be obtained from the websites: www. dh.gov.uk/Home/fs/en and www.audit-commission.gov.uk.

What are the principles of safe practice for giving medication?
Annie Law

In 1986 the UKCC produced an advisory paper on the administration of medicine, which stated that first-level nurses and midwives should be considered competent to administer medicines on their own, and be responsible for their actions in so doing. Involvement of a second person would need to occur only if a learner was being taught, the patient's condition made it necessary, or in some exceptional circumstances. Healthcare institutions vary in their policies regarding the checking procedures for drugs and the number of people who should be involved. Children's services often require two people to check drugs before administration, because of the often complex calculations required. In addition, many institutions require two people to check intravenous (IV) and cytotoxic drugs because of the rapid effect of the drugs, and the implications should an error occur.

Table 2.2 provides a step-by-step guide to the stages that should be followed in the checking and administration of medicines.

Table 2.2. Stages in checking and administrating medications	
Drug Administration Flow Chart	
Action	*Rationale*
Before administration, read prescription chart carefully. Ensure that you know what the drug is for, the usual dose, side-effects, contraindications and any special instructions or precautions	To check that the prescription is written clearly (in indelible ink) and accurately. It is part of the nurse's role to act as the last line of defence against drug errors. The doctor may have overlooked potential interactions and may have made a mistake in the dose or route (*Nursing Times* 1994, NMC 2010)
If the prescription chart is unclear in any way, return it to the prescriber for clarification	To reduce the risk of error (Dimond 2004; *Nursing Times* 1994)
Check that the patient's details are clearly written on the chart. If there are patients with the same or similar name, a warning label should be attached to the chart	To provide sufficient information to check that medicines are given to the correct patient
If more than one chart, ensure that charts are clearly marked '1 of 2' or '2 of 2' as appropriate – merge all onto one chart at the earliest opportunity	Ensures that everyone is aware of the existence of more than one chart to reduce the risk of missed doses
Check that the patient's weight is clearly written if any medicine is prescribed where the dose is related to weight	

Check each prescribed medication for: • Name of drug • Route of administration • Dose • Start date • Signature of doctor • Any special instructions (e.g. with food) • Time of last administration • Time due for administration (NMC 2010)	To ensure that the correct drug is given by the correct route in the right dose at the right time. Some drugs, e.g. antibiotics, are only given for a short course; as the nurse administering the drugs you should request a review of the need for a drug if it has been given for a long time
Check for any co-existing therapy, particularly in the 'as required' section	To ensure the same drug or constituent of the drug has not been prescribed in more than one section – risk of overdose (NMC 2010)
Check drug against prescription: • Name of drug • Dose of tablet/capsule/syrup, etc. • Calculation (if any) • Expiry date (NMC, 2010)	To ensure that correct dose and drug are given
Check patient's identity against prescription chart and any name bracelet. Where appropriate, ask the patient to state their name, address and date of birth. Do not ask, 'Are you Mr ....' as a confused, hard-of hearing, or anxious patient may answer yes to this question when it is not their identity. This may not always be practical in learning disability services, but you must ensure you are confident the person you are administering to is the right person	To ensure that the correct patient receives the correct drug (*Nursing Times* 1994, NMC 2010)
Obtain patient's consent and administer the drug	Patient's consent is required for all treatment (NMC 2010)
	Table 2.2 contl

Record that the drug has been administered. Where supervising a student in the administration of medicines, you should clearly countersign the signature of the student (NMC 2010)	To indicate that the drug has been given and to prevent the dose being given again
Record if the drug has not been given for any reason and inform the prescriber	It may be necessary to alter the route of administration or review the need for the drug (NMC 2010)
Instruction by telephone to administer a previously un-prescribed substance is *not* acceptable (NMC 2010)	Risk of unclear instructions or misunderstanding. If absolutely necessary, repeat instructions back to prescriber and ensure that you have a second witness; both of you should record the instructions.

The NMC (2010) Standards for medicines management provides the minimum standard of practice and should be used in conjunction with local policies and procedures.

Nurses should incorporate the five 'rights' of drug administration (*Nursing Times* 1994) into their practice:

- Use the right drug.
- Give to the right patient,
- In the right dose,
- By the right route,
- At the right time.

Some common problems in the administration of medicines

Conflict with the prescriber

What would you do if you felt that the dose of the drug that was prescribed for a patient was unusually high, and when you questioned the doctor who had prescribed it he or she confirmed that this was the intended dose? You are personally accountable for your actions: If you are still concerned, you should check with a more senior doctor and seek advice from a pharmacist. Other sources of information that are available to you include the *British National Formulary* (BNF) and any local prescribing guidelines (Dimond 2004).

Illegible writing

You cannot read clearly the name of the drug that has been prescribed, but it has been administered by several of your colleagues at previous administration times. If you are in any doubt, do not administer the drug, and check with the prescriber, senior doctor or pharmacist first. If you do not check any illegible prescription and an error occurs, you will be equally liable (Dimond 2004). After checking with the prescriber, always request that the prescription is rewritten. Many institutions clearly state in their drug policies that prescriptions must be written in capital letters in indelible ink.

PRN (as required) medication

These are drugs prescribed by a doctor, but administered to the patient at the nurse's discretion based on the nurse's assessment of the patient. They typically include analgesics, sleeping tablets, indigestion medicines, aperients and, particularly in learning disability, medications to reduce anxiety and challenging behaviour. Often, insufficient information is provided when these drugs are prescribed, such as the maximum amount that can be given in 24 hours and intervals at which they can be given (Dimond 2004). You must be aware of the limitations of these drugs. You should check not only the time of the last dose, but also the total that has been given in the last 24 hour period. When administering drugs prescribed on the PRN part of the prescription chart, you should always check the regularly prescribed drugs to be certain that there are no contraindications. An example of this would be the prescribing of PRN paracetamol and a regular prescription for co-codamol, which could result in a paracetamol overdose.

Remote orders

Standard 11 of the NMC (2010) states that:

> In exceptional circumstances, where the medication (NOT including controlled drugs) has been previously prescribed and the prescriber is unable to issue a new prescription, but where changes to the dose are considered necessary, the use of information technology (IT) (such as fax, text message or email) may be used but must confirm any change to the original prescription.

The NMC makes it clear that if a medication has not been previously prescribed, remote prescribing is not permitted if the prescriber has not assessed the patient, except in life-threatening situations. The key points to remember are:

- A verbal order is not acceptable on its own.
- The fax/email must be stapled to the patient's drug chart.

A new prescription must be signed by the prescriber who sent the fax/email within 24 hours.

A dose is missed

If a dose is missed, for whatever reason, this should be recorded and reported as soon as possible. The implications for a missed dose are:

- Recurrence of symptoms,
- Lower plasma levels of the drug,
- Diminished effect of the drug.

This is especially important for drugs such as insulin, anticoagulants, and drugs for epilepsy, myasthenia gravis and Parkinson's disease (*Nursing Times* 1994). Some of the most common reasons for missing a dose are:

- Nil by mouth,
- Nausea/vomiting,
- Patient's refusal.

If patients state that they do not want their medication, an assessment should be made as to whether the drug should be changed to a PRN medication, whether the patient requires educating about the need to take the drug regularly for maximum benefit, and whether or not the person has capacity to make an informed choice over medication refusal.

When patients refuse their drugs, nurses face a dilemma: should they disguise the medicines in food or drink or just not give the medication, which might result in deterioration of the patient's health? Is covert administration ethical or legal? This method of administration has been common practice over the years in many settings where the nurse is acting alone. The NMC (2007) produced a statement on disguising medicine in food and drink in an attempt to assist practitioners in decision making. As a registered nurse it is your professional duty to familiarise yourself with this document.

There are ethical, legal and pharmaceutical issues that need to be considered in the covert administration of drugs. Ethically, is it right to trick a patient into taking medication? There may be circumstances when, by so doing, you save a life or avoid substantial harm. If you did administer a medication covertly, can you be prosecuted under criminal law or the Human Rights Act (Treloar et al 2000, 2001)? The NMC (2010) advises that disguising medicines in the absence of informed consent may be regarded as a deception. A clear distinction should always be made between those who have capacity to refuse medication, whose refusal should be respected, even if the decision adversely affects their health, and those who lack this capacity. In addition, the pharmaceutical properties of a drug may be changed if the preparation is crushed and added to food or drink.

You should never feel that you have to make a decision alone to administer drugs covertly, and it is recommended you follow the following steps if the patient does not have the capacity to make an informed decision:

- Discuss with the multiprofessional team.
- Discuss with the patient's relatives.
- Respect any previous instruction left by the patient.
- Consult local policies or, if not available, ask to see them.
- Seek advice from your employer's legal advisors.
- Maintain good records of decisions and actions taken.
- Agree a method of administration with the pharmacist.
- Remember, capacity to consent can fluctuate and should be regularly assessed.
- Remember that you are accountable for your actions.

(NMC 2007)

Can a learning disability nurse become an independent nurse prescriber?
Karen Ford

Learning disability nurses can train to become independent and supplementary prescribers. The types of areas where they might use this advance qualification and skill is, for example, with young people who have attention deficit disorder or autism who require prescribed medication. Another area is for epilepsy. It is important that the nurse working in the field of learning disability can support their clients with everyday health problems. Therefore to be a prescriber can open up support for minor illnesses and sexual healthcare. Because a nurse prescriber has access to the BNF does not mean that drugs should be prescribed without consideration of competence with the drugs and the clinical indication. For non-medical prescribers working in learning disability, further skills may need to be acquired and training undertaken, which can only further enhance the reward for the nurse alongside the responsibility which comes with this extended role.

Consider the case of a female client with Down's syndrome who asks for contraceptive advice and support. This could be undertaken by a nurse who works closely with the client, having built a trusting relationship with her. Nurses are ideally placed if they are prescribers and have also undertaken a sexual health course to enable them to prescribe competently for this indication.

To become prescribers nurses must have been qualified as registered nurses for more than three years, work for more than a year in the area in which they plan to prescribe, and there must be a clinical need for them to be a prescriber (NMC 2006). It is not a course that suits everyone as it is academically demanding, but it delivers great professional and personal rewards. The qualification (V300) is annotated onto the professional register upon successful completion of the course. The course itself challenges the nurse due to the diverse contents which include pharmacology, numeracy, consultation skills, and professional, legal and ethical elements as well as critical appraisal of systems in practice.

How do I contact relatives/carers following a death?
Martyn Geary

Informing relatives that a loved one has died is stressful for all practitioners, whatever their level of experience. The following guidance may be helpful.

Before the death

- Record the name and contact telephone number of a person to be contacted in the event of a patient's deterioration. Do not assume that this will be the same as the next of kin. Consider recording two names to ensure that the name of an additional contact is known should the first be unavailable.
- Record the person's full name, not simply their surname – there may be people in the same house with the same surname.
- Clarify when this person might not wish to be contacted. For example, does he or she wish to be contacted during the night? If not, ascertain the time after which they do not wish to be contacted and if there is anyone else who should be contacted in their place.

Contacting relatives/carers over the telephone

- Collect all of the relevant documentation together.
- Find a private and quiet place (preferably an office or room separate from the rest of the ward or unit) where you can make the telephone call.
- Inform colleagues of what you are about to do so that you will not be disturbed.
- Check and double check that you are about to contact the right relative or carer about the right patient – mistakes can and do happen.
- Before you dial the number, mentally rehearse what you are going to say.
- When the phone is answered, introduce yourself and ask to speak to the person concerned.
- Clarify that you are speaking to the right person. Instead of saying, 'Is that Mrs Smith?', say instead something along the lines of, 'Is that Mrs Pat Smith, Jack's wife?'
- The phone call itself will cause alarm so do not delay in giving the news. Try to convey the information slowly and sensitively without the use of euphemisms. For example, after having established that you are speaking to the right person, you might say, 'Mrs Smith, I'm afraid I've got some bad news. There's no easy way to say this. I'm sorry to say Mr Smith has died.'
- Be prepared for a range of possible responses.
- If the person wishes to come into the hospital/ward/unit/home, ensure that you make it clear how to gain access, particularly at night if the usual entrances are closed.
- Ask if the person is fit to drive.
- Ask if you could telephone anyone on their behalf.
- If they are not intending to leave for the hospital immediately, explain that you will phone back in half an hour to check on them.
- If they choose not to come in during the night, explain what needs to be done the following day.

Preparing for relatives'/carers' arrival

- Ensure that all staff members are aware of the patient's death and that relatives/carers are expected.
- If at all possible, try to ensure that a member of staff is allocated to the care of relatives.
- If relatives/carers are expected to arrive during the night, arrange for

hospital security or portering staff to meet them at the hospital entrance and show them to the ward/unit.

- Ensure that the allocated staff member is waiting for them on the ward/unit and is there to escort them to a prepared office or quiet room. Ensure that there are sufficient chairs available and tissues are at hand in the room. If there is a phone in the office, divert calls to a different extension. A busy ward office is not the ideal place.

- Ensure that the nurse allocated to the patient's care is appraised of the circumstances surrounding the death – relatives/carers are likely to have questions about what happened and the order of events. Documenting the details of events surrounding a death can also be of value if the ward or unit operates a bereavement support programme where relatives may meet with practitioners in the months following the death. Unless recorded, events around a death can be forgotten by health professionals, especially if they were not directly involved in care delivery at the time.

Being with relatives/carers

- Be sensitive to the range of possible reactions people may display.
- Remember that there is likely to be little or nothing a practitioner can say that will ease the pain that people experience. Attempting to 'reassure' can, albeit unintentionally, be interpreted as talking in platitudes.
- Recognise and accommodate religious and cultural diversity in the way that people express their grief.
- Take your lead from the bereaved. Even if people have arrived at the hospital, check that they will wish to view the body. If so, explain beforehand what they will see when they enter the bed area or side-room. Some people may never have seen a dead body and may be apprehensive as to what to expect.
- Accompany carers/relatives to the bedside.
- Check with relatives if they wish to spend time alone. Providing chairs at the bedside gives them reassurance that they will not be rushed.
- How people wish to act with the deceased will vary. Religious and cultural factors as well as personality and the effect of grief itself will influence what people wish to say or do.
- Offer the opportunity for relatives/carers to speak to a member of the medical staff to discuss events surrounding the death.
- Some people may wish to kiss, hold or lie with the deceased; others may

choose not to, while some may be reticent and appreciate the nurse taking the lead in touching and 'speaking' to the person who has died.

- While providing time for relatives to be alone if they wish, check regularly whether there is anything they need. Remember to point out the location of toilets and telephone facilities and offer refreshments.
- Before they leave the ward/unit, ensure that they are given information (reinforced with written details) as to what to do and where to go to collect the death certificate and any property of the deceased. A list of support organisations should also be given.
- Ensure that all details of the visit are entered in the nursing notes.

What if I am unable to contact the person over the telephone?

In addition to trying the number at a later time, check to see if there is an alternative contact number. If no telephone number is recorded, check with directory enquiries. Failing that, you may have to consider contacting the patient's GP, if appropriate, to request a visit to the deceased's relatives, or contact the police service who can arrange for officers to visit the address to convey the information personally. There will be a procedure for contacting the police – this will need to be checked with your organisation's own policy.

What if there is an answering machine attached to the telephone?

As soon as you realise that an answering machine is attached to the telephone, replace the receiver without leaving a message. This will give you time to compose yourself and rehearse what you wish to say. Call back, but in the message you do leave, be sure *not* to tell the relative/carer about the death, but ask them to contact the ward/unit as soon as possible, giving the name of the person with whom they should speak.

What are my responsibilities in reporting malpractice?
Kevin Power

There are two types of situation that may lead you to report malpractice. The first relates specifically to those whose names appear on a professional register, such as nurses and doctors, and is usually termed professional misconduct. The second is malpractice by anyone within the care area, or concerns about poor standards.

Professional misconduct

Nurses are advised to discuss any concerns they have about a registered colleague with their employer in the first instance (NMC 2008b). *Table 2.3* lists the most common types of professional misconduct reported to the NMC.

You need to be sure of your facts and give a clear factual account of your concerns. That means stating what has actually occurred rather than what you suspect may have occurred. If you can get other witnesses to support your concerns, all the better. If there are no other witnesses, record all the facts including date and time and precisely what you observed. Remember to write down what you saw, not what you think happened.

Many nurses are afraid to report poor standards and malpractice because of the potential for recriminations and possibly even loss of their job (O'Dowd 2002). Certainly, students that I teach often say they would be unlikely to complain about poor standards of care that they witness, out of fear of being failed by their

Table 2.3. The most common types of professional misconduct allegations reported to the NMC		
	2006–2007	*2007–2008*
Dishonesty (this includes theft, fraud and false claim to registration, claiming sick pay fraudulently, falsification of records, dishonesty about previous employment and misappropriation of drugs)	19.23%	17.32%
Patient abuse (physical, sexual, verbal, inappropriate relationship)	17.09%	14.30%
Failure to maintain adequate records	7.48%	10.37%
Maladministration of drugs	10.47%	9.87%
Neglect of basic care	10.04%	9.16%
Unsafe clinical practice	7.48%	7.75%
Failure to collaborate with colleagues	4.06%	6.95%
Colleague abuse (physical, sexual, verbal, inappropriate relationship)	4.27%	2.72%
Failure to report incidents	3.42%	2.62%
Failure to act in an emergency	3.21%	1.91%
Pornography – adult	2.35%	1.01%
		From NMC (2008c)

assessor as a reprisal. This culture of fear of reprisals seems to persist for qualified nurses (Nazarko 1998, Health Which 1999, Wallis 2001, Ferns and Chojnacka 2005). This appears to remain the case despite the enactment of the Public Interest Disclosure Act, 1998, which protects the whistleblower if victimised or dismissed as a result of disclosing malpractice.

To whom should I report malpractice?

Under the Public Interest Disclosure Act 1998, protection from victimisation and dismissal by an employer is given to those who speak out against any malpractice. Areas covered by the Public Interest Disclosure Act 1998 are listed in *Box 2.3*.

However, this does not give a carte blanche for anyone to go directly to the press with a complaint. All other reasonable attempts should be made to rectify a situation before going to the media. You should first raise any concerns internally with your employer, and if no progress is made you may take those concerns to a prescribed regulator; only then, if no progress is made, should concerns be raised externally to your employer. You are, however, allowed to seek legal advice and still be protected by the Act. If you decide to go to the media in the first instance, there is likely to be less protection from some sanctions, such as dismissal by your employer (RCN 2004).

Box 2.3. Areas covered by the Public Interest Disclosure Act 1998

- A criminal act
- A failure to comply with legal obligation (this includes negligence, breach of contract, including contract of employment, and breach of administrative law)
- A miscarriage of justice
- Danger to health and safety
- Damage to the environment
- An attempt to cover up any of these

Malpractice covered by the Public Interest Disclosure Act 1998

Concerns should first be raised with your employer, such as your line manager, senior colleague or supervisor. For example, if you are a staff nurse then you should raise the issue with the charge nurse or more senior nurse. If the person you have concerns about is your manager and you work in the NHS, you have the right to raise concerns with the trust board, the health authority or even a health minister (RCN 2004).

Prescribed regulator

If you work in the independent sector, such as a nursing home or private hospital, concerns can be raised with a prescribed regulator. Regulators include the Health and Safety Executive, the Inland Revenue, the Audit Commission and the local authority. You may also report concerns to a prescribed regulator if you feel that those concerns have not been acted upon by an NHS employer.

Legal adviser

Should you need independent and confidential advice about a concern of malpractice, disclosures to a legal adviser are protected under the Act. This means that you can seek a legal opinion without being accused of breaching confidentiality.

Reporting malpractice externally

The Act does allow for reporting malpractice to the police, media, MPs, etc., under exceptional circumstances, i.e. where one of the following conditions is satisfied:

- Reasonable belief that the person reporting malpractice would be victimised if he or she raised the matter internally or with a prescribed person.
- There is no prescribed person, and reasonable belief that the evidence would be concealed or destroyed.
- The concern had already been raised with the employer or prescribed person (RCN 2004).

It may also be advisable to seek advice from a representative of your union. However, the law does give the greatest protection for internal disclosure, which includes reports made to Government ministers. If you decided to take your concerns to the media before raising them with your employer, the Act would provide less protection from dismissal than if you had used the institution's grievance procedures.

There is a good deal of useful advice on reporting malpractice on the Public Concern at Work website (http://www.pcaw.co.uk). See *Box 2.4* lists some of the tips given on this website.

Box 2.4. Whistleblowing advice

- Stay calm
- Remember that you are a witness, and not a complainant
- Think about the risks and outcomes before you act
- Let the facts speak for themselves – don't make ill-considered allegations
- Remember that you may be mistaken or that there may be an innocent or good explanation
- Do not become a private detective
- Recognise that you may not be thanked

(Public Concern at Work 2009)

What are my rights and responsibilities regarding risk management?

Paul Rigby

The assessment and management of risk, partly as a result of clinical governance requirements, now has a high profile within clinical practice and is an important part of the nurse's role (Torgesen 2008). The identification of any potential threats to patient safety and the introduction of measures which aim to eliminate or reduce risk are now part of everyday clinical practice (Bird and Dennis 2005). The NMC Code (2008a) outlines clearly the responsibilities that registered nurses have to act to identify and minimise the risk to patients and clients:

- *You must act without delay if you believe that you, a colleague or anyone else may be putting someone else at risk.*
- *You must inform someone in authority if you experience problems that prevent you from working within the NMC Code or other nationally agreed standards.*
- *You must report your concerns in writing if problems in the environment of care are putting people at risk.*

Risk assessment and risk management

People often confuse the very different concepts of risk assessment and risk management, and a clear understanding of the differences is a useful starting point for any examination of risk.

39

- *Risk assessment* involves identifying risk, through the systematic collection of information, defining what can go wrong in a situation, and predicting and measuring the likelihood of harm occurring.
- *Risk management* includes the measures taken to control risks or to minimise their occurrence.

While it is not possible to eliminate all risks, nurses have a duty to avoid taking unnecessary risks and to protect patients in their care as far as they are able to do so (National Patient Safety Agency 2007). Doyle (1998) has described a cycle of risk management which can provide a useful frame of reference when considering the management of risk in clinical practice (see *Figure 2.1*).

Aims of risk assessment and risk management

Raven (1999) identified four basic aims of risk assessment/management:

- Protection and safety of the patient/family/community.
- Minimising/reducing risk.
- Minimising litigation risk (personal/organisational).
- Involvement of the patient/carer in the risk assessment/management process.

Figure 2.1. Risk management cycle (Doyle 1998).

40

While there is an increasing number of clinical risk assessment tools available for the nurse to use, it is important to bear in mind certain principles that accompany the process:

- Clinical risk assessment often involves patients and therefore can be an interpersonal process.
- Although clinical risk assessment tools can be very useful, you do need to draw from a wide variety of sources for your information.
- Risk assessments should be grounded in history and based on empirical evidence.
- You need to focus upon probability rather than certainty.
- Rather than focusing upon at risk people, you should focus upon at risk situations (Ryrie 2000).
- Risk assessment and risk management responsibilities should be shared within the multiprofessional team.

Effective team working and decision making are essential components of successful risk management. Risk assessment is an ongoing process and the opinions of all team members should be sought on a regular basis. Use reflection and clinical supervision to seek support, share ideas and solve problems.

Clear, objective and accurate record keeping is an important responsibility for all nurses (NMC 2008a). To maintain public confidence it is important that practice is seen to be not only professional and evidence based, but also accountable (Department of Health 2000b). Even if mistakes are made, it is important that the appropriate lessons are learnt and the necessary changes to practice are made.

As a registered nurse, you have a responsibility to highlight deficiencies in training, communication, teamwork and clinical supervision. It is important to bear in mind that all of these factors can affect the process of assessing and managing risk.

What do I do if someone presents an immediate risk to themselves or others?

Russell Woolgar

Nurses have a duty to safeguard clients/patients and themselves. The Health and Safety at Work Act 1974 is the primary piece of legislation covering work-related health and safety in the United Kingdom. It sets out your employer's responsibilities for your health and safety at work.

Your employer has a duty under health and safety law to protect you (the nurse) and as far as possible, to have any risks to your health and safety properly controlled. This will be met principally through the use of an appropriate clinical risk assessment. Risk assessments will inform your actions relating to client/patient contact including where that contact takes place, for how long and in what circumstances.

Under mental health law, section 136 of the Mental Health Act 1983 gives the police powers to remove a person who appears to be suffering from mental disorder and who is 'in immediate need of care or control' from a public place to a place of safety. Removal may take place if a police officer believes it is necessary in the interests of that person, or for the protection of others. The purpose of removing a person to a place of safety (usually a police station cell or hospital emergency department) is to enable him or her to be assessed by a doctor or interviewed by an allied mental health professional.

As such, dependent on the actions/threat of action relating to immediate risk, as a nurse you would have a duty to take 'reasonable action' to ensure your own and others' continued safety.

Under common law you have a right to use reasonable force when defending yourself from an assault or risk of injury.

Reasonable force

A person may use such force as is reasonable in the circumstances for the purposes of self-defence, the defence of another, the defence of property, the prevention of crime, or lawful arrest.

In assessing the reasonableness of the force used, prosecutors should ask two questions:

- Was the use of force necessary in the circumstances, i.e. was there a need for any force at all? *and*
- Was the force used reasonable in the circumstances?

From: http://www.cps.gov.uk/legal/s_to_u/self_defence/

References

Bird D, Dennis S (2005) Integrating risk management into working practice. *Nursing Standard* **20**(13): 51–4

Department for Constitutional Affairs (2005) *Mental Capacity Act.* HMSO, London

Department of Health (2000a) *No secrets: Guidance on developing and implementing multi-agency policies and procedures to protect vulnerable adults from abuse.* HMSO, London

Department of Health (2000b) *An organisation with a memory: Report of an expert group on learning from adverse events in the NHS.* HMSO, London

Department of Health (2008a) *Code of Practice, Mental Health Act 1983.* TSO, London

Department of Health (2008b) *The Mental Capacity Act 2005, Deprivation of Liberty Safeguards Addendum to the Mental Capacity Act Code of Practice.* DH, London

Department of Health (2009) *Guidance issued to GPs and oncology departments regarding cancer.* Available from: http://www.nhsbsa.nhs.uk/Documents/HealthCosts/Guidance_ issued_to_GPs_and_oncology_departments_regarding_cancer

Department of Health/National Practitioner Programme (2006) *A Guide to the mechanisms for the prescribing, supply and administration of medicine.* HMSO, London

Dimond B (2004) *Legal aspects of nursing* (4th edn). Prentice Hall, New York

Doyle M (1998) Clinical risk assessment for mental health nurses. *Nursing Times* **94**(17): 47–9

Ferns T, Chojnacka I (2005) Reporting incidents of violence and aggression towards NHS staff. *Nursing Standard* **19**(38): 51–6

Health Which? (1999) Blowing the whistle. *Health Which?* **April**: 16–17

Healthcare Commission (2007a) *Investigation into services for people with learning disabilities at Cornwall Partnership NHS Trust.* Healthcare Commission, London. Available from: www.healthcarecommission.org.uk

Healthcare Commission (2007b) *Investigation into services for people with learning disabilities provided by Sutton and Merton Primary Care Trust.* Healthcare Commission, London. Available from: www.healthcarecommission.org.uk

Ministry of Justice (2008) *Deprivation of liberty safeguards. Code of practice to supplement the main Mental Capacity Act 2005 code of practice.* TSO, London.

National Patient Safety Agency (2007) *Healthcare risk made easy.* NPSA, London

Nazarko L (1998) Breaking the silence. *Elder Care* **10**(3): 44

NMC (2006) *Standards of proficiency for nurse and midwife prescribers.* Nursing and Midwifery Council, London

NMC (2007) *Covert administration of medicines – disguising medicine in food and drink. Advice Sheet.* Available from: http://www.nmc-uk.org

NMC (2008a) *The Code: Standards of conduct, performance and ethics for nurses and midwives.* NMC, London

NMC (2008b) *Environment of care advice sheet.* NMC, London. Available from: http://www. Nursing and Midwifery Council-uk.org/aDisplayDocument.aspx?documentID=3987

NMC (2008c) *Fitness to practice annual report 1 April 2007 to 31 March 2008.* NMC, London

NMC (2010) *Standards for medicines management.* NMC, London

Nursing Times (1994) Professional development. Medication: The role of the nurse. *Nursing Times* **90**(37 Suppl): 1–4

O'Dowd A (2002) Is legislation protecting nurses who blow the whistle? *Nursing Times*

98(46): 10–11

Public Concern at Work (2009) *How do I blow the whistle?* Available from: http://www.pcaw. co.uk/FAQ_individuals.htm

Raven J (1999) Managing the unmanageable: Risk assessment and risk management in contemporary professional practice. *Journal of Nursing Management* **7**(4): 201–6

Royal College of Nursing (2004) *Blowing the whistle.* RCN, London

Ryrie I (2000) Assessing risk. In Gamble C, Brennan G (eds). *Working with serious mental illness: A manual for clinical practice.* Baillière Tindall/RCN, London

Shepherd M (2002) Managing medicines. *Nursing Times* **98**(17): 43–6

Torgesen I (2008) Risk management. *Nursing Times* **104**(17): 12–13

Treloar A, Beats B, Philpot M (2000) A pill in the sandwich: Covert medication in food and drink. *Journal of the Royal Society of Medicine* **93**(8): 408–11

Treloar A, Philpot M, Beats B (2001) Concealing medicines in patients' food. *Lancet* **357**(9249): 62–4

Wallis L (2001) Protecting the whistleblower. *Nursing Standard* **13**(47): 16–17

NOTES

Chapter 3

Mental health

Sharon Clay, Catherine Hart, Dorothy Hemel and Chris Knifton

- How common are mental health problems in people with learning disabilities?
- What are the principles of carrying out mental health assessments?
- What do I need to consider when assessing mental health problems?
- How important is a physical health examination in suspected mental health problems, and what might this include?
- How are mental health assessments carried out?
- How do I assess psychiatric symptoms?
- Which diagnostic criteria or system should be used in learning disability?
- What is meant by the term 'diagnostic overshadowing'?
- What is the role of the clinical psychologist?
- What are the common mental health problems experienced by people with a learning disability?
- What psychological interventions can be used?
- What social interventions can be used?
- Are mental disorders associated with specific learning disability phenotypes?
- Should generic mental health or specialist mental health and learning disability services be used?
- What is meant by the Green Light Toolkit, and what is the learning disability nurse's role in its use?
- Is there any published guidance for nurses working in this area?

How common are mental health problems in people with learning disabilities?
Catherine Hart and Chris Knifton

As recently as the 1980s it was still generally believed that individuals with a learning disability did not possess the cognitive capacity to experience mental health problems and that any behavioural disturbances exhibited were caused by their learning disability. Fortunately, understanding has improved in this area and it is now recognised that although mental health and learning disabilities are two separate diagnoses, people with a learning disability can experience the full range of mental health problems exhibited by the general population. It is estimated that up to 40% of all users of learning disability services have mental health problems (Emerson et al 2001, Raghavan and Patel 2005), with prevalence rates actually higher than that found in the general population (Borthwick-Duffy 1994, Day and Jancar 1994). Common forms of mental health problems experienced by people with learning disabilities might include schizophrenia (occurring in approximately 3% of people with a learning disability) (Clarke 1999); cyclical behaviour and mood changes (4%, Deb and Hunter 1991); depression (3–8%, Clarke 1999); personality disorders (10–13%, Weissman 1993), dementia (up to 22%, Cooper 1997), and anxiety disorders (28%, Day 1985).

What are the principles of carrying out mental health assessments?
Catherine Hart and Chris Knifton

The whole assessment should be carefully planned in advance, ideally with someone who knows the person well, so discussion about the most appropriate venue, time of day, visual aids/cues, timing of the assessment (including breaks), refreshments, support from a significant other, etc, can all be considered. An additional issue is how you may come across during the assessment. Your own body language, tone of voice, the way you dress, socio-cultural practices, manners and respect, even how you address the person, need careful thought. Strategies exist to put the person at ease when carrying out your assessment. Paramount, perhaps, are effective communication strategies that take into account the individual needs of the person. This includes consideration of communication aids, interpreters, using language/terminology the person is familiar with, allowing sufficient time, use of augmented communication strategies if relevant, avoidance of metaphors, and asking patients to explain to you what they have understood.

Choosing an appropriate assessment tool or modifying a standardised assessment may need to be considered. Check with local protocol. If a standardised assessment is modified then this needs to be made clear in the assessment report, as well as the reasons for the modification. It may be that you have needed to alter wording or use examples with an individual, and this all adds to the qualitative elements of a mental health assessment. You should only use assessment tools that you are trained or supported to use and that are licensed to be used within your organisation.

What do I need to consider when assessing mental health problems?
Catherine Hart, Chris Knifton and Dorothy Hemel

Assessment needs to follow a biopsychosocial approach, be comprehensive, and remain multidisciplinary (Hardy and Holt 2005). People with mild learning disabilities are likely to display similar signs and symptoms to those of the general population, whereas people with severe forms are more likely to show atypical signs and symptoms, often behavioural in nature (Hardy and Holt 2005).

Hardy and Holt (2005) suggest that the process of mental health assessment should address the issues listed in *Box 3.1*.

Box 3.1. Mental health assessment

- What is the problem?
- What is happening now?
- What has caused or contributed to the problem?
- What are the vulnerability factors?
- What does the service user want to do about the problem?

In addition, we also need to ask, 'What protective factors or adaptive coping skills does this person have?'

Careful history taking, as well as reviewing the current situation and any presenting issues, becomes an essential part of this assessment. The assessment must include not only the person him or herself, but also relevant family, carers, significant others and other professionals.

An essential part of the assessment will include discussion with the client, sometimes taking the form of interviewing. When this is undertaken, some important considerations need to be borne in mind:

- If the interviewer is in a position of authority, people with a learning disability may say what they feel the interviewer wants them to say.
- Be aware of the attention span of the client, and adjust the interview as appropriate.
- Use open-ended questions where possible, although closed questions may be necessary in cases of poor verbal communication, confusion or extreme anxiety and stress.
- Where the client has difficulty remembering the timing of events (such as

date of onset of symptoms, duration, etc), focus on significant life events, such as birthdays.
- Guard against suggestibility and acquiescence.
- Try to explain the assessment fully, as well as the possible outcomes of the assessment. It is often a daunting process for an individual, so building a trusting rapport early in the interview helps you to elicit useful information. It may help to assess individuals where they feel comfortable if such a place is available to you and risk issues allow.
- Many standardised or formal mental health assessments may not be suitable for someone who has a learning disability, therefore choosing a suitable assessment tool as well as clinical judgement are both essential.

The nurse will also need to consider the level of functioning of the person, including skills, abilities, emotions, expression, communication, performance in activities of daily living, and individual nuances in behaviour 'usually' associated with the person. This establishes a baseline from which behaviour deviances can be measured. In addition it is important to establish that the person has no underlying physical health problem, for example, infection or pain.

How important is a physical health examination in suspected mental health problems, and what might this include?
Chris Knifton and Dorothy Hemel

A physical health examination and assessment is important. The Royal College of Nursing (RCN) (2007) notes that undiagnosed physical health problems may predispose, precipitate or maintain a mental health problem. Indeed, some physical health problems produce a similar clinical presentation to mental health disorders (Hardy and Holt 2005).

Symptoms of some mental health problems may be caused by delirium, and this may confuse diagnosis. Delirium is a confusional state with an underlying physical health cause. Once the physical health cause is treated, the symptoms of delirium usually subside. Symptoms of delirium may include hallucinations and delusions, irritability, depressed mood, over- or under-active behaviour, agitation, withdrawal, memory difficulties, etc. Many of these symptoms appear in common mental problems such as anxiety, depression, bi-polar disorder and even dementia. Some common causes of delirium include infection, metabolic disorders, trauma, hypoxia, nutritional deficiencies, including dehydration, over- or under-active thyroid, constipation, and some medication side effects/toxicity. A physical examination to rule out possible causes of delirium is essential. All registered nurses need to ensure they are familiar with the current National Institute for Health and Clinical Excellence (NICE) guidance on delirium (NICE 2010).

Physical examinations may vary slightly, but ideally should include the cardiovascular system, detailed neurological examination (focal deficits, gait abnormalities, speech abnormalities), endocrine system (hypothyroidism), vital sign monitoring (temperature, pulse, respiration and blood pressure), full blood count, urea and electrolyte checks, tests for blood sugar, liver function, and thyroid function, B12 and folate levels, lipid profiles, and sensory screening (British Psychological Society and Royal College of Psychiatrists, 2009). Weight changes, nutritional assessments and consideration of elimination needs (e.g. constipation, urine infections, or even vomiting/nausea) may be indicated. In addition, medication checks, including polypharmacy, drug sensitivity, contraindications and toxicity levels all need to be checked carefully.

The registered nurse needs to be aware of these procedures and must support the person with learning disabilities, and sometimes his or her carers, in understanding what is required. This may include understanding the individual needs of the person and that some clinical procedures may need to be adapted. Examples of this may include using an appropriately sized leg cuff to take blood pressure where taking it on the arm would be inappropriate or impossible. In addition, the nurse should also work closely with the person and carers to obtain appropriately informed consent before investigations can commence. Where this is not obtained, the nurse must follow guidance as found within the Mental Capacity Act 2005 (Department for Constitutional Affairs 2005) based on the best interests of the person.

There is an additional relationship between physical health risks and mental health problems. In particular there are increased health risks for endocrine, gastrointestinal, respiratory and coronary heart disease, diabetes and infections (Mentality and NIMHE, 2004). Reasons for this are diverse, and may include deliberate avoidance by some health professionals (Phelan et al 2001) or lack of knowledge and experience of physical health issues amongst mental healthcare professionals (Day 2008).

How are mental health assessments carried out?
Catherine Hart

All mental health assessments are carried out using systematic history taking. Accessing previous medical notes and nursing records may be necessary, and consent for this may be required. If the person has been in residential care, records would have been kept by staff and may prove useful. In addition, consultation with family and carers is of importance – even if the person is in residential care. The person may have lived at home for a number of years before requiring residential care, and family members may therefore have a wealth of knowledge about the person, including being able to fill in the gaps where the person has been moved from one facility to another. It is through this understanding held by the family, that the picture of what constitutes 'normal' for the person can be developed. This is essential when distinguishing between the person's learning disability and any mental health problem.

A holistic approach to mental health assessment is seen as good practice, and encourages consideration of a whole range of issues including environment, significant life events, current care practices, changes (such as transitions, staff changes, routine changes, day service changes, etc), evidence of traumatic experiences, and so on. Physical ill-health should also be carefully assessed; as well as potentially being overshadowed as a mental health problem, some conditions may cause secondary mental health problems. Physical illness and medication may be an underlying cause for a range of symptoms (Deb et al 2001).

Having a format in mind for carrying out an assessment, means you are less likely to forget to ask about a specific area. A suggested format is shown in *Box 3.2.*

Box 3.2. Suggested assessment format

- *History:* Presenting a good history relies upon having all the pertinent information, which can seem difficult when you have so many things to think about. It may be that you need to write things down under headings or draw diagrams/family trees.
- *Referral and where your information has come from:* Where was the patient seen? (At their GP/family home/inpatient setting, etc) Who referred them? (GP/police/consultant etc) Whose reports have you gained information from?
- *Presenting complaints:* Why has this person been referred to you? And why now? What has changed for this person? Record what they feel their problems are and how long they have been present.
- *History of difficulties:* Record the information as the individual's complaints are explored, taking note of whether they are following a train of thought or seem quite jumbled. If, for example, a patient complains of hearing voices then this needs to be explored in the same way that a complaint of pain would be. It is also important to remember to ask how much of an impact these problems are having on the individual's life and the lives of loved ones and carers.

- *Past psychiatric history:* Explore any previous contact with mental health services. If possible, gain information regarding when they were seen, by whom, including their profession, what type of work they engaged in, and the outcome.
- *Past medical history:* This includes a detailed history of physical health ailments, hospital appointments, long-term conditions, acute health problems, including regular episodes of recurrent infections, and medication.
- *Family history:* For assessment to be holistic, a bio-psycho-social formulation should be drawn upon that includes family history, where known. Here it is important to gain information regarding any family history of psychiatric or relevant medical conditions. Remember to include any neurological disorders, suicides, abuse, drug and/or alcohol misuse, criminal behaviour, etc.
- *Personal history:* Topics to be covered may include early development, childhood behaviour, school/educational history, occupational history including day centre or similar facilities, sexual relationships, marriage history, children/stepchildren, types of residential accommodation, changes in settings, and forensic history. This list is not exhaustive and other details particular to the individual may need to be considered.
- *Premorbid personality:* What were the individuals like before things changed for them? What was their mood like and what were they like as a person?
- *Current social circumstances:* Consider how they are managing with social relationships, do they have any hobbies or interests? Who do they live with? What social support do they have? Consider social networks available in their work place, day centre or college, or if they choose not to attend. Finally, consider the relationship they have with staff members. There may be changes in their social circumstances – have people left the home? Has there been a change in key worker?
- *Medication:* List all medication, prescribed and otherwise. This may also be an opportunity to ask about drug and/or alcohol use.
- *Mental state examination:* You will be assessing someone's mental state from the minute you meet them and all the questions that you have asked will give you an indication of their mental state. Be aware of how the patient is responding to you, are they shy and passive or are they shouting and abusive? Do they seem to be clean and tidy or dishevelled and chaotic? Your examination of the patient's mental state is at the time that you see them and not the history of their past experiences. So, if you see a patient who was hallucinating the day before, their morbid experiences would be described in their history, not in the mental state examination.

How do I assess psychiatric symptoms?
Catherine Hart and Chris Knifton

A wide range of assessment tools is available, and some of these have been designed specifically for people with learning disabilities. It is important to note however that assessment tools are not diagnostic tools. Individual organisations and services will have their own routine assessment tools, some of which require specific training in their use. It is your responsibility to familiarise yourself with your organisation's own assessment policy/guidance and the assessment tools in use. A range of different professionals may be involved in carrying out assessment, as well as nurses. Examples of specific assessment tools specifically designed for people with learning disabilities that screen for a wide range of mental health problems are listed in *Table 3.1*.

Table 3.1. Specific mental health assessment tools used in learning disability		
Assessment of Dual Diagnosis (ADD) Matson and Bamburg (1998)	79 item screening instrument for people with mild/moderate learning disabilities.13 subscales	Healthcare professionals can use, after training. Takes approximately 20 minutes to complete
Camberwell Assessment of Need for Adults with Developmental and/ or Intellectual Disability (CANDID) Xenitidis et al (2003)	Semi-structured interview. 25 areas of need considered	Formal training not required, although experience of clinical assessment is. Takes 10–15 minutes to complete
Cardinal Needs Schedule – Learning Disability Version (LDCNS) Raghaven et al (2004)	23 assessed areas of functioning. Includes interviews and rating scales	Can be used by nurses.Training required for data input and needs analysis

Dementia Scale for Down's Syndrome (DSDS) Gedye (1995)	Measures early, middle and late stages of dementia.	Use restricted to clinical psychologists and trained psychometricians
Dementia Questionnaire for People with Learning Disabilities (DLD) (formerly known as DMR) Evenhuis et al (2007)	Screening tool for early detection of dementia. 50 items based around 8 sub-scales	Completed by carers
Diagnostic Assessment for the Severely Handicapped – II (DASH-II) Matson (1995)	84 items based around 13 diagnostic categories. Similar to ADD, but designed specifically for people with a severe/ profound learning disability. Based on an interview with a carer who has known the client for at least 6 months	Can be carried out by a healthcare professional. Takes 20–30 minutes to complete
Psychiatric Assessment Schedule for Adults with Developmental Disabilities (PAS-ADD) Moss (2002)	3 different formats, including a semi-structured interview and a checklist. 29 identifiable psychiatric symptoms in the previous 4 weeks. Includes PAS-ADD Checklist, Mini PAS-ADD 9 informant-rated screening tool and PAS-ADD interview	The interview takes 30 minutes to complete, possibly more
Psychopathology Instrument for Mentally Retarded Adults (PIMRA) Matson (1988)	Rating scale	
Reiss Screen for Maladaptive Behaviour Reiss (1994)	38 items covering 8 scales	Takes 20 minutes to complete

Which diagnostic criteria or system should be used in learning disability?
Catherine Hart

Different systems are currently in place to classify, and therefore to reach a diagnosis for, a mental health disorder. These include the International Classification of Diseases (ICD-10) (World Health Organisation 1993), and the Diagnostic and Statistical Manual of Mental disorders (DSM-IV) (American Psychiatric Association 1994). These systems are used to classify mental disorder in the general population, and as such may not be as sensitive to the potentially atypical presentation of signs and symptoms among people with learning disabilities. A further system, DC-LD was therefore developed by the Royal College of Psychiatrists (2001). DC-LD stands for 'Diagnostic Criteria for Psychiatric Disorders for use with Adults with Learning Disabilities/Mental Retardation'. It is designed to be used alongside the ICD-10 for people with mild learning disabilities, or as a standalone tool for people with moderate, severe, and profound learning disabilities. The nearest equivalent DSM-IV codes can also be cross referenced with the DC-LD.

Choice over systems may vary between organisations. However, in general (but not exclusively), most European countries favour ICD-10, whilst American countries favour DSM-IV. Although there is much similarity between these systems, differences do occur and this can have a big impact on diagnosis. One example of this can be found with dementia where Strydom et al (2007) found that DSM-IV dementia criteria were more inclusive than ICD-10 in recognising dementia signs and symptoms.

It is important that you familiarise yourself with the diagnostic tool used within your own organisation.

The usefulness of someone receiving a 'diagnosis' may be viewed differently by different people. In some cases the individual may find it useful to have a description of their difficulties that sums them up well and easily describes their difficulties to other people and health professionals. For example, someone who may have struggled to cope with significant mood swings from feeling quite low and lethargic to elated and full of energy, along with impulsive behaviour, may feel relief at having a diagnosis of bi-polar disorder. Diagnosis helps them to understand their symptoms, and allows them access to appropriate services and interventions. However, there are some schools of thought that suggest that receiving a mental health diagnosis is labelling and stigmatising for individuals. Receiving a diagnosis for some people may make them feel that they have been reduced to a label or an ICD-10 code without anyone really understanding their difficulties. There is also an argument which suggests that some people may find it hard to take ownership of their difficulties if they were given a diagnosis, although others may feel that not having so much responsibility for their difficulties makes them easier to live with.

A complete psychological formulation would take into account biological, social, psychological and interactional factors, within the broader social/cultural and environmental context. In this way, a person's mental health difficulties can be understood from a number of perspectives and may help individuals to gain understanding about their difficulties, without stigmatising them.

What is meant by the term 'diagnostic overshadowing'?
Chris Knifton

Diagnostic overshadowing refers to the person's learning disability traits being inappropriately viewed as signs/symptoms of a mental health disorder, or even the reverse when signs/symptoms of a mental health disorder are left unrecognised and inappropriately attributed to an individual's learning disability. One interesting example of diagnostic overshadowing can be seen in distinguishing between the negative symptoms of schizophrenia (such as withdrawal, reduced communication, flattened mood) and autism.

What is the role of the clinical psychologist?
Catherine Hart

Psychologists aim to reduce psychological distress, and enhance and promote psychological wellbeing (Harvey 2001). The strengths of the role of clinical psychologists lie in the breadth and depth of knowledge that they possess as well as the experience and skills they bring to their role. The core skills highlighted in the document: *Core purpose and philosophy of the profession* (Division of Clinical Psychology, British Psychological Society 2001) outlines the core skill areas that chartered psychologists work in. These are listed below.

Assessment

The assessment process underpins the work of a clinical psychologist. Assessments may be in the form of admission assessments, regular outcome measures to assess change in a client, or standardised psychometric assessment. Assessing and collating data relating to behavioural analysis also identifies targets at which interventions can be aimed, as well as assessing the level of effectiveness of a treatment.

Formulation

Psychological formulations are an integral aspect of the clinical psychologist's role. Collaborative formulations may be used to assist the multidisciplinary team to be aware of many factors that affect clients' presentation as well as any outstanding issues with their care and treatment. Formulation also ensures that clients are not treated in a symptom–technique matching way; this is especially important when working with severe cases where individuals display multiple disorders. Ideally, these are also reviewed with clients and form important guidelines for their treatment.

Intervention

Psychologists work in a range of different clinical areas, therefore utilising different treatment approaches and therapeutic models. However, despite the differences in treatment models, many psychologists will work on many levels, including individual and group therapy, consultation with the care system and with the wider system dynamics.

What are the common mental health problems experienced by people with a learning disability?
Catherine Hart and Chris Knifton

Anxiety disorders

Anxiety is common amongst most people and is generally limited to a specific event, such as an exam, a driving test, or starting a new job. However, if the anxiety shows no signs of abating and starts to interfere with normal activities of daily living and routine, an anxiety disorder might need to be considered. A range of anxiety disorders may be diagnosed, including generalised anxiety disorders, phobic anxiety disorders, panic disorders, post-traumatic stress disorders and obsessive-compulsive disorders. Common signs and symptoms of anxiety disorders may include:

- A constant feeling of 'tenseness' or feeling on edge all the time.

- A level of anxiety that is interfering with school/work/day-to-day responsibilities.
- The experience of irrational fears with an inability to rationalise the fear.
- Avoidance of everyday situations or activities because of the anxious feelings they engender.
- Sudden, unexpected attacks of panic.

Because anxiety disorders are a group of related conditions rather than a single disorder, they can present very differently from person to person. But despite their different forms, all anxiety disorders share one major symptom: persistent or severe fear or worry in situations where most people would not feel threatened.

It is important to note that, for people with autistic disorders, when routines are disrupted and result in anxiety, this should not be diagnosed as a new anxiety disorder (Deb et al 2001). It is important to differentiate between the symptoms of anxiety disorders and symptoms such as irritability and over-activity which may occur in mania or hypomania (Deb et al 2001) (see below).

NICE Clinical Guidance 113 (2011) for the management of generalised anxiety disorders (GAD) suggests a stepped model of care in collaboration with a person-centred approach to treatment. Registered nurses working with people with a GAD need to familiarise themselves with this guideline.

If someone is presenting with their first episode of GAD or this has just been brought to your attention, then the first step is to correctly identify and communicate this in order to help the individual understand the impact of the disorder and to start effective treatment as soon as possible.

In individuals with a learning disability, consider the diagnosis of GAD if their mood alters unexpectedly and they are displaying a high level of anxiety or significant worry. Somatic complaints may have become more noticeable as they may have increased in frequency. Sometimes individuals are not able to verbalise their feelings and may instead complain of unexplainable pains in their body, etc.

NICE (2011) guidance recommends that if GAD does not seem to have improved after psycho-education and active monitoring then low intensity interventions may be tried. These may include:

- Individual non-facilitated self-help.
- Individual guided self-help.
- Psycho-educational groups.

If marked functional impairment is still evident then treatment options may include either:

• An individual high-intensity psychological intervention (e.g. CBT/applied relaxation), *or*
• Drug treatment (e.g. an SSRI).

Interventions may need to be adapted to suit an individual's needs, although, unless the individual has a severe learning disability, interventions outlined above can be used.

Bi-polar, mania and hypomania disorders

Bi-polar is the preferred terminology for a disorder sometimes referred to as manic-depression. Here, a person will alternate in mood between periods of elation (mania) and depression. During periods of elation, referred to as manic episodes, the person may appear excitable and there is an accompanying change in behaviour. This usually involves an increase in activity and may include reckless behaviours such as over-spending or promiscuity in some instances. There is an accompanying lack of insight and grandiose ideas. Agitation may frequently accompany manic episodes. Mania, as a diagnosis, refers to people who do not have accompanying depression, and hypomania may be viewed as a milder form of mania in people with a learning disability, in whom evidence of elated mood may also be associated with aggression (Deb et al 2001). It may be possible to diagnose mania in people with severe and profound learning disability, as symptoms can still be evidenced through observation and family/care-giver accounts (Deb et al 2001, Reid 1972). Vanstraelen et al (2003) note importantly that vomiting, regression, confusion, aggression and self-injury may be signs of such affective disorders.

As a registered nurse, it is important you follow NICE (2006) guidance in ensuring provision for an annual physical health review that includes: lipid levels, including cholesterol in all patients aged over 40; plasma glucose levels; weight; smoking status; alcohol use; and blood pressure.

Important guidance for nurses working with clients with mania or bipolar disorders is available in NICE Clinical Guidance 38 (2006).

Dementia

Dementia is an umbrella term for a condition causing progressive deterioration to the brain, and may take several forms. The commonest form of dementia is Alzheimer's disease, but a great many other forms exist including vascular dementias and dementia with Lewy bodies. It is important to note that people with a learning disability are at higher risk of developing dementia then the general population. People with Down's syndrome, in particular, are at greater risk (British Psychological Society and Royal College of Psychiatrists 2009). In addition, people with Down's syndrome are more likely to develop dementia at a younger age then the general population (Alzheimer's Society 2000) with the peak incidence occurring in their early 50s (British Psychological Society and Royal College of Psychiatrists 2009).

In particular, people with Down's syndrome are at higher risk of developing Alzheimer's disease (Oliver and Holland 1986; Janicki and Dalton 2000). Perhaps the biggest difficulty in terms of diagnosing dementia in people with a learning disability is the lack of reliable and standardised criteria, diagnostic procedures (Deb et al 2001) and appropriate baseline comparisons. Previously, general population neuropsychological assessments have been used, sometimes adapted, for people with learning disabilities. This has caused difficulties due to variability in the degree of learning disability, as it is impossible to apply normative data to these assessments. A poor performance on these types of test, which would usually indicate dementia, may just be picking up the underlying learning disability.

Routine day-to-day activities of people with a learning disability place very little demand on their cognitive abilities. This lack of change and challenge may make early, and often more subtle, signs of dementia very difficult to detect. This also makes it difficult to collect baseline and background information on individuals if they live in care environments, since the high turnover of staff means that the person's 'normal' level of functioning and subtle changes to this may be missed.

The British Psychological Society and Royal College of Psychiatrists (2009) advise that every adult with Down's syndrome should be assessed at the age of 30 to establish a baseline. This can then be used to compare any future changes when dementia is suspected (see, for example, Kalsy et al 2005, Jervis and Prinsloo 2007).

Best practice shows that assessment over time is essential and should incorporate both neuropsychological assessment with the person with learning disability (if appropriate) and information from other people who know the individual well. It also remains important for the individual to have a full health screen and further investigations so as to rule out any other physical conditions which may be impacting on cognitive functioning. Examples of assessment tools include:

- Dementia Questionnaire for People with Learning Disabilities (DLD) (Evenhuis et al 2007)
- Dementia Screening Questionnaire for Individuals with Intellectual Disabilities (DSQIID) (Deb et al 2007)
- Dementia Scale for Down's Syndrome (DSDS) (Gedye 1995).

The NICE guidelines state that people with dementia should not be excluded from any services because of their diagnosis, age (whether designated too young or too old) or due to a coexisting learning disability.

Treatment interventions may include:

- Memory assessment services (which may be provided by a memory assessment clinic or by a community mental health team) are the single point of referral for all people with a possible diagnosis of dementia.
- Structural imaging should be used to exclude other cerebral pathologies and to help establish the subtype diagnosis. Magnetic resonance imaging (MRI) may be the preferred option to assist with early diagnosis and detect subcortical vascular changes, although computed tomography (CT) scanning can also be used. Specialist advice should be taken when interpreting scans in people with learning disabilities.
- People with dementia who develop non-cognitive symptoms that cause them significant distress or who develop behaviour that challenges should be offered assessment to establish factors that may generate, aggravate or improve such behaviour. The assessment should be comprehensive and include:
  - the person's physical health
  - depression
  - possible undetected pain or discomfort
  - side effects of medication
  - individual biography, including religious beliefs and spiritual and cultural identity
  - psychosocial factors
  - physical environmental factors
  - behavioural and functional analysis conducted by professionals with specific skills, in conjunction with carers and care workers.

Health and social care managers should ensure that all staff working with older adults with learning disabilities have access to dementia care training consistent with their roles and responsibilities.

Registered nurses working with people with learning disabilities and dementia need to be familiar with NICE Clinical Guidance 42 (2006, revised March 2011) on dementia, and the British Psychological Society and Royal College of Psychiatrists (2009) guidance on the assessment, diagnosis, treatment and support of people with learning disabilities who develop dementia.

Depression

In mild to moderate learning disability, individuals may be able to describe their symptoms. In profound or severe learning disability, this may not be as possible. The nurse must pay careful attention to outward signs that may manifest in behaviour and/or appearance. This may include changes in posture, restlessness, agitation, self-neglect, sleep disturbances, appetite changes, withdrawal, reduced energy/initiative, marked loss of interest, worsening mood in the morning, etc. Vanstraelen et al (2003) note importantly that vomiting, as well as regression, confusion, aggression and self-injury may be signs of such disorders. Priest and Gibbs (2004) note that depression may also manifest in physical symptoms, including headache or fatigue.

Debate continues as to whether rates of depression are higher in people with Down's syndrome (Collacott et al 1992) or lower (Haveman et al 1994).

Tools specifically designed for assessing depression, and thus of use when evaluating treatment, include the Hamilton Rating Scale for Depression (Hamilton 1967), the Beck Depression Inventory (Beck et al 1996), and the Zung Self-Rating Depression Scale (Zung 1965). There is evidence that these tools have successfully been used with people with learning disabilities (Priest and Gibbs 2004).

Personality disorders

Personality disorders remain a controversial area of psychiatry. One of the theories of the development of personality disorders, and of relevance to people with learning disabilities, is attachment theory.

Attachment is described as an emotional bond to another person. John Bowlby was the first attachment theorist, describing attachment as a 'lasting psychological connectedness between human beings' (Bowlby 1969: 194). Bowlby believed that the earliest bonds formed by children with their caregivers had a tremendous impact that continued throughout their life. According to Bowlby, attachment also serves to keep the infant close to the mother, thus improving the child's chances of survival.

The central theme of attachment theory is that mothers who are available and responsive to their infant's needs establish a sense of security. The infant knows that the caregiver is dependable, which creates a secure base for the child to then explore the world. However, when a child does not experience his or her caregiver as a 'secure base' then difficulties in the child's attachment pattern may become evident. Theorists have suggested that a difficulty with attachments (or disorganised attachments) in early life can develop into more serious difficulties relating to people expressing and managing emotions in later life. Children diagnosed with oppositional-defiant disorder (ODD), conduct disorder (CD), or post-traumatic stress disorder (PTSD) frequently display attachment problems, possibly due to early abuse, neglect, or trauma. Clinicians also suggest that children adopted after the age of six months have a higher risk of problems with attachment than the general population.

While attachment styles displayed in adulthood are not necessarily the same as those seen in infancy, research suggests that early attachments can have a serious impact on later relationships. Often, what may have been described as attachment difficulties in childhood develop into persistent personality difficulties in adulthood. These types of difficulties are sometimes given the title 'personality disorders'. This diagnosis really describes a cluster of symptoms that may have their roots in disorganised attachments. People who have received this diagnosis may find that they have disturbances in self-image; have difficulty with making and sustaining successful interpersonal relationships; find it hard to understand or display an appropriate range of emotion; perceive themselves, others, and the world differently; and have difficulty possessing an adequate level of impulse control.

Attachment theory and the development of personality difficulties is pertinent in the field of learning disability as individuals with a learning disability may, in some cases, be more susceptible to the factors which can lead to the development of a disorganised attachment style, and ultimately pervasive personality difficulties. These factors may include:

- Inconsistent parenting.
- Experience of rejection/abandonment at home or at school.
- Communication difficulties.
- Challenging behaviours.
- 'Special' schooling.

Deb et al (2001) note that making a diagnosis of personality disorder in a person with severe learning disability is difficult, arguing that it may only be possible to give a good description of the behaviours observed, and assess the circumstances around them.

Communication problems and physical, sensory and behavioural disorders associated with learning disability affect the ability to diagnose a personality disorder (Khan et al 1997). The diagnosis of personality disorders often requires subjective information about thoughts and emotions, difficult to elicit in those with severe degrees of learning disability. Consequently, difficulties arise and a particular pattern of behaviour diagnosed as 'personality disorder' in those with mild or moderate learning disability may be perceived as 'behavioural disorder' in those with severe or profound disability.

The criteria for several personality disorders assume a level of cognitive ability which may be absent in those with learning disability. Dissocial (Goldberg et al 1995) and paranoid personality disorders are examples. Difficulties in establishing concepts such as preoccupation with unsubstantiated, conspiratorial explanations of events either immediate to the patient or 'in the world at large' in a group with significant cognitive limitations are self-evident.

Further problems include the lack of valid, reliable instruments (Khan et al 1997), differences between ICD-10 and DSM-IV criteria, confusion of definition, different personality theories (Goldberg et al 1995), and the difficulty in distinguishing personality disorders from late effects of childhood psychosis (Corbett 1979).

People with a learning disability often display behaviours that overlap with features of some personality disorders. For example, earlier studies (Craft 1959) suggested that schizoid personalities were very common in people with learning disability. A significant proportion of those so labelled may actually have had autism (Deb and Hunter 1991). Autistic traits also overlap significantly with features of anankastic personality disorder.

Features of borderline personality disorder, such as self-injurious behaviour, impulsiveness and affective lability, occur commonly in learning disability (Mavromatis 2000). Consequently, additional features should be sought before making this diagnosis (Wilson 2001). Affective disorders commonly found in learning disability also mimic features of emotionally unstable personalities (Deb and Hunter, 1991).

Some examples of personality disorders are given in *Table 3.2.*

Table 3.2. Examples of personality disorders	
Disorder	*Short description*
Borderline personality disorder	Borderline personality disorder is a mental illness characterised by pervasive instability in moods, interpersonal relationships, self-image, and behaviour (often associated with high levels of self-harm and para-suicidal behaviours)
Schizoid personality	Schizoid personality disorder is a psychiatric condition characterised by a lifelong pattern of indifference to others and social isolation
Schizotypal personality	Schizotypal personality disorder is primarily characterised by peculiarities of thinking, odd beliefs, and eccentricities of appearance, behaviour, interpersonal style, and thought
Paranoid personality	Paranoid personality disorder is a psychiatric condition characterised by extreme distrust and suspicion of others
Antisocial personality	Antisocial personality disorder is a psychiatric condition characterised by chronic behaviour that manipulates, exploits, or violates the rights of others
Avoidant personality disorder	Avoidant personality disorder is an active-detached personality pattern, meaning that individuals may purposefully avoid others due to fears of humiliation and rejection
Narcissistic personality	Narcissistic personality disorder is characterised by self-centredness. Like histrionic disorder, people with this disorder seek attention and praise
Histrionic (hysterical) personality	Histrionic personality disorder involves a pattern of excessive emotional expression and care-seeking behaviours, including an excessive need for approval and inappropriate seductiveness
Passive-aggressive (negativistic) personality	Passive-aggressive personality disorder is characterised by an individual appearing to acquiesce to the desires and needs of others, but actually passively resisting them and becoming increasingly hostile and angry
Dependent personality	Dependent personality disorder is described as an over-reliance on others to meet emotional and physical needs
Personality disorder NOS	Personality disorder not otherwise specified is reserved for disorders that do not fit into the other personality disorder categories.

Obsessive-compulsive personality disorder	Obsessive-compulsive personality disorder is a condition characterised by a chronic preoccupation with rules, orderliness, and control

Schizophrenia

The diagnosis of schizophrenia remains, in part, a recognition of subjective symptoms that include alterations to thought processes and perceptions. Essentially this diagnosis is used when there are disrupted beliefs and/or experiences and where the person's perception of the world does not match reality. Examples may include delusions, hallucinations and thought broadcasting. In general, the signs and symptoms of schizophrenia are usually divided into positive and negative symptoms. Positive symptoms include delusions and hallucinations, and negative symptoms include withdrawal, reduced motivation, and self-neglect, although this list is not exhaustive. Impaired communication, particularly limited verbal skills, may make these features difficult to identify in people with a learning disability (Gravestock et al 2005). It may also be difficult to differentiate between the negative symptoms of schizophrenia and other mental health problems such as depression. Diagnosing schizophrenia in people with a moderate to severe learning disability is difficult (Royal College of Psychiatrists 2001). A particular difficulty may be found in autism, where 'fantasy thinking', a possible symptom in autism spectrum disorder, needs distinguishing from psychotic symptoms (Deb et al 2001). 'Imaginary friends', a feature not uncommon in learning disability may be confused with psychotic symptoms. Indeed there is difficulty in being absolutely certain if hallucinations are actually being experienced (Royal College of Psychiatrists 2001).

In people with a learning disability, Gravestock et al (2005) argue, psychopathology (i.e. persecutory delusions, thought disorders, etc.) is lessened, although there is a risk of increased displays of bizarre behaviour. In addition, they note that delusion content is more bland.

Schizophrenia may occur in approximately 3% of the learning disability population (Deb 2001).

What psychological interventions can be used?
Catherine Hart

Psychological interventions are perhaps best known as 'talking therapies', and there remains a growing awareness that they can be equally effective for people with learning disabilities. However, there remains a lack of research in determining the most effective type (Hatton 2002). Currently, psychological interventions most often used with people with learning disabilities include behavioural approaches, cognitive-behavioural therapy (CBT), systemic approaches, humanistic counselling, and psychodynamic approaches. Both group and individual sessions may be used after careful assessment based on individual need. These approaches are particularly useful with people who have depression, anxiety disorders, eating disorders, and psychotic symptoms. Some learning disability nurses may choose to undertake further training to qualify in psychological therapies such as CBT.

What social interventions can be used?
Chris Knifton

Hardy et al (2005) divide social interventions into community, individual (such as coping skills, social skills and communication, assertiveness, etc.), home interventions, and interventions that focus on how individuals spend their day. Other examples also include family therapy (Association for Family Therapy 2003). Some learning disability nurses may choose to undertake further training to qualify as family therapists and others become particularly adept in facilitating social skills or assertiveness training.

Are mental health disorders associated with specific learning disability phenotypes?
Catherine Hart and Chris Knifton

Great care needs to be taken when considering this question. Associating a mental health disorder with a form/type of learning disability opens up very real concerns for diagnostic overshadowing. For example, if one considers the clear evidence on the correlation between Alzheimer's disease and Down's syndrome, there is a risk that deterioration in the behaviour and performance of activities of daily living of someone in their 40s with Down's syndrome will be attributed to dementia. However, other vulnerability factors may be the reason, and could include a change in environment, bereavement/attachment losses (including key worker/staff changes), medication changes, hypothyroidism/physical ill-health, or depression.

However, the literature does point to some phenotypes as perhaps associated with mental health problems and these are summarised in *Table 3.3*. (See *Chapter 1* for further discussion on phenotypes or types of learning disability).

However, the Royal College of Psychiatrists (2001) also notes that several

Table 3.3. Mental health disorders and learning disability phenotypes	
Mental health problem	*Associated phenotype*
Anxiety	Fragile X Syndrome (Bregman et al 1988, Royal College of Psychiatrists 2001), Phenylketonuria (Royal College of Psychiatrists 2001)
Dementia	Down's syndrome (Cooper and Collacott 1994, Deb et al 2001, Khan et al 2002)
Depression	Down's syndrome (Collacott et al 1992) Turner syndrome (Royal College of Psychiatrists 2001)
Mood disorders	Foetal alcohol syndrome (particularly in children), Prader-Willi syndrome Rubenstein-Taybi syndrome (Royal College of Psychiatrists 2001)
Cycloid psychosis (acute polymorphic psychotic disorder without symptoms of schizophrenia)	Prader-Willi syndrome (Verhoeven et al 1998)
Schizophrenia	Prader-Willi syndrome

causes of learning disability are also associated with characteristic behaviours. Here, any symptoms, they argue, that are necessary clinical features of a learning disability phenotype, should *not* then also be recorded as a separate mental health disorder. They provide the example of over-eating in Prader-Willi syndrome; overeating is a necessary feature when diagnosing Prader-Willi, and, as such, making an additional diagnosis to include eating disorder, is not necessary.

Should generic mental health or specialist mental health and learning disability services be used?
Chris Knifton

There is still much debate as to whether people with a learning disability who have additional mental health needs should access mainstream or generic mental health services. Priest and Gibbs (2004) suggest that argument for the use of generic services stems from normalisation philosophy, noting that this includes access to 'culturally normative experiences of society', such as the use of generic services available to the general population. Day (1995) however has argued that current mental health services cannot satisfactorily meet the needs of this client group.

Alexander et al (2001) provide some interesting discussion about the differences between these two services. It is indeed reasonable to suggest that people with mild learning disabilities may be appropriately served by generic services, whilst those with more moderate, severe or profound learning disability may have their needs more appropriately met through specialist services. Priest and Gibbs (2004) indeed propose: 'It is likely, then, for the foreseeable future that as "one size does not fit all", both approaches to service delivery for this client group will be required' (2004: 171).

What is the meant by the Green Light Toolkit and what is the learning disability nurse's role?
Sharon Clay

The National Service Framework for Mental Health (Department of Health 1999) aimed to improve quality and effectiveness of care, challenge inequalities in accessing care and enhance service user and carer experience of mental health services. Those with a learning disability who also have a mental illness should be able to access service with reasonable adjustments.

Reports such as the Michael Inquiry, *Healthcare for all* (Michael 2008) and Mencap's *Death by indifference* (2009) highlighted unmet healthcare needs for people with a learning disability. The evidence and recommendations from such reports are equally appropriate to mental health trusts.

Green Light is a framework and self-audit for the improvement of mental health support services for those with learning disabilities. The Green Light Toolkit was developed by the Valuing People Support Team to assist mental health services with assessing the standard of accessibility of services to people with a learning disability (Foundation for People with Learning Disabilities et al 2004).

What is the role of the learning disability nurse in using this?

Learning disability nurses have a valued part to play in the implementation of the Green Light Toolkit within mental health services. They will often have worked across a wide variety of community, acute and primary care settings and have played an integral part in health promotion and in improving access to mainstream community services, including mental health services for those with learning disabilities. This is an opportunity for learning disability nurses to embrace further collaborative working with other healthcare professionals in mental health services and to share their specialist knowledge, skills, and flexible approaches to communication and assessment to meet people's healthcare needs.

Hopefully, this will encourage and expand knowledge of other professionals and positively change attitudes and beliefs around supporting and caring for individuals with a learning disability, thus enabling them to access mental health services.

Is there any published guidance for nurses working in this area?
Chris Knifton

A useful practice guideline produced by the European Association for Mental Health in Mental Retardation (EAMHMR), published in 2001, offers a systematic collection of evidence-based practice within this area (Deb et al 2001). In 2007 the RCN produced guidance for nurses in mental health services delivering healthcare to people with learning disabilities (Royal College of Nursing 2007). Where dual diagnosis is also linked to offending behaviour, the Care Services Improvement Partnership has produced additional guidance (Betts and Zammit 2007). For people with a dual diagnosis including dementia, the British Psychological Society and the Royal College of Psychiatrists (2009) jointly produced *Dementia and people with learning disabilities – Guidance on the assessment, diagnosis, treatment and support of people with learning disabilities who develop dementia*. In addition NICE has produced a series of guidance papers on a wide range of issues affecting mental health that are equally applicable to people with learning disabilities. The Estia Centre and Turning Point have also jointly produced an excellent practical guide for staff working in this area entitled, *Supporting complex needs: A practical guide for support staff working with people with a learning disability who have mental health needs* (Hardy et al 2006). Registered nurses may also find the Code of Practice for the Mental Health Act 1983 (Department of Health 2008), and the Code of Practice for the Mental Capacity Act 2005 (Department for Constitutional Affairs 2007) important considerations.

References

Alexander RT, Piachaud J, Singh I (2001) Two districts, two models: In-patient care in the psychiatry of learning disabilities. *British Journal of Developmental Disabilities* **47**(2):105–10

Alzheimer's Society (2000) *Learning disabilities and dementia*. Alzheimer's Society, Brighton, Sussex

American Psychiatric Association (1994) *Diagnostic statistical manual IV.* American Psychiatric Publishing Inc, Arlington

Association for Family Therapy (2003) *What is family therapy?* Available from: http://www.aft.org.uk

Beck A, Steer R, Brown G (1996) *The Beck Depression Inventory II.* Harcourt Brace and Co, San Antonio

Betts N, Zammit B (2007) *Positive practice, positive outcomes: A handbook for professionals in the criminal justice system working with offenders with learning disabilities.* Care Services Improvement Partnership, London

Borthwick-Duffy S-A (1994) Epidemiology and prevalence of psychopathology in people with mental retardation. *Journal of Consulting and Clinical Psychology* **62**:17–27

Bowlby J (1969/1999) *Attachment (2nd edn.) Attachment and Loss, Vol 1.* Basic Books, New York

Bregman JD, Leckman JF, Ort SI (1988) Fragile X syndrome; genetic predisposition to psychopathology. *Journal of Autism and Developmental Disorders* **18**: 343–54

British Psychological Society (2001) *The core purpose and philosophy of the profession.* British Psychological Society, Leicester

British Psychological Society and the Royal College of Psychiatrists (2009) *Dementia and people with learning disabilities – Guidance on the assessment, diagnosis, treatment and support of people with learning disabilities who develop dementia.* British Psychological Society, Leicester

Clarke D (1999) Functional psychoses in people with mental retardation. In Bouras N (ed) *Psychiatric and behavioural disorders in developmental disabilities.* Cambridge University Press, Cambridge

Collacott RA, Cooper S-A, Lewis KR (1992) Differential rates of psychiatric disorders in adults with Down's syndrome compared with other mentally handicapped adults. *British Journal of Psychiatry* **161**: 671–4

Cooper S-A (1997) High prevalence of dementia among people with learning disabilities not attributable to Down's syndrome. *Psychological Medicine* **27**: 609–16

Cooper S-A, Collacott R (1994) Clinical features and diagnostic criteria of depression in Down's syndrome. *British Journal of Psychiatry* **165**: 399–403

Corbett JA (1979) Psychiatric morbidity and mental retardation. In James FE, Snaith RP (eds) *Psychiatric illness and mental handicap.* Royal College of Psychiatrists, London

Craft M (1959) Mental disorder in the defective: A psychiatric survey among in-patients. *American Journal of Mental Deficiency* **63**: 829–34

Day J (2008) The relationship between physical health and mental health. In Dooher J (ed) *Fundamental aspects of mental health nursing* (pp. 147–63). Quay Books, London

Day K (1985) Psychiatric disorders in the middle aged and elderly mentally handicapped. *British Journal of Psychiatry* **147**: 660–7

Day K (1995) Psychiatric services in mental retardation: Generic or specialised provision? In Bouras N (ed) *Mental health in mental retardation: Recent advances and practices* (pp. 275–92). Cambridge University Press, Cambridge,

Day K, Jancar J (1994) Mental and physical health and ageing in mental handicap; a review. *Journal of Intellectual Disability Research* **38**: 241–56

Deb S (2001) Epidemiology of psychiatric illness in adults with intellectual disability. In Hamilton-Kirkwood L, Ahmed Z, Deb S et al (eds) *Health evidence bulletins – Learning disabilities (Intellectual disability)* (pp. 14–17). NHS, Cardiff

Deb S, Hare M, Prior L, Bhaumik S (2007) The dementia screening questionnaire for individuals with intellectual disabilities. *British Journal of Psychiatry* **190**: 440–44

Deb S, Hunter D (1991) Psychopathology of people with mental handicap and epilepsy. II Psychiatric illness. *British Journal of Psychiatry* **159**: 826–30

Deb S, Mathews T, Holt G, Bouras N (2001) *Practice guidelines for the assessment and diagnosis of mental health problems in adults with intellectual disability.* Pavilion, Brighton

Department for Constitutional Affairs (2005) *Mental Capacity Act 2005.* DCA, London

Department for Constitutional Affairs (2007) C*ode of Practice for the Mental Capacity Act 2005.* TSO, London

Department of Health (1999) *Mental health: National service framework.* Stationery Office, London

Department of Health (2001) *Building a safer NHS for patients: Implementing an organisation with a memory.* DH, London

Department of Health (2008) *Mental Health Act 1983: Code of Practice.* TSO, London

Emerson E, Hatton C, Felce D, et al (2001) *Learning disabilities: The fundamental facts.* Mental Health Foundation, London

Evenhuis HM, Kengen MMF, Eurlings HAL.(2007) *Dementia questionnaire for people with learning disabilities (DLD).* UK adaptation. Harcourt Assessment, San Antonio

Foundation for People with Learning Disabilities, Valuing People Support Team and National Institute for Mental Health in England (2004) *Green Light: How good are your mental health services for people with learning disabilities? A service improvement toolkit.* Turning Point, London

Gedye A (1995) *Dementia scale for Down's syndrome – Manual.* Gedye Research and Consulting, Vancouver

Goldberg B, Gitta MZ, Puddephatt A (1995) Personality and trait disturbances in an adult mental retardation population: significance for psychiatric management. *Journal of Intellectual Disability Research* **39**: 284–94

Gravestock S, Flynn A, Hemmings C (2005) Psychiatric disorders in adults with learning disabilities. In Holt G, Hardy S, Bouras N (eds) *Mental health in learning disabilities – A reader* (pp. 7–17). Pavilion Publishing, Brighton

Hamilton M (1967) Development of a rating scale for primary depressive illness. British *Journal of Social and Clinical Psychology* **6**: 278–96

Hardy S, Holt G (2005) Assessment of mental health problems. In Holt G, Hardy S,

Bouras N (eds) *Mental health in learning disabilities – A reader* (pp. 19–26). Pavilion Publishing, Brighton

Hardy S, Kramer R, Holt G, Woodward P, Chaplin E, Janjua A (2006) *Supporting complex needs: A practical guide for support staff working with people with a learning disability who have mental health needs.* Turning Point, London

Hardy S, Woodward P , Barnes J (2005) Social Interventions. In Holt G, Hardy S, Bouras N (eds) *Mental health in learning disabilities – A reader* (pp. 49–56). Pavilion Publishing, Brighton

Harvey P (2001) *The core purpose and philosophy of the profession.* British Psychological Society, Leicester

Hatton C (2002) Psychosocial interventions for adults with intellectual disabilities and mental health problems: A review. *Journal of Mental Health* **11**(4): 357–73

Haveman MJ, Maaskant MA, Van Schrojenstein HM, Urlings HFJ, Kessels AGH (1994) Mental health problems in elderly people with and without Down's syndrome. *Journal of Intellectual Disability Research* **38**(3): 341–55

Janicki MP, Dalton AJ (2000) Prevalence of dementia and impact on intellectual disability services. *Mental Retardation* **38**: 276–88

Jervis N, Prinsloo L (2007) How we developed a multidisciplinary screening project for people with Down's syndrome given the increased prevalence of early onset dementia. *British Journal of Learning Disability* **36**: 13–21

Kalsy S, McQuillan S, Adams D, Basra T, Konstantinidi E, Broquard M, Peters S, Lloyd V, Oliver C (2005) A proactive psychological strategy for determining the presence of dementia in adults with Down syndrome: Preliminary description of service use and evaluation. *Journal of Policy and Practice in Intellectual Disabilities* **2**(2): 116–25

Khan A, Cowan C, Roy A (1997) Personality disorders in people with learning disabilities. A community survey. *Journal of Intellectual Disability Research* **41**: 324–30

Khan S, Osinowo T, Pary R (2002) Down syndrome and major depressive disorder: A review. *Mental Health Aspects of Developmental Disabilities* **5**(2): 46–52

Matson JL (1988) *The PIMRA manual.* International Diagnostic Systems, Los Angeles.

Matson JL (1995) *The diagnostic assessment for the severely handicapped II.* Scientific Publishers, Baton Rouge

Matson JL, Bamburg J (1998) Reliability of the assessment of dual diagnosis (ADD). *Research in Developmental Disabilities* **20**: 89–95

Mavromatis M (2000) The diagnosis and treatment of borderline personality disorder in persons with developmental disability – 3 case reports. *Mental Health Aspects of Developmental Disabilities* **3**: 89–97

Mentality and NIMHE (2004) *Healthy body and mind: Promoting healthy living for people who experience mental distress: A guide for people working in primary health care teams supporting people working with severe and enduring mental illness.* Mentality and NIMHE.

Michael J (2008) *Healthcare for all: Report of the independent inquiry into access to healthcare for people with learning disabilities.* DH, London

Moss S (2002) *The mini PAS-ADD interview pack.* Pavilion Publishing, Brighton

NICE (2006) *Clinical guidelines: Bipolar disorder. The management of bi-polar disorder in adults, children and adolescents in primary and secondary care.* NICE, London

NICE (2010) *Delirium: Diagnosis, prevention and management.* NICE, London

NICE (2011) *Clinical guidelines: Generalised anxiety disorder and panic disorder (with or without agoraphobia) in adults. Management in primary, secondary and community care.* National Collaborating Centre for Mental Health and the National Collaborating Centre for Primary Care, London

NICE/SCIE (2006) *Clinical guidelines: Dementia. Supporting people with dementia and their carers in health and social care.* NICE/SCIE, London

Oliver C, Holland AJ (1986) Down's syndrome and Alzheimer's disease: A review. *Psychological Medicine* **16**: 307–22

Phelan M, Stradins L, Morrison S (2001) Physical health of people with severe mental illness can be improved if primary care and mental health professionals pay attention to it. *British Medical Journal* **322**: 43–4

Priest H, Gibbs M (2004) *Mental health care for people with learning disabilities.* Churchill Livingstone, London

Raghavan R, Marshall M, Lockwood L, Duggan L (2004) Assessing the needs of people with learning disabilities and mental illness: Development of the Learning Disability version of the Cardinal Needs Schedule. *Journal of Intellectual Disability Research* **48**: 25–37

Raghavan R, Patel P (2005) *Learning disabilities and mental health.* Oxford Blackwell, London

Reid AH (1972) Psychoses in adult mental defectives: I. Manic depressive psychosis. *British Journal of Psychiatry* **120**: 205–12

Reiss S (1994) *The Reiss screen for maladaptive behaviour test manual* (2nd edn). IDS Publishing, Worthington, OH

Royal College of Nursing (2007) *Mental health nursing of adults with learning disabilities. RCN guidance.* Royal College of Nursing, London

Royal College of Psychiatrists (2001) *DC-LD: Diagnostic criteria for psychiatric disorders for use with adults with learning disabilities/mental retardation.* Gaskell, London

Strydom A, Livingston G, King M, Hassiotis A (2007) Prevalence of dementia in intellectual disability using different diagnostic criteria. *British Journal of Psychiatry* **191**: 150–7

Vanstralen M, Holt G, Bouras N (2003) Adults with learning disabilities and psychiatric problems. In Fraser W, Kerr M (eds) *Seminars in the psychiatry of learning disabilities (2nd edn).* Gaskell and the Royal College of Psychiatrists, London

Verhoeven WMA, Curfs LMG, Tuinier S (1998) Prader-Willi syndrome and cycloid psychosis. *Journal of Intellectual Disability Research* **42**: 455–62

Weissman MM (1993) The epidemiology of personality disorders: An update. *Journal of Personality Disorders* **Suppl**: 44–62

Wilson SR (2001) A four stage model for management of borderline personality disorder in people with mental retardation. *Mental Health Aspects of Developmental Disabilities* **4**: 68–76

World Health Organization (1993) *The ICD-10 classification of mental and behavioural disorders: Clinical descriptions and diagnostic guidelines.* WHO, Geneva

Xenitidis K, Slade M, Thornicroft G, Bouras N (2003) *CANIDID: Camberwell Assessment of need for adults with developmental and intellectual disabilities.* Gaskell, London.

Zung WK (1965) A self-rating scale for depression. *Archives of General Psychiatry* **12**: 63–7

NOTES

Chapter 4

Physical health

Nicola Brooks, Jamie Hart, Dorothy Hemel, Amelia Henry, Julia Kew, Tina Kirk, Chris Knifton, Sue Lyons, Kevin Power, Sam Screaton, Daniel Senior, Penny Tremayne, Trish Sealy and Laura Smith

- What are annual health checks?
- What is a Health Action Plan (HAP)?
- What is health facilitation?
- What is a communication passport?
- What should I know about clinical observations for vital signs?
- What do I need to know about enteral feeding?
- What nutrients are essential for a balanced diet, and what foods do they come from?
- How prevalent is obesity, and how would I assess/screen someone for obesity?
- How is obesity managed?
- How would I assess capability for physical activity?
- How can I prepare someone for their first exercise session?
- What does a personal trainer/exercise therapist need to know when a client is referred?
- What are the risks of exercise or prolonged physical activity?
- What is catheterisation?
- How do I deal with healthcare associated infections?
- What do I need to know about pressure ulcers?
- How do I recognise acute ill-health?
- What do I need to know about wound dressings?
- What does an aseptic technique involve?
- What do I do if one of my clients is diagnosed with cancer (or another terminal illness)?

What are annual health checks?
Chris Knifton

People with learning disabilities are less likely to receive regular health checks or routine screening (Mencap 2004, Disability Rights Commission 2006). However,

---

**Box 4.1. Areas to be considered in annual health checks
for people with a learning disability**

- Baseline observations of height and weight
- Baseline observations of vital signs
- Continence support if necessary
- Contraception advice if necessary
- Dental health
- Eye test
- Family history
- General fitness
- Hearing test
- Management of long-term conditions (i.e. asthma, epilepsy, diabetes)
- Medical history
- Medication
- Mental health
- Mobility and posture
- Screening, appropriate to age and gender
- Sexual health

---

there is clear evidence to suggest that people with learning disabilities experience a range of health problems. A response to this has been the introduction of annual health checks which inform Health Action Plans (see below). Annual health checks may be carried out by the person's GP or practice nurse. However, as a learning disability nurse you may be expected to support some aspects of a health check. Examples of what may be included are shown in *Box 4.1*.

What is a Health Action Plan (HAP)?
Sam Screaton, Amelia Henry, Julia Kew and Laura Smith

Health Action Plans originated from the document *Valuing people* (Department of Health 2001). They form part of a person-centred plan and are often developed by the healthcare facilitator (which can often be a learning disability nurse). Examples of areas covered in a HAP include mental health, medication, nutrition, vision, hearing, oral care, sexual health, etc. This list is not exhaustive and it is important that the HAP reflects the person's own lifestyle and choices. They are not static plans, and need to be carried out during important transition periods in the person's life, including changes in service provider and changes in health status. Guidance on HAPs and the role of the health facilitator can be found in the document *Action for health – Health action plans and health facilitation* (Department of Health 2002).

In this guidance, a Health Action Plan is described as:

The actions needed to maintain and improve the health of an individual and any help needed to accomplish these. It is a mechanism to link the individual and the range of services and supports they need, if they are to have better health. Health Action Plans need to be supported by wider changes that assist and sustain this individual approach. The Plan is primarily for the person with learning disabilities and is usually co-produced with them.

(Department of Health 2002:7)

There are five key components to a good Health Action Plan:

* The Plan says what things the person is doing to look after his or her health.
* The Plan belongs to the person and is co-produced with him or her as much as possible; there must be evidence of using person-centred approaches to gather any information.
* The Plan is in a format that the person can understand wherever possible; attempts have been made to make the key actions accessible to the person.
* There is evidence that planned actions have been carried out.
* The Plan has been reviewed as part of an annual health check.

The Health Action Plan should encourage people with a learning disability to think about their health and take more control over meeting their own health needs and planning their lifestyle. For people who do not have capacity, the Health Action Plan should be used as a tool to assess the person's current health, and to identify what actions need to be taken or are already being taken in the person's best interest to improve/maintain good health. This should be done with the people who know the individual best, using the Circle of Support tool. This is a tool used to identify who is important to the person; it usually identifies family and friends and paid/voluntary people, e.g. community nurse and people from work and daytime activities, significant to the individual. It can be used to identify who is the best person to help facilitate a plan with the person but also to ensure that people work together for the person, or to identify who should be involved if it is a 'best interests' plan. It is recognised that it is not always possible to make a plan fully accessible to an individual; in these circumstances it is important that attempts are made to engage with the individual, and that person-centred approaches have been used to develop the person's plan.

It is important to remember that all adults must be assumed to have capacity until proven otherwise. A blanket decision of a person's capacity cannot be made and, therefore, when completing a Health Action Plan with a person who has a learning disability, the person's capacity should be assessed for each health need. A person may be able to make an informed choice about one area of health and be involved in that part of the plan, but may not have capacity in other areas. Therefore, people may have a mixture of Health Action Plan profiles, some that they have been involved in and some that have been drawn up in their best interests.

What is health facilitation?
Sam Screaton, Amelia Henry, Julia Kew and Laura Smith

Health facilitation is about supporting people with a learning disability to have good health and wellbeing. It involves ensuring people with a learning disability receive equal access to health services and that they are put at the centre of any decisions about their health. It is about making it easy for them to be involved.

There are three types of health facilitator:

- *Type 1: Strategic health facilitators* are members of the learning disability health facilitation team employed by the primary care trust. Strategic health facilitators are involved in service development work and in informing the planning and commissioning of health services specifically relating to meeting the needs of people with learning disabilities.
- *Type 2: Specialist health facilitators* include all health professionals, such as learning disability and mental health professionals and primary and secondary care health professionals. Their role is to provide treatment, guidance and advice on specific health issues, usually on a short-term basis in partnership with patients and their individual health facilitators.
- *Type 3: Individual health facilitators* are usually friends, paid workers, family carers, parents or volunteers. Their role is to provide direct support to the individual in terms of meeting their health needs. Some individual health facilitators will support a person to complete a Health Action Plan and to

access health services, whilst others will solely support the person in terms carrying out the actions within the plan.

Health action planning and health facilitation cannot be seen as isolated processes and much of their effectiveness and success depends on good collaboration between individuals and all types of health facilitators.

What is a communication passport?
Sue Lyons

Communication passports were first developed by Sally Millar in the 1990s at the CALL centre, University of Scotland. They are now in use across the country. These passports are a way of collecting together information about how a person communicates and they detail what help or support the person needs to communicate. Everyone who knows the person well should be involved in putting together the passport. This information can then be shared with people in the individual's life. This will help everyone to make sure they communicate in the best ways for the person.

If, as a learning disability nurse, you think someone could benefit from having a communication passport, contact your local speech and language therapist or learning disability team for support or training.

It could take the form of:

* A booklet,
* A DVD, or
* A computer.

It can help with things like:

* Meeting new people,
* Starting a new job,
* Going to meetings, or
* Drawing up a Health Action Plan or person-centred plan.

A communication passport can help individuals to communicate and be more fully involved in their lives. More information can be found in *Personal Communication Passports: Guidelines for good practice* (Millar and Aitken, 2003).

What should I know about clinical observations for vital signs?
Chris Knifton

As a registered nurse you will have already been assessed as competent in carrying out, monitoring and responding to vital signs or clinical observations when you were a student. However, depending on where you are working, it may have been some time since you practised these skills. It is worthwhile therefore examining some of these essential skills again. Sometimes referred to as vital signs, these are measures of physiological functioning that are required for life, and include pulse, respiration, temperature, blood pressure and, where appropriate, pulse oximetry readings. If, when taking clinical observations or measurements, you are unsure about the findings, you must seek advice. Any abnormalities must be recorded and reported to medical staff or senior nursing colleagues and always need to be acted upon. A number of organisations may use electronic devices for recording measurements – ensure you have personally read and understood the manufacturer's guidance for any such device and make sure these are accessible for staff. In addition, some service users may prefer the 'manual' recording of measurements, and as such it is important you keep up-to-date with these basic skills. Average ranges for vital signs in adults are shown in *Table 4.1*.

Blood pressure measurement

This is the measurement of the force exerted to the walls of blood vessels as blood is pumped by the heart and flows around the body. High readings (hypertension) is a sustained blood pressure reading over 140/90 mmHg (NICE 2006a). Low readings (hypotension) is where the systolic measurement (top value) is below 100 mmHg (Marieb and Hoehn 2010). What may be regarded as normal readings however will vary from person to person, and is dependent

Table 4.1. Normal ranges of vital signs for the average adult (adapted from Dougherty and Lister 2011)	
Vital sign	*Range*
Blood pressure	110/70 to140/80 mmHg, although variable
Pulse	55–90 beats/min
Temperature	36–37.5°C
Respiration	12–18 breaths/min

on a number of factors including age, activity, weight, emotion, and diet. It is important therefore to have baseline measurements for people under your care. When high blood pressure is recorded, this is usually associated with physical health problems, including obesity. It is important to act on observations of abnormalities as, if left untreated, there is an increase in the risk of stroke, heart problems and some forms of dementia (particularly vascular dementias and Alzheimer's disease). Management includes identifying and responding to the cause of the hypertension (i.e. medication, diabetes, stress), making appropriate lifestyle changes (i.e. appropriate exercise, healthy eating, alcohol reduction, caffeine reduction, smoking cessation), using relaxation techniques, and possibly taking medication (anti-hypertensives). Hypotension may be a side effect of medication, dehydration, or, in extreme cases, internal bleeding.

As a registered nurse you need to ensure you are able to take a blood pressure reading and respond effectively to the observations found. There are a number of clinical devices available for taking blood pressure, ranging from manual to electronic. Ensure you are familiar with the devices used in your organisation. It is important to also consider the diversity of your clients, as sometimes adaptations need to be made when, for example, brachial artery blood pressure measurement is inappropriate. Alternative sites for taking blood pressure, such as the thigh, may need to be considered (Bickley and Szilagyi 2009). It is also worth knowing that stethoscopes are now available to support nurses who are hard of hearing so the Korotkoff sounds can be heard.

Pulse rate

This measures the rate at which the heart is pumping blood around the body. A number of factors may affect the pulse, including age, exercise, anxiety, pain, medication and even emotion. The pulse can be detected in arteries that lie close to the surface of the body through light compression. There are various sites for taking the pulse, but the more common are:

*   Distal aspect of the wrist (radial artery).
*   Lateral to the larynx in the neck (common carotid artery).
*   Medial side of the bicep brachii muscle in the upper arm (brachial).

Other sites where a pulse can be felt include:

*   Lateral to the orbit of the eye (superficial temporal artery).

- Inferior to the inguinal ligament (femoral artery).
- Posterior to the knee (popliteal artery).
- Superior to the instep of the foot (dorsalis pedis artery).

It is important you are familiar with a range of pulse sites. The radial pulse is the most frequently used site, but where access to the wrist is compromised (e.g. by dressings/bandages or where limbs are missing), alternative sites need to be considered. Pulse measurements should include rate (beats per minute felt), strength (strong, weak) and rhythm (irregular, regular). It is important that you count the pulse for one minute using your fingers (not your thumb). Feeling for less than this time (i.e. 30 seconds and doubling results) may lead to missed irregular beats. Advise people to breathe normally when taking the pulse – breath holding can affect pulse rate. A pulse rate of over 100 beats per minute is known as tachycardia, and slower than 60 beats as bradycardia (Marieb and Hoehn 2010).

Temperature measurement

A raised or lowered temperature can be an indication of infection, injury, medication reaction or an acute condition (hypothermia or hyperthermia). A number of factors can affect a person's temperature, including exercise, ill-health, hormone levels, environment or circadian rhythm. There is a range of devices available for recording body temperature and choice of device often depends on where on the body the measurement is being taken.

Examples include:

- *Oral temperature*: Glass mercury thermometers (now used rarely if at all), digital thermometers for oral use, or disposable single-use thermometers. Most oral thermometers need to be placed in the sublingual pocket of the mouth. Check with manufacturer's guidance on how long the device needs to remain *in situ*, but this is usually three minutes. If the thermometer is in the wrong place then readings can be inaccurate. If the person has eaten, drunk or smoked you will need to wait at least 15 minutes before taking the measurement. It may not be appropriate to take oral temperatures in people likely to have a seizure or in people who are confused and unable to understand or comply with the procedure.
- *Aural temperature*: Temperature can be taken in the ear with a tympanic thermometer. Tympanic thermometers are electronic and the manufacturer's

guidance needs to be followed carefully. Readings are usually between 0.5°C–1°C higher than an oral reading. You will need to consider how use of the thermometer may be interpreted or understood by your client and ensure that this would cause no undue distress. If the patient has been lying on one side, where possible use the other ear, or wait at least 20 minutes. Avoid this method if there is evidence of an ear infection or ear trauma.

- *Temporal temperature*: This refers to temperature readings taken from the temporal artery. This is done by running the thermometer over the forehead and temples to behind the ear. Again, you will need to consider how the thermometer may be interpreted or understood by clients. The thermometer will make sounds and some have a light on the device. Consideration of the person's mental health (such as psychosis and beliefs of 'thought transmissions') may affect compliance or anxiety.
- *Skin temperature*: This includes liquid crystal or chemical dot thermometers. It is important you follow the manufacturer's guidance and are able to read and interpret the measurement correctly.

Respiration measurement

This measures the number and quality of breaths a person takes in one minute. In particular, the measurement involves the rate (the number of times they breathe), depth (deep or shallow breathing), pattern of chest movement, rhythm (regular or irregular breaths), effort exerted by the person to breathe and other observations (e.g. associated cough; nasal flaring; facial expression, such as pursuing of lips; use of accessory muscles, such as neck/shoulders; noises made; etc). A number of factors can affect the respiratory rate and include exercise, environment, health, age, and emotional state. When assessing individuals' respiration it is important to remember that it is easy for them to alter their breathing pattern if they feel they are being watched.

What do I need to know about enteral feeding?
Tina Kirk

What is enteral feeding?

The term 'enteral feeding' refers to the practice of delivering nutritionally complete food via a tube which goes directly into the stomach, duodenum or jejunum (NICE 2006b). If clients are fed this way then they will almost certainly receive all or part of their hydration (called flushes) and medication, if required, by this route.

Why would this be necessary?

The usual reason why clients in the learning disability services require enteral feeding is because they are unable to swallow safely and are at risk of aspiration (food/drink going into the lungs). This is usually due to the level of disability which affects consciousness, but may also be due to disorders of swallowing and cognitive impairment. In other services it can be necessary because of head injuries, mouth and throat cancers, throat obstructions, etc.

Who would decide about this?

The decision to instigate enteral feeding would be made by a 'best interest' multidisciplinary team, taking into account capacity and consent issues. The medical team would decide what type of tube should be installed. Following this, the dietician would decide what liquid food would be required for the person's needs (there are several), how it should be given (there are two methods), how much water (flushes) is needed to keep the patient hydrated and what he or she requires for medication administration. A feeding plan would be devised giving comprehensive instructions. Following this the Home Enteral Nutrition Service (HENS) would be contacted to provide the feed, equipment and advice to carers.

Types of enteral tubes

- *Nasogastric tubes.* These are only suitable for short-term use, often post-operatively. They are not indicated for the long-term feeding requirements of people with profound or severe physical disability or learning disabilities.
- *Percutaneous endoscopic gastrostomy (PEG) tube.* These are by far the most common and are surgically placed under sedation, local or general anaesthesia. There are several types and they are fixed by a balloon, cross bar or disc. Occasionally they are surgically sewn into place. They are inserted directly through the stomach wall.
- *Percutaneous jejunostomy (PEJ) tube.* These are similar to PEG tubes but are inserted through the stomach into the jejunum. This is a more difficult procedure and has more complications, but is useful in clients at severe risk of reflux. They are used much less commonly than PEG tubes.

- *MIC-KEY tube/button.* This is a small button positioned externally on the stomach into which an 'extension tube' is clicked into place for all administrations. This extension tube is then removed when not being used.

Both PEG and PEJ have a tube permanently hanging outside the body with ports for the administration of food, water or medication. In the case of MIC-KEY buttons, however, have the advantage of no permanent external tube which could potentially get caught in clothing or by fingers and be dislodged.

Types of feeds

There are several types of feeds and these are provided in either a small plastic bottle or a bag, depending on how they are given (see below). All are nutritionally complete and prescribed individually for each patient by the dietician, who will take into account weight, tolerance, physical health, etc. Some feeds contain extra fibre; some are 'compact' for clients who cannot tolerate large amounts; and some have extra nutrients for clients who are deficient. Some feeds are given at various times throughout the day and some people are fed overnight.

It must be noted that some clients continue to eat and/or drink at times whilst having some feed/drink given enterally and all of these situations are highly individual and should be reflected in care plans.

Pump or bolus feeds?

In pump feeding the food is administered by a small pump device which is usually hung on the back of a wheelchair or on a bedside table, dependent on when the food is to be given. The pump must be 'set' by the carer for the delivery of the food. This will be the amount (ml) of food to be given, sometimes the whole bag, sometimes part of it, and the rate at which it is to be given (ml per hour). For each delivery of food a 'giving set' needs to be attached to the food bag through the pump and into the PEG or PEJ site tube (or MIC-KEY extension tube). These giving sets are supplied by the HENS team and are single use. An on line teaching session on setting up pump feeds is available at www.nutriciaflocare.com.

Bolus feeds, sometimes called Kangaroo feeds, are administered manually. Bolus giving sets consist of a long tube that attaches to the PEG or PEJ site tube (or MIC-KEY extension tube) with a 60 ml port into which the prescribed amount and type of food is manually poured from a bottle. The rate of delivery is determined by gravity; if you hold the port higher it will be dispensed more quickly. There is also a small valve on the tube which can affect the rate of delivery by effectively closing the tube by degrees. This leaves the carer in charge of how quickly the food is dispensed. This not always ideal as busy carers may be tempted to deliver it too quickly, which may not be good for the client. It is also worth noting that whilst it would be possible to hang these bolus feeds on drip stands, it is considered very bad practice since the carer needs to constantly monitor the intake. Bolus giving sets are single use and are supplied by the HENS team. All syringes for enteral feeding have purple markings.

Whichever system is used, there are three important issues to note.

- The client should be at least slightly upright when receiving the feed to prevent reflux. This is true even for clients who are fed overnight.
- The tubes must be 'primed', i.e. water must be syringed into the tubes so that air is not introduced into the stomach.
- Oral hygiene still needs to be maintained for these clients and it is important that this is adhered to.

Flushes

Flushes are the equivalent of drinking and all clients will have been assessed as to how much water they require on a daily basis to keep them sufficiently hydrated. This will be detailed on their feeding plan. Flushes will be administered at regular times during the day, often, but not always, to coincide with medication administration. Flushes are usually administered by syringe directly into the hanging tube or via the extension tube for MIC-KEY buttons. Flushes are also given before and after every feed, primarily to keep the tubes clean and to prevent them clogging up. They can therefore be given by bolus set before and following administration of food. They are also given before, after, and in between all medication administrations. Some clients are very intolerant of a large volume of fluid and their flushes may be minimal. Cooled boiled water (referred to as CBW) should always be used. In most residential establishments jugs of CBW are prepared in advance. Some clients have bags of sterile water for their specific needs.

Giving medication

Medication may be administered by either a PEG or a PEJ, and in some rare cases clients have both and medication is split between the two. Care is needed in this circumstance to ensure correct administration. Drugs are always given by enteral syringes which have purple markings to distinguish them. There are several syringe types and some may need adapters to fit onto the client's tube. It is useful to have bottle bungs which enable medicine to be drawn up from the bottle. In most cases drugs are supplied in liquid form but some are dispersible. On occasion, drugs need to be crushed and mixed with water, or powder/liquid emptied from capsules; in these cases advice and permission from the pharmacist is required. It must be reiterated that a flush needs to be given before and after medication administration and also in between every different drug.

Clamping of tubes

All the enteral tubes, whether the permanent hanging types or the MIC-KEY extension tubes, have a small clamping device on them. This is very simple and is simply flicked into place to cut off the flow into the tube. This enables carers to 'shut' the tube whilst changing syringes during medication administration or when detaching a feed, etc. In the hanging tube devices there is a small screw top to stop the flow out of the tube when it is not in use. It is important that when this top is in place the clamp is taken off, as leaving the clamp permanently on can damage the tube.

Care of stoma sites

Stoma sites need to be cleaned daily with mild soap and water and dried thoroughly. No creams, lotions or powder should be used around them. Any swelling, redness, leakage, irritation, etc, should be reported to the GP, dietician or HENS team. If the device is not sutured in place it should be gently rotated regularly to prevent any 'sticking'. In balloon retained devices the water in the balloon needs checking about once a week and changed if necessary. This means using a 5 ml syringe in the side port (the one not used for anything else) to very gently draw off the water; it will do this itself once started. You will then need to discard this and replace with a further 5 ml of cooled boiled water.

Hygiene

It is very important to ensure good hygiene around enteral feeding. Gloves should be worn for all contact with stoma sites whether cleaning, flushing or when administering food or medication. Gloves should be disposed of appropriately and hands washed using the six point system. Equipment for enteral feeding is client specific and should not be shared. Syringes, etc, have their own shelf life and systems should be in place to deal with these. They are as follows:

- Baxa 30 uses
- Medicina 1 week
- Enteralok 1 week
- MIC-KEY extension tubes and all adapters 30 uses.

Following their use all equipment should be washed using soapy water, rinsed thoroughly and allowed to air dry. They should be washed separately to domestic washing up.

Problems with enteral feeding

- *The tube is clogged and nothing will go down it*:
  - Ensure clamps are not on.
  - Try putting a small flush down it.
  - Try unblocking the tube with warm sterile water using a very gentle push/pull motion with a 50 ml syringe, but avoid excessive force. Instil 10–15 ml soda water, leave for 30 minutes and try again. If all fails contact dieticians, HENS or the A & E department.
- *The PEG/PEJ has fallen out.* If anyone is appropriately trained to replace it they will do so, if not a Penine tube should be available (see the patient's care plan) to insert into the stoma to prevent it from closing, this must be taped into place and the area dressed. If there is no Penine tube system, just dress the site. In both scenarios immediate assistance should be sought from HENS or A & E.
- *The client keeps being sick.* Ensure client is properly positioned to receive feed. Get HENS or dieticians to check feeding rate if on a pump. Discuss with doctor if there is a need for an anti-emetic.
- *The client is losing/gaining weight.* Discuss with dieticians regarding feeding regime.
- *The client is constipated/has diarrhoea.* Discuss with dieticians regarding type of feed/flushes. Review hygiene procedures. Review medication with GP.
- *The stoma site is red/sore/leaking.* Check water in balloon-retained devices. Ensure hygiene procedures are being adhered to. Check non-surgically retained devices can be gently rotated. Ensure area is cleaned. Contact GP or HENS for advice.

- *The client has a dry mouth.* Ensure adequate oral hygiene. Consider lip salves/soft paraffin. Artificial saliva can be prescribed if necessary. Discuss flushes with dieticians.

What nutrients are essential for a balanced daily diet, and what foods do they come from?
Daniel Senior and Jamie Hart

Nutrients are chemicals or substances that the body needs to metabolise in order to function correctly. They are usually grouped together in categories known as macronutrients (including proteins, carbohydrates and fats) and micronutrients (such as water, vitamins, minerals, and phytonutrients). A fundamental aspect of cellular function for the 100 trillion cells in a typical adult is optimal nutrient intake. Both nutrient excesses, and deficiencies, can disrupt cellular function resulting in decreases in both physical and mental health performance and behaviour. The aim of a balanced diet is to provide the right amount of nutrients so that cellular functioning is maintained and all the systems of the body can perform their role in a range of circumstances.

As a registered nurse, it is important that you understand what makes a balanced diet, which foods to include and which to avoid. The amount of nutrients required will vary between people and depends on many factors. Current and long-term health conditions, somatotype (body type) and how active a person is can all have an impact on the volume of nutrients needed. The number of calories consumed will have a direct impact on an individual's weight; manipulating this allows for effective weight management.

A balanced diet, however, is a little more difficult to understand; someone can easily be consuming the correct number of calories but still be deficient in vitamins and minerals. This is why having a good idea of which foods will deliver a balanced diet is so important. The human body has evolved in order to extract energy from carbohydrates, proteins and fats (macronutrients). As a basic rule a person should be looking to consume a diet consisting of 50% carbohydrate, 30% proteins and 20% fats. When trying to advise people on eating a healthy diet there are some basic points which can be adhered to. These include promoting fresh food where possible and steering people away from processed food. A daily diet should consist of foods low in sugar (less than 20 g per 100 g of food) and salt (less than 6 g per day).

Table 4.2 lists some foods where macro and micronutrients are found. As many different combinations as possible should be included to increase the likelihood of achieving a balanced diet.

Table 4.2. Foods containing essential macro and micronutrients	
Proteins	Beef, chicken, turkey, pork Fish Eggs Nuts
Carbohydrates	Pasta, bread, rice Fruits Vegetables
Fats	Vegetable oil Olive oil Nut oils Fish oils

How prevalent is obesity, and how would I assess/screen someone for obesity?

Jamie Hart and Daniel Senior

Turner (2001) notes that, in the UK, obesity is more common among people with a learning disability than among the general population. This has a number of service implications; obesity increases the risk of long-term health conditions, including cardiovascular disease, pulmonary disease, metabolic disorders and osteoarthritis, as well as having psychological, emotional and economic consequences (Bhaumik et al 2008). In particular, Turner (2001) notes that obesity rates are higher among women and follows trends noted by Rimmer et al (1993), Wood (1994) and Bell and Bhate (1992). In addition Bhaumik et al (2008) found that, compared with the general population, women and people with Down's syndrome were particularly more likely to be obese. An overall prevalence of obesity in people with learning disability is 21% (range 2–35%) (Bhaumik et al 2008). It is worthwhile noting that the same researchers also found being underweight in this population was 19% more common in men, and was associated with a younger age, with not taking medication and having learning disabilities other than Down's syndrome (Bhaumik et al 2008).

Assessing or screening for obesity often uses markers such as body mass index (BMI). Burkhart et al (1985) however advise that, due to some of the physical characteristics or make-up of some forms of learning disability, using BMI may not be suitable, i.e., in Down's syndrome. A more precise method may be through the use of skin folds and callipers. These methods should however

Table 4.3. Hip–waist ratio		
Risk	Ratio male	Ratio female
High	> 1.0	> 0.85
Moderate	0.96–1.00	0.81–0.85
Low	< 0.95	< 0.80
		National Institute of Health

only be carried out by a person trained in their use and they should include the measurement of skin folds taken from different areas of the body. There are a number of different equations to calculate body fat percentage using different skin fold sites. The most common is the calculations developed by Jackson and Pollock in the 1970s. They proposed calculations based on three and seven skin fold assessments to provide a reasonably accurate management tool for clinicians to monitor body mass and fat changes. Problems with this technique are related to the experience and consistency of the assessors. Katch and McArdle (1983) suggested that investigators needed to have performed several thousand skin fold measurements for research purposes.

With this in mind, a more suitable method to assess for obesity, that nurses are able to perform, is to compare hip and waist measurements (hip–waist ratio). If the person's waist circumference is larger than the hip circumference then he or she will be at a higher risk of obesity and will probably be categorised as overweight. Dividing the waist measurement by the hip measurement gives the person's hip to waist ratio.

As can be seen from *Table 4.3*, hip to waist ratios have very slight differences between genders. However, the measurement is still indicative of the risk for obesity-related disorders, and can be used as a reliable assessment tool. The hip measurement is normally taken around the widest part of the buttocks (below the anterior supra-iliac spine). The waist measurement is normally taken just above the line of the navel at the widest part of the stomach.

How is obesity managed?
Jamie Hart and Daniel Senior

A balanced and healthy diet together with a moderate level of appropriate physical exercise are the fundamental principles for managing obesity. When working with people with a learning disability this may not be as straightforward as it would seem. As has already been noted, obesity in this group is associated with people living in the community, particularly those living either independently or with family (Bhaumik et al 2008). This may be due, as the authors point out, to a lack of education and practical support afforded to the family, over-protection by care givers, or difficulty resisting demands to challenging behaviour. In addition, socio-economic status of people living independently might lead to cheaper or 'easier' diet choices taking the form of processed and unhealthy options. Appropriate budgeting advice and support with shopping lists may be just as important as healthy eating educational packages in such instances.

For people in residential settings, awareness by care staff about the importance of diet is crucial. As a learning disability nurse, there may be a need to review menu options available to clients. Where food is prepared by care staff, consideration needs to be given to recognising the knowledge, skills and time of staff to give appropriate regard to the importance of diet, including an awareness of healthy eating.

An additional concern in obesity management within this population is the risk of psychiatric medication-induced obesity (Schwartz et al 2004). This requires particular management, including medication review and careful consideration of the risks versus benefits on the person's physical and mental health. Medication commonly associated with weight gain is shown in *Table 4.4*. An increase in weight as a result of antidepressants may, for example, affect self-esteem and exacerbate depressive symptoms.

Potential interventions used for people with learning disabilities for managing obesity include:

- Weight loss interventions, focusing on calorie intake/energy expenditure.
- Physical exercise interventions, focusing on calorie use.
- Behavioural interventions.
- Health promotional programmes, focusing on education (Hamilton et al 2007).

Table 4.4. Medication commonly associated with weight gain (Adapted from Schwartz et al 2004)	
Antipsychotics	Chlorpromazine Clozapine Olanzapine
Antidepressants	Amitryptyline Mirtazapine Selective serotonin reuptake inhibitors (such as fluoxetine)
Mood stabilisers	Valporate Lithium

Weight loss intervention

Weight management interventions are hard to prescribe and deliver, because of the natural psychological relationship afforded to food by most human beings. We need it to survive of course, but the emotional attachments are all-encompassing. So with the learning disabled population this is an even bigger challenge. A basic understanding of what constitutes a balanced diet is something that nurses should be aware of. In addition the nurse should be aware that a slightly hypo-calorific diet (reducing daily intake by 500 calories) should be enough to effect a healthy weight loss in any population. Many diets available at present use starvation techniques in order to drop weight quickly (reducing diet by 1000 cal or more); however, these reduced calorie diets can have adverse health risks and can ultimately, due to the effect on metabolism, lead to poor weight control, more commonly known as yo-yo dieting.

Exercise prescription

Exercise among people with a learning disability can also be challenging. Even professional physical trainers may not be aware of problems associated with some forms of learning disability. Therefore it is important for parents and carers to be made aware of places they can go to obtain good advice when trying to integrate exercise into the lives of people with a learning disability. There can be many exercises that are contraindicated and any professional exercise therapist/trainer must be made aware of the physical problems that can be associated with learning disability. Therefore you should try to have an awareness of your patient's physical problems so that you can pass information on to parents, carers and professionals.

Nurses need to have a basic understanding of the services available to families and carers in the geographical area and, where possible, qualified and experienced professionals should always be used.

How would I assess capability for physical activity?
Jamie Hart and Daniel Senior

Most people are able to take part in appropriate physical exercise. Basic tests for readiness for physical exercise are numerous. However, blood pressure is the most important health marker that needs to be checked to make sure the person is healthy enough to start. If the person has particularly high (persistently over 140/90 mmHg) or low (persistently under 90/60 mmHg) blood pressure, the advice of a general practitioner would always be needed before commencing an exercise regime.

How can I prepare someone for their first exercise session?
Jamie Hart and Daniel Senior

Adequate preparation for an exercise session is essential, as without, the experience can be difficult for all involved. It may be useful to discuss what may be involved and perhaps arrange a couple of visits to the leisure centre or gym to familiarise the person with what may be a new environment. If a personal trainer is involved it may be useful to arrange an informal chat so all parties feel comfortable. Here there needs to be a focus on supporting the person with a learning disability to feel relaxed about the exercise programmes and routines being offered and establish realistic goals and, importantly, boundaries. Clear boundaries as to conduct and behaviour may need to be clearly articulated. This may include discussion about social proximities, and touching. Latterly this may be an important feature of guiding a client through an exercise class, and it is important that this is neither misinterpreted nor causes offence. The role of a personal trainer must always be clarified, as this avoids potential further confusion, with relationships being misconstrued. Personal trainers may have little knowledge or experience of learning disability, and fears, prejudices and myths may need to be addressed appropriately.

Anyone using a gym for the first time will be made aware of basic health and safety and will need to be wearing suitable clothing which is neither loose nor baggy, together with appropriate footwear.

What does a personal trainer/exercise therapist need to know when a client is referred?
Jamie Hart and Daniel Senior

During the referral stage, it is important that you consult with the client's GP, particularly if the person has not participated in exercise classes for a long time, or at all. A health screen, which includes weight, height, and vital signs (temperature, pulse, and lying and standing blood pressure) may be taken.

The information you give to physical trainers about the person's health status and lifestyle needs important consideration, and requires consent from the person first. You may need to get further advice on what you can and cannot disclose from your manager. In general, it is useful for a personal trainer to know about the person's medical history, recent surgery, physical disabilities and/or syndromes and their effect on movements. If the person has a particular genetic syndrome which has led to obesity (such as Prader-Willi syndrome, Cohen syndrome, Bardet-Biedl syndrome or Down's syndrome) then additional information on this condition may need to be offered. There may be some particular health problems commonly associated with some conditions (such as atlanto-axial instability in Down's syndrome, or osteoarthritis in Turner's syndrome) which would require investigation or discussion prior to exercise classes.

As discussed elsewhere, communication difficulties may be apparent in many people with learning disabilities. Understanding the communication system used by the client is important, and this may not always be verbal. Many people with communication difficulties have a 'communication passport' which may need to be discussed at the referral.

What are the risks of exercise or prolonged physical activity?

Jamie Hart and Daniel Senior

The risks of prolonged, regular, and, importantly, appropriate physical exercise are minimal. However, appropriate physical exercise is the most difficult part to quantify. Therefore professionals should be aware of possible problems to look out for.

Physical injuries

Injuries can occur at any time and for a number of reasons. These may be due to sudden trauma when exercising too hard (muscle tears and strains) and/or aches and pains that develop over a period of time (overuse injury).

Overuse injuries can be as simple as a repetitive strain injury or, more seriously, joint degeneration. It should be recognised that the latter is likely only in subjects who are predisposed to degenerative joint problems, which are usually congenital. Injuries can all be helped by various qualified therapists including physiotherapists, chiropractors, osteopaths and sports therapists. However, the level of moderate physical exercise that is needed for a normal healthy body should not cause problems. If an injury is sustained, however, the person may be exercising too hard or too often. This can sometimes cause both physical and psychological problems. People predisposed to obsessional behaviour can easily become over-attached to the positive feelings that exercise can provide.

It must be stressed that in most populations, appropriate exercise is now being prescribed. The health benefits seem always to outweigh the costs. Nurses cannot be expected to be health and fitness professionals so it is therefore important to reiterate that, for nurses, a basic understanding of how and where to get good advice in the geographical area is the main prerequisite to affecting the health of people in the learning disability population.

What is catheterisation?
Penny Tremayne

Urinary catheterisation is the 'insertion of a hollow tube using an aseptic technique to enable drainage of urine or instillation of fluids as part of medical treatment' (Robinson 2007: 48).

Catheterisation may be carried out for the following reasons:

- To empty the bladder pre-operatively, post-operatively or before a specific investigation.
- To relieve urine retention.
- To determine residual urine.
- To measure accurately urine output.
- To bypass obstruction.
- To relieve incontinence, as a last resort where there are no other practicable means.

If catheterisation is going to be inevitable then Bissett (2005) considers that a thorough risk assessment must be completed before the insertion. This should include the patient's viewpoint and attitude towards the insertion, which might be influenced by age, gender, sexual activity and body image. You also have to assess the patient's level of knowledge and understanding about the insertion. Some patients with a learning disability may continually pull at the catheter, causing trauma. Never presume a person with a learning disability lacks capacity to consent to this procedure. If someone does lack capacity, you must be able to demonstrate that it is in their best interests.

A wide variety of catheters is available: careful assessment of the correct size and appropriate material will help to minimise complications. The main criteria for the selection of an appropriate catheter are the material it is made from, its size and length. As a registered nurse you need to ensure that you are able to provide a rationale regarding your selection.

- *Material*: Here you must consider the length of time the catheter may be in use, to avoid repeated re-catheterisation. Examples of materials used include polyvinyl chloride (PVC) (7 days); Teflon-coated with a latex core (28 days); Silicone (12 weeks); Hydrogel-coated latex (12 weeks); Hydrogel-coated silicone (12 weeks). You need to be aware, however, of any product allergies, such as a latex allergy, that the patient may have. Other materials exist and some of these are more costly (silver/silver-coated catheters).

- *Size*: People are all unique and that includes in all dimensions, including that of the urethra. This may be particularly relevant to people with profound and multiple learning disabilities or congenital abnormalities. This means that one size does not fit all. Catheter size is usually measured in Charrière (Ch). This refers to the external diameter of the catheter; 1 Ch is equivalent to 0.3 mm and hence external diameter of a 20 Ch catheter is 6 mm. Sometimes you may see the measurement of the catheter as Fg, meaning French gauge. As a general rule you should opt for the smallest catheter possible, usually 12–14 Ch (Madeo and Roodhouse 2009). However with suprapubic catheters, the size should be no smaller than 16 Ch as this facilitates maintenance of a tract between the skin and bladder (Bond and Harris 2005). A final consideration is the past medical history of the person. If, for example, the person has previously had a catheter inserted, this may have dilated the urethra. If the person has haematuria and clots in the urine then a larger catheter will be required to drain the bladder.

- *Length*: You may have heard of the terms 'male' and 'female' catheter. These terms are to be avoided, but they can refer to the length of catheter. The female urethra is shorter than the male and therefore the catheter required for a woman will usually be shorter, the usual length being 20–26 cm. A longer catheter is used for men (up to 45 cm), although longer catheters can also be used for women who have genital oedema, since the valve of a shorter catheter can cause friction and trauma. A longer catheter may afford the patient greater freedom and mobility, so the patient should be assessed carefully.

Catheterisation must follow an aseptic technique. You are advised to attend a catheterisation update course if this procedure is unfamiliar to you or if you have not carried out the procedure recently. It is important to remember that catheterisation should always be a last option unless the intervention is part of emergency care.

How do I deal with healthcare associated infections?
Kevin Power

Antibiotic-resistant bacteria are a constant worry in the health service. The media regularly report outbreaks of 'superbugs'. So how should you tackle this problem? Meticillin-resistant *Staphylococcus aureus* (MRSA) and *Clostridium difficile* (*C. diff*) are the two causative agents that are of most concern, but this should not obscure the fact that there are many potential sources of infection in healthcare institutions and the home. There is helpful specific advice on the Department of Health website which deals specifically with both MRSA and *C. diff*.

MRSA

The following advice is taken from the Department of Health (2007a). More detailed information is available on its website.

- To reduce the likelihood of spreading infection, you should always wash your hands or use an antibacterial hand rub after you have had any physical contact with a patient – whether or not the patient has a wound. Remember that healthcare workers can be carriers of the bacteria even if they are not infected themselves.
- You should always encourage patients to wash their hands after using the toilet and before and after eating.
- If you suspect infection, there is a simple test which involves taking a swab or other sample from the suspected site of the infection and sending it for laboratory analysis. Also, check patients' antibiotics to make sure their treatment is appropriate for MRSA.
- If patients are infected, always use gloves when treating them and consider moving them away from other patients to help stop the bacteria spreading.
- In high-risk situations (e.g. patients admitted for major surgery, such as hip replacement or heart surgery) if pre-screening shows MRSA carriage, decontamination with skin and nose treatment is recommended before patients are operated on.

C. difficile

The following advice is taken from the Department of Health's (2009) website:

- All staff should apply the following mnemonic protocol (SIGHT) when managing suspected potentially infectious diarrhoea:

S Suspect that a case may be infective where there is no clear alternative cause for diarrhoea.

I   Include the patient and consult with the infection control team (ICT) while determining the cause of the diarrhoea.

G Gloves and aprons must be used for all contacts with the patient and his or her environment.

H Hand washing with soap and water should be carried out before and after each contact with the patient and the patient's environment.

T Test the stool for toxin, by sending a specimen immediately.

Further guidance is offered by the Department of Health (2007b):

- Always wash your hands after you have had any physical contact with a patient. Do not rely solely on alcohol gel as this does not kill *C. difficile* spores.
- To keep cases of *C. difficile* down, healthcare workers should try to avoid prescribing broad spectrum antibiotics, as far as possible, so that patients' natural protection is not weakened.
- If you suspect infection, there is a simple test for diarrhoeal faeces to see if *C. difficile* toxins are present. It gives a result within a few hours. In outbreaks, or for surveillance of the different strains circulating in the population, *C. difficile* can be cultured from faeces and the isolates sent to the Anaerobe Reference Laboratory (National Public Health Service, Wales; Microbiology, Cardiff) or HPA Regional Laboratories for typing and testing for susceptibility to antibiotics.
- Infected patients should be isolated and healthcare workers dealing with them should wear gloves and aprons, especially when dealing with bedpans, etc.
- Environments should be kept clean at all times. Where there are cases of *C. difficile* infection, a disinfectant containing chlorine or other sporicidal agent should be used to reduce environmental contamination with the spores.

The Department of Health (2006) provides specific guidance for nursing and residential homes in dealing with healthcare associated infections.

Final points

Remember that if a patient cannot mobilise and is confined to a side room with a label of 'infectious', he or she is probably going to feel isolated and stigmatised. You can help the patient by encouraging visitors to stagger the times of their visits. Make sure that the patient understands his or her condition and is not isolated, unless absolutely essential. All trusts will have an infection control nurse or team, which will be an invaluable source of information and support to both staff and patient.

What do I need to know about pressure ulcers?
Penny Tremayne

Pressure ulcer assessments are commonly used within the clinical practice setting, although Saleh et al (2009) consider that clinical judgement may be as effective as employing a risk assessment scale to assess risk. For example, have you ever undertaken a pressure ulcer risk assessment and the result indicates that the individual is not at risk, yet you still think they are? In this situation, you are professionally accountable and responsible for your actions and omissions and you should implement interventions, despite the result of the assessment. The Royal College of Nursing (RCN) (2005) indicates that ulcer assessment should include the following:

- Appearance of the surrounding skin and the wound
- Cause of the ulcer
- Dimensions
- Evidence of undermining or tracking – sinus/fistula
- Exudate – amount and type
- Involvement of the tissue viability nurse
- Odour
- Pain
- Signs of local infection
- Site and location
- Stage.

People with learning disabilities may be at particular risk of developing pressure sores when they become seriously ill, have impaired mobility, poor nutrition, are obese or frail/thin, have limited communication skills, or have poor posture. Other risks that may more generally be applied, as noted by the RCN

(2005) include having a spinal cord injury, being neurologically compromised, elderly or pregnant, or having an infection.

What are the grades of a pressure ulcer and what do they mean?

The European Pressure Ulcer Advisory Panel (2003) in the RCN (2005: 26–27) guideline identifies the following grades of pressure ulcer:

- *Grade 1.* Non-blanchable erythema of intact skin. Discoloration of the skin, warmth, oedema and indurations or hardness may also be indicators, particularly in people with darker skin.
- *Grade 2.* Partial thickness skin loss involving epidermis, dermis or both. The ulcer is superficial and presents clinically as an abrasion or blister.
- *Grade 3.* Full thickness skin loss involving damage to or necrosis of subcutaneous tissue that may extend down to, but not through underlying fascia.
- *Grade 4.* Extensive destruction, tissue necrosis, or damage to muscle, bone or supporting structures with or without full thickness skin loss.

Practice points for pressure ulcers are shown in *Box 4.1*.

What care does the RCN guideline suggest regarding mobilising and re-positioning?

The RCN (2005) indicates that care should be individualised. Mobilising should be actively encouraged and if mobilising is not an option the positioning and re-positioning should be 'frequent' and recorded. Positioning on the bony

---

Box 4.1. Practice points for pressure ulcers

- Are pressure ulcer dressings changed according to the care plan?
- What does the pressure ulcer look like?
- Is there any exudate?
- If so, is it mild, moderate or heavy?
- Is the pressure ulcer epithelialising, granulating, sloughy, necrotic, infected or fungating/malodorous?
- Compare the appearance with the photograph or original measurement template

---

prominences, back of the head, temporal region of the skull, ear, shoulders, elbows, hip, thigh, leg, buttocks, rib cage, sacrum, knees, heels and toes should be avoided. This can also include the ischial tuberosities, parts of the body affected by anti-embolic stockings (ensure correctly measured for and fitted), parts of the body where pressure, friction and shear are exerted in the course of daily activities, and parts of the body where there is external force from clothing or equipment. Nasal cannulae, for example, can cause possible breakdown of skin integrity around the bridge of the nose, inside the nose, on the cheeks, and in the ear. In those who are immobile passive limb movements should be given (RCN 2005).

If the patient is at risk of developing a pressure ulcer, then follow the stages of the nursing process, and ensure that there is a realistic, accurate and individualised care plan agreed and that this is implemented and evaluated accordingly. The care plan will include a goal – what is to be achieved. This can be immediate, but is more usually medium-term or even ongoing, and must include a review/goal date.

The care plan should be evidence based and can include care such as that outlined below (this list is not exhaustive):

- Adoption of an appropriate moving and handling procedure to reduce damage to the skin from shearing and friction, applying local protocol/policy for patient handling.
- The use of pressure cushions and appropriate mattresses, the RCN (2005) stipulate the following:
  - *Grade 1–2*: a minimum of a high specification foam mattress or cushion with pressure-reducing properties. If the ulcer deteriorates then an alternative pressure mattress with a continuous low pressure system should be used.
  - *Grade 3–4*: the minimum provision should be an alternating air pressure mattress or continuous low pressure system. The RCN (2005) guidelines go on to clarify that the first choice of an alternating air pressure mattress should be an overlay system unless there are contra-indications such as the weight of the individual.
- Maintain or promote a balanced diet and adequate hydration – to minimise the patient's vulnerability to pressure as well as maintain elasticity of the tissues.
- Make sure that the skin is clean, dry and well moisturised. Cleanse skin as soon as possible after soiling, using mild detergents in conjunction with warm water to prevent drying and irritation, and apply moisturiser to any dry skin. There are also some non-water based foams available which clean and moisten the skin.

- If the patient requires a dressing for a pressure ulcer, as a registered nurse you should select one that is clinically effective. The RCN (2005) considers that dressing choice should be 'modern'. Dressings should:
  - Allow excess exudate to be removed from the wound surface.
  - Provide a moist micro-environment.
  - Be sterile/contaminant free.
  - Not shed dressing material in the wound.
  - Reduce wound pain.
  - Be easy to remove and apply.
  - Not cause allergic reactions.
  - Not cause any trauma when removed.
  - Be impermeable to micro-organisms.
  - Provide thermal insulation.

Evaluation

A judgement on the effectiveness of the delivery of care should be made if the patient's condition improves or deteriorates, or on the review/goal date. Thus the previous stages, such as assessment and planning, might have to be revisited.

How do I recognise acute ill-health?
Chris Knifton and Dorothy Hemel

It is the nurse's responsibility to both recognise and respond appropriately to signs and symptoms of acute ill-health. At times this may include emergency care. Subbe et al (2001) note that acute deterioration is usually preceded by a decline in physiological parameters. As a registered nurse, it is important therefore that you are able accurately to assess the person for changes in:

- Appearance, including skin colour, e.g. flushed, pale, ashen, sweating, clammy.
- Temperature.
- Pulse.
- Respiration rate.
- Blood pressure.
- Level of consciousness.
- Oxygen saturation levels.
- Blood glucose levels.

In particular, when working with people with learning disabilities, additional observations need to be considered as possible markers of acute ill-health:

- Behaviour changes, e.g. aggression, anxiety, withdrawal.
- Changes in activities of daily living (ADL).
- Changes in communication.
- Environment manipulation, e.g. light fitting destruction during cases of migraine.
- Confusion.
- Hallucinations and or delusions.

Additional investigations of which you need to be aware include:

- Urine testing.
- Bowel assessment, e.g. use of the Bristol stool chart for possible constipation.
- Medication side effect monitoring, e.g. use of Liverpool University Neuroleptic Side Effect Rating Scale (LUNSERS) for antipsychotic medication).
- Vomiting.
- Weight assessments.
- Nutrition, e.g. use of the Malnutrition Universal Screening Tool (MUST).
- Tissue viability, e.g. use of the Waterlow tool.

It is usual to take a full range of vital sign observations (temperature, pulse, respiration, blood pressure), weight, height, urine testing, tissue viability and nutrition assessment/screening on admission. This will provide a useful baseline to work from. Fluctuations from the person's usual ranges may highlight the possibility of acute ill-health.

It is paramount that, as a registered nurse, you are familiar with what is normal for the person. However, as well as having baseline observations, it is also important to record how the person behaves when he or she is unwell. Some people may exhibit a specific behaviour associated with feeling unwell. This may take the form of bizarre or challenging behaviour, or withdrawal and avoidance behaviours (see *Table 4.5*). Indeed, when challenging/complex behaviour or mental disorder is being assessed, a physical health assessment for acute ill-health should always be carried out.

Documentation of regular observations is essential. Once a change, or sign

Table 4.5. Examples of behaviours that may indicate ill-health in patients with a learning disability

Behaviour	Health complaint
Bill has recently started to lie with his left cheek on the cold bathroom floor. He becomes aggressive if moved	Bill has toothache but cannot effectively communicate this. He has found the coldness of the bathroom floor relives the pain
Jane hit her head with her fists, and sometimes banged her head against the walls. Staff felt this was attention-seeking behaviour	Jane's behaviour was a result of headaches, and the behaviour stopped when analgesia was given
Sanjay started to poke items such as pencils and his toothbrush in his left ear. Staff felt this was self-injurious behaviour and was part of his learning disability phenotype	On investigation he was found to have earache
After meals, Lin would regularly punch herself in the abdomen and make herself sick. Staff felt this was either behavioural or the start of an eating disorder such as bulimia	Following a hospital referral due to excessive weight loss, Lin was found to have a hiatus hernia. The behaviour noted was Lin's attempt to relieve the painful symptoms
Pat has a past history of faecal smearing. In recent weeks this behaviour has returned and she now regularly smears her faeces in her bedroom	There is a danger of diagnostic overshadowing. Although in the past this was behavioural, upon investigation it was found her current smearing coincided with constipation as a side effect of a newly prescribed medication - this had gone unrecognised by staff

of acute ill-health has been identified, you need to act immediately. This may be to report to a senior colleague or to the person's GP. If the person looks unwell, but all observations are within normal limits, it is advisable still to report your concerns to a senior colleague.

Some clinical areas may use a physiological track and trigger system to identify the early deterioration of a person's condition. These systems are commonly known as Early Warning Scores (EWS) or Modified Early Warning

Scores (MEWS). You need to be familiar with these tools if they are used within your clinical setting.

Sometimes, however, when patients are asked if they are unwell, they may communicate that they are all right. It is important that, if you think there is something wrong, you undertake further investigation. Patients may say they are all right because they have an underlying fear of doctors, of going into hospital or of having investigations in an unfamiliar environment, possibly due to previous experiences.

Consultation with carers, which may include family members, is crucial. There is a need to obtain information about patients' usual behaviour (baseline), how they behave when they are unwell, and if there are any underlying maladaptive strategies during ill-health. These maladaptive strategies may be used by individuals to manage the problem themselves and avoid early interventions they do not understand would be of benefit. This should be recorded in the individual's health action plan.

What do I need to know about wound dressings?
Nicola Brooks

It is important that you follow local guidelines on wound dressings, and liaise and follow guidance from the trust or organisation's tissue viability nurse.

There is a huge variety of wound dressings available, with companies competing with each other to produce the ideal. Dressings are split into two categories: primary and secondary. A primary dressing is one that is in direct contact with the wound, and a secondary dressing is one that is superimposed over a primary dressing.

Factors to consider when selecting a dressing include:

* Ritualistic practice: Is the dressing something that has always been used?
* Evidence-based practice.
* Clinical experience.
* Resources available (expense, availability).
* Patient preference (comfort).
* Where the wound is situated and its size.
* What will work for which type of wound.

Characteristics of the optimum wound dressing

The ideal dressing in wound care is one that provides optimal conditions for wound healing and prevents further damage to the surrounding areas. Turner (1985) identifies several classic characteristics of the optimum dressing. Such a dressing would need to:

- Maintain a high humidity between the wound and dressing (to promote a faster rate of epithelialisation).
- Remove excess exudate and toxic compounds.
- Allow gaseous exchange.
- Provide thermal insulation at the wound surface.
- Be impermeable to wound bacteria.
- Be free from particles and wound contaminants.
- Allow removal without causing trauma at dressing change.

Types of wound dressing

The main types of wound dressing are:

- *Hydrocolloids.* These interact with wound exudates when in contact with the wound. They slowly absorb fluid to change the state of the dressing by forming a gel. The dressing should extend approximately 2 cm around the wound edge.
- *Hydrogels.* Used to deslough/debride wounds. When in contact with the wound they absorb exudates to provide a moist environment. These dressings are available as a flat sheet or gel, but require a secondary dressing to keep them in place.
- *Alginates.* Manufactured from seaweed, they form a gel when in contact with a wound. Suitable for use on exudating wounds.
- *Hydrofibres.* Used to deslough/debride wounds as a primary dressing for moderate to heavily exudating wounds. Available as a woven pad or ribbon of hydrocolloid fibres.
- *Foams.* Used for exudating flat or cavity wounds with differing absorbencies. Should not be used on dry wounds because of the risk of adherence.
- *Vapour-permeable films.* These are used to treat shallow wounds, or prophylactically to prevent pressure damage, or as a retention dressing. They can be left in place for up to seven days; however, care must be taken on removal to prevent trauma to fragile skin. The skin around the wound must be kept clean and dry.
- *Tulles.* An open-weave cotton dressing impregnated with paraffin, which

requires frequent changes to prevent it drying out. It is difficult to remove if adherent, and becomes embedded in granulation tissue.

- *Iodine-based products.* These dressings contain an antiseptic, although the effects of the dressing may be reduced by the presence of pus or exudates. They can cause sensitivity in some patients.
- *Silver-based products.* These dressings have antibacterial properties contained in a dressing or cream form. Side-effects have been reported with the long-term use of silver. The dressings can be used prophylactically as a dressing on line insertion sites, e.g. Hickman lines.
- *Wound manager bags.* These products are used to control exudate on high output wounds and protect the surrounding skin. Ideally they are used to monitor the yield of exudate from a wound. They can be left in place for a long period.
- *Larval therapy.* Larvae are not often a first-line choice of wound dressing. The sterile larvae of the common greenbottle (*Lucilia sericate*) are used to debride the wound and remove bacteria. They are used and disposed of according to strict protocol, and ordered specifically for single patient use.
- *Vacuum-assisted closure (VAC) therapy.* VAC is used to apply negative pressure to a specialised dressing positioned in the wound cavity. Nursing staff will require extra training in the use of VAC pumps and equipment to use them effectively. The dressings can be left *in situ* for a few days.
- *Paste bandages.* These products consist of cotton bandages impregnated with a medical paste. Secondary dressings are required to secure them in place. Allergic reactions are common. Paste bandages are often used in the treatment of thrombophlebitis.

When using any form of wound dressing, careful patient assessment is essential. It is advisable to use a wound assessment tool to ensure reliable and consistent documentation. Wounds should be reassessed regularly to evaluate the treatment given, as no single product is suitable for all wound types or all stages of healing. A flexible approach to the selection of wound care products is required to optimise the healing process.

What does an aseptic technique involve?
Nicola Brooks

An aseptic technique is a method of preventing micro-organisms from reaching vulnerable sites (Dougherty and Lister 2008). It is used to prevent contamination of wounds that could lead to infection, and is achieved by ensuring that only sterile equipment is used during an invasive procedure. The aseptic technique procedure has continually evolved from ritualistic and evidence-based practice and is skills based (Preston 2005).

The equipment required consists of:

- Sterile dressing pack.
- Fluid for insertion (if required).
- Appropriate dressing.
- Hand hygiene preparation (according to local policy).
- Dressing trolley.
- Scissors.
- Tape.
- Plastic apron.

See *Box 4.2* for the procedure for an aseptic technique.

Box 4.2. Procedure for aseptic technique

- Explain the procedure to the patient and gain his/her consent.
- Ensure patient consent before the procedure
- Clean the dressing trolley with alcoholic preparation (according to local policy)
- Place required equipment on the bottom shelf of the trolley
- Take all equipment to the patient's bedside (or treatment room as appropriate) and put on plastic apron
- Loosen the dressing around the wound
- Wash your hands and apply bacterial hand rub
- Check the sterility of all equipment – open the sterile field using only the corners of the paper.
- Open all other sterile packs and tip contents onto the sterile field
- Wash your hands again and apply bacterial hand rub
- Place your hand in the disposable bag (found inside the dressing pack) and use to remove the used dressing. Invert the bag and stick on the dressing trolley using its own adhesive strip
- Put on sterile gloves, touching only the wrist of the gloves
- Irrigate or clean the wound as necessary
- Change the dressing as required
- Dispose of all used equipment in the clinical waste after the procedure

---

What do I do if one of my clients is diagnosed with cancer (or another terminal illness)?
Trish Sealy

Consider the following case of Mr W.

Case study

Mr W, aged 68, had been resident in a long-term care facility for over 30 years. A long-term smoker, he was diagnosed with lung cancer as an incidental finding on chest X-ray when he was admitted to hospital with a chest infection. His case was discussed in the local respiratory-oncology multidisciplinary team meeting and as he had no symptoms from his lung cancer it was decided to manage him with 'best supportive care'. (This is a term used to cover ongoing monitoring and a symptomatic approach to problems as they arise, rather than actively treating with chemotherapy and/or radiotherapy.)

What did that mean for Mr W?

It quickly became apparent to those caring for Mr W that clarity of communications and continuity of carers would be crucial in ensuring he maintained the best quality of life possible. It was decided to hold a multiprofessional meeting to discuss issues around his care. This meeting was attended by the manager, nursing and care staff, physical health and psychiatric medical professionals who knew Mr W, the pharmacist covering the unit, an independent mental capacity advocate (IMCA) and representatives from the local community specialist palliative care team.

Specialist palliative care is the holistic care of anyone with a life-limiting illness. Teams can provide support and advice, both directly and indirectly into a patient's care and they work across acute, community and hospice settings.

Capacity issues

Consider the Mental Capacity Act (2005). Although having capacity for some day-to-day decisions, Mr W was deemed not to have capacity to retain and process information relating to his lung cancer. The physician with the closest long-term relationship with Mr W did tell him about his cancer and explain to him that it could not be cured but he quickly forgot the conversation and it was deemed inappropriate to keep repeating it. Hence an IMCA was present at the multiprofessional meetings to ensure that W's best interests were central at all times.

In Mr W's case the specialist palliative care team was able to provide advice regarding how to plan for future care for him and to answer questions regarding likely progression of his illness, signs to look out for and possible symptoms that could occur. This allowed for timely prescribing of appropriate anticipatory 'if required' medicines, such as analgesia and nebulisers. The care team was also provided with contact details for ongoing support and signposted towards other appropriate resources for information and education.

During the multiprofessional meeting, the team decided they would want to aim to keep Mr W at the care facility until his death, unless extreme circumstances prevented it (in that case the back up options of local hospice or community hospital were considered, as everyone was keen to avoid an admission to the acute sector). A do not attempt cardiopulmonary resuscitation (DNA CPR) form was completed and held in Mr W's records as it was felt it would be futile to attempt CPR in the event of sudden collapse.

Over several months Mr W's condition steadily deteriorated with gradual weight loss and reduction in energy levels and mobility. His care team gained advice and support from the palliative care team and was able to care for Mr W until his death. A few days before he died, Mr W told a member of the care staff that he felt he was dying, and they were able to provide gentle, honest and appropriate support for him as that possibility had been pre-emptively discussed with staff at educational sessions provided by the palliative care team clinical nurse specialist.

After Mr W's death, staff at the care facility were able to inform the other residents about what had happened and the specialist palliative care team facilitated a 'debrief' session, to allow staff time and space to reflect on a period of care which some had felt had been outside their 'usual' skills but they had identified as being a crucial role for them in caring for Mr W.

References

Bell A, Bhate M (1992) Prevalence of overweight and obesity in Down's syndrome and other mentally handicapped adults living in the community. *Journal of Intellectual Disability Research* **36**: 359–64

Bhaumik S, Watson JM, Thorp CF, Tryer F, McGrother CW (2008) Body mass index in adults with intellectual disability: Distribution, associations and service implications: A population-based prevalence study. *Journal of Intellectual Disability Research* **52**: 287–98

Bickley LS, Szilagyi PG (2009) *Bates' guide to physical examination and history taking*, 10th edn. Lippincott Williams and Wilkins, London

Bissett L (2005) Reducing the risk of catheter-related urinary tract infection. *Nursing Times Supplement* **101**(12): 64–7

Bond P, Harris C (2005) Best practice in urinary catheterisation and catheter care. *Nursing Times Supplement* **101**(8): 54–8

Burkhart J, Fox R, Rotatori A (1985) Obesity of mentally retarded individuals: Prevalence, characteristics and intervention. *American Journal of Mental Deficiency* **90**: 502–11

Department for Constitutional Affairs (2005) *Mental Capacity Act 2005*. DCA, London

Department of Health (2001) *Valuing people. A new strategy for learning disability for 21st century*. DH, London

Department of Health (2002) *Action for health: Health action plans and health facilitation*. DH, London

Department of Health (2006) *Essential steps to safe, clean care: Reducing healthcare-associated infections*. Available from: http://www.dh.gov.uk/en/ Publicationsandstatistics/Publications/PublicationsPolicyAndGuidance/DH_4136212

Department of Health (2007a) *A simple guide to MRSA*. DH, London

Department of Health (2007b) *A simple guide to C. Difficile*. DH, London

Department of Health (2009) *Clostridium difficile infection: How to deal with the problem*. DH, London

Disability Rights Commission (2006) *Report of the DRC Formal Inquiry Panel to the DRC's formal investigation into the inequalities in physical health experienced by people with mental health problems and people with learning disabilities*. DRC, London

Dougherty L, Lister S (eds) (2008) *The Royal Marsden Hospital manual of clinical nursing procedures*. Student edn (7th edn). Wiley Blackwell, London

Dougherty L Lister S (eds) (2011) *The Royal Marsden Hospital manual of clinical nursing procedures*. (8th edn). Wiley Blackwell, London

Hamilton S, Hankey CR, Miller S, Boyle S, Melville CA (2007) A review of weight loss interventions for adults with intellectual disabilities. *Obesity Reviews* **8**: 339–45

Katch FI, McArdle WD (1983) *Nutrition, weight control and exercise*. Lea and Febiger, Philadelphia

Madeo M, Roodhouse AJ (2009) Reducing the risks associated with urinary catheters. *Nursing Standard* **23**(9): 47–55

Marieb EM, Hoehn K (2010) *Human anatomy and physiology* (8th edn). Pearson Benjamin Cummings, San Francisco

Mencap (2004) *Treat me right! Better health care for people with a learning disability*. Mencap, London

Millar S, Aitken S (2003) *Personal Communication Passports. Guidelines for good prac-*

tice. CALL centre, Edinburgh

NICE (2006a) *Hypertension: Management of hypertension in adults in primary care (a partial update of NICE Clinical Guideline 18).* NICE, London

NICE (2006b) *Nutrition support in adults, oral nutrition, enteral tube feeding and parenteral nutrition. Methods, evidence and guidance. Clinical Guidance 32.* National Institute for Health and Clinical Excellence, London. Available from: www.nice.org. uk.

Preston RM (2005) Aseptic technique: Evidence-based approach for patients' safety. *British Journal of Nursing* **14**(10): 540–2

Rimmer JH, Braddock D, Fujirua G (1993) Prevalence of obesity in adults with mental retardation: Implications for health promotion and disease prevention. *Mental Retardation* **31**: 103–10

Robinson J (2007) Female urethral catheterisation. *Nursing Standard* **22**(8): 48–56

Royal College of Nursing (2005) *The management of pressure sore ulcers in primary and secondary care: A clinical practice guideline.* RCN/NICE, London

Saleh M, Anthony D, Parboteeah S (2009) The impact of pressure ulcer risk assessment on patient outcomes among hospitalised patients. *Journal of Clinical Nursing* **18**: 1923–9

Schwartz TL, Nihalani N, Jindal S, Virk S, Jones N (2004) Psychiatric medication-induced obesity: A review. *Obesity reviews* **5**: 115–21

Subbe C, Kruger M, Rutherford P, Gemmel L (2001) Validation of a modified early warning score in medical admissions. *Quarterly Journal of Medicine* **94**: 521–6

Turner S (2001) Health needs of people who have a learning disability. In Thompson J, Pickering S (eds) *Meeting the health needs of people who have a learning disability* (pp. 63–88). Ballière Tindall, London

Turner T D (1985) Which dressing and why? In Westaby S (ed) *Wound care.* London: Heinem

Wood T (1994) Weight reduction of a group of adults with learning disabilities. *British Journal of Learning Disabilities* **22**: 97–9

NOTES

Chapter 5

Long-term conditions

Catherine Hart, Chris Knifton, Kathleen McNicholas and Nikki Welyczko

- What do I need to know about thyroid disorders?
- What do I need to know about diabetes mellitus?
- What do I need to know about cardiovascular disease?
- What do I need to know about dementia?
- What do I need to know about epilepsy?

What do I need to know about thyroid disorders?
Nikki Welyczko

Hypothyroidism

The endocrine system is made up of glands that produce and secrete hormones. These include the thyroid, the pituitary gland, the adrenal glands, the pancreas and many others. The thyroid gland lies just in front of the trachea in the neck and is the largest endocrine gland in the body. The major hormone secreted by the thyroid gland is thyroxine, also called T4. The amount of T4 produced by the thyroid gland is controlled by another hormone, which is made in the pituitary gland located at the base of the brain, called thyroid stimulating hormone (TSH).

The most common type of thyroid problem is hypothyroidism. Hypothyroidism means that the thyroid gland does not make enough of the hormone thyroxine. It is often called an underactive thyroid. This causes many of the body's functions to slow down.

Hypothyroidism is classified as either primary or secondary. The primary form is caused by a disorder with the thyroid gland itself. The secondary form is caused by a failure to stimulate normal thyroid function (Scott 2012).

Prevalence

The disorder is most prevalent in women (it is estimated that about 1 in 50 women develop it during their lives) and in individuals with Down's syndrome (hypothyroidism develops in one in three people with Down's syndrome before the age of 25 years) (Clinical Knowledge Summaries 2011). Incidence is increasing in the UK population, particularly in the 40–50 age group (Scott 2012).

However, routine screening for thyroid disorders in the general adult population is not recommended (BTA et al 2006).

People with diabetes, especially type 1 diabetes, are at an increased risk of developing thyroid disease. Most people with diabetes who develop new thyroid disease are hypothyroid, however, there is a small increased risk of developing hyperthyroidism (Clinical Knowledge Summaries 2011). Hypothyroidism, occurs in 1 in 4000 live births (Vaidya and Pearce 2008) and can be a serious problem if left untreated. It is therefore important that all children, and particularly those with Down's syndrome, be tested at birth (with the heel prick or 'Guthrie test') and then on a yearly basis to ensure that the thyroid is working correctly.

Symptoms

Many clinical signs and symptoms can be caused by a low level of thyroxine. Essentially, everything in the body 'slows down'. However, not all symptoms develop in all cases. Symptoms that commonly occur include tiredness, weight gain, constipation, aches, feeling cold, dry skin, lifeless hair, fluid retention, mental slowing, and depression. Less common symptoms include a hoarse voice, irregular or heavy menstrual periods in women, infertility, loss of sex drive, carpal tunnel syndrome (which causes pains and numbness in the hand), and memory loss or confusion in the elderly (Scott 2012). However, all these symptoms can be caused by other conditions, and sometimes, particularly in the elderly and people with a learning disability, the diagnosis is not obvious. Symptoms usually develop slowly and gradually become worse over months or years as the level of thyroxine in the body gradually falls.

Untreated

Untreated, hypothyroidism can lead to an increased risk of developing heart disease. This is because a low thyroxine level causes the blood lipids (cholesterol, etc) to rise, particularly if the person is younger than 65 years of age (Hak et al 2000, Surks et al 2004, Mariotti and Cambuli 2007, Razvi et al 2008, Rodondi et al 2010).

During pregnancy there is an increased risk of developing some pregnancy complications, for example, pre-eclampsia, anaemia, premature labour, low birth weight, stillbirth, and serious bleeding after the birth (Reid et al 2010). A rare complication of untreated hypothyroidism is hypothyroid coma (myxoedema coma) (Weetman 2003). This is a medical emergency and is generally fatal. Progression is usually gradual but when the body is under physiological stress, such as infection, exposure to cold, or trauma, this exacerbates severe or prolonged hypothyroidism and coma may rapidly develop (Scott 2012).

Causes

The most common causes of hypothyroidism are an autoimmune disease called 'autoimmune thyroiditis' and thyroid damage due to surgery or radioactive iodine therapy (Biondi and Cooper 2008). The immune system in the body normally makes antibodies to attack bacteria and viruses. However, in autoimmune disease, the immune system makes antibodies against certain tissues of the body. With autoimmune thyroiditis, the body makes antibodies that attach to the thyroid gland and this affects its function. The thyroid gland is then not able to make enough thyroxine, and hypothyroidism gradually develops. It is thought that something triggers the immune system to make antibodies against the thyroid, but the 'trigger' is not fully understood (Scott 2012).

Autoimmune thyroiditis is more common than usual in people with:

* A family history of hypothyroidism caused by autoimmune thyroiditis.
* Down's syndrome.
* Turner's syndrome. (The lack, partial lack, or abnormal formation of the second X chromosome produces the condition called Turner syndrome.)
* An enlarged thyroid gland (diffuse goitre).
* A past history of Graves' disease, or thyroiditis following childbirth.
* A personal or family history of other autoimmune disorder. For example, vitiligo, pernicious anaemia, Addison's disease, Type 1 diabetes, premature ovarian failure, coeliac disease, Sjogren's syndrome.

Some people with autoimmune thyroiditis also develop a swollen thyroid gland (goitre). Autoimmune thyroiditis with a goitre is called Hashimoto's disease. In addition, people with autoimmune thyroiditis have a small increased risk of developing other autoimmune conditions such as vitiligo (depigmentation of the skin) and pernicious anaemia (lack of vitamin B12) (Clinical Knowledge Summaries 2011).

Other causes of hypothyroidism are less common and include:

* Worldwide, iodine deficiency is the most common cause of hypothyroidism (the body needs iodine to make thyroxine). However, it is rare for a diet in Western countries to lack sufficient iodine (Weetman 2003).
* A side-effect of some medicines. For example, amiodarone and lithium (Clinical Knowledge Summaries 2011).
* Other types of 'thyroiditis' (thyroid inflammation) caused by various rare conditions.

- A pituitary gland problem is a rare cause. The pituitary is situated just under the brain and it produces TSH which stimulates the thyroid gland to make thyroxine. If the pituitary does not make TSH, then the thyroid cannot make enough thyroxine.
- Some children are born with an underactive thyroid gland (congenital hypothyroidism) (Vaidya and Pearce 2008).

Diagnosis

A blood test, known as a thyroid function test (TFT), is used to identify problems with thyroid gland function and measures levels of thyroid-stimulating hormone (TSH) and thyroxine (T4).

- *Thyroid-stimulating hormone (TSH).* This hormone stimulates the thyroid gland to make thyroxine. If the level of thyroxine in the blood is low, then the pituitary releases more TSH to try and stimulate the thyroid gland to make more thyroxine. Therefore, a raised TSH level means the thyroid gland is underactive and is not making enough thyroxine. A high TSH level indicates that the thyroid gland is failing because of a problem that is directly affecting the thyroid (primary hypothyroidism). The opposite scenario, in which the TSH level is low, usually indicates that the person has an overactive thyroid that is producing too much thyroid hormone (hyperthyroidism). Occasionally, a low TSH may result from an abnormality in the pituitary gland, which prevents it from making enough TSH to stimulate the thyroid (secondary hypothyroidism). In most healthy individuals, a normal TSH value means that the thyroid is functioning normally.
- *Thyroxine (T4).* A low level of T4 confirms hypothyroidism.

In some cases, people may have a raised TSH but have a normal T4. This means that whilst the body is making enough thyroxine, the thyroid gland needs extra 'stimulation' from TSH to make the required amount of thyroxine. This is known as 'sub-clinical hypothyroidism' and means that there is an increased risk of developing hypothyroidism in the future, and continued regular blood tests are required.

Treatment

Fortunately, hypothyroidism can be easily treated by oral medication with the synthetic hormone levothyroxine. This is an inexpensive drug which serves to replace the missing hormones. With treatment, symptoms are usually quickly alleviated and complications are unlikely to develop (Weetman 2003).

Most adults require between 50 and 150 micrograms daily (British National Formulary 2011).

A low dose is sometimes prescribed at first, especially in those over 60 or with heart problems, and this is then gradually increased over a period of time. Blood tests are usually taken every 2–3 months, and the dose may be adjusted accordingly. The blood test measures TSH (see above). Once the blood TSH level is normal it means that the correct amount of levothyroxine is being taken. It is then common practice to check the TSH blood level once a year. The dose may need adjustment in the early stages of pregnancy and in late middle age and onwards.

Ideally, levothyroxine should be taken on an empty stomach (before breakfast). This is because some foods rich in calcium or iron may interfere with the absorption of the drug from the gut. (For the same reason, levothyroxine tablets should not be taken at the same time of day as calcium or iron tablets.) (British National Formulary 2011).

As levothyroxine tablets replace the body's natural hormone, side-effects are relatively uncommon (British National Formulary 2011). However, people with angina sometimes find that their angina becomes exacerbated after first starting the drug. This should be reported to a doctor.

Too high a dose of levothyroxine can lead to symptoms and problems of an overactive thyroid. For example, palpitations, diarrhoea, irritability, sweating, and an increased risk of developing osteoporosis.

Other medicines may interfere with the action of levothyroxine. For example, carbamazepine, iron tablets, phenytoin, rifampicin and warfarin. People with hypothyroidism are entitled to free prescriptions for all medicines, whether related to the hypothyroidism or not.

Hyperthyroidism (thyrotoxicosis)

Hyperthyroidism or thyrotoxicosis is a condition where the thyroid gland produces too much thyroid hormone (Weetman 2003). The additional thyroxine creates a metabolic imbalance that causes many of the body's functions to speed up.

Symptoms

Symptoms include restlessness, nervousness, feeling emotional, irritability, insomnia, being 'always on the go', tremor of the hands, palpitations (atrial fibrillation and flutter) (Frost et al 2004), weight loss despite an increased appetite, increased perspiration, an intolerance of heat, an increased thirst, diarrhoea or needing to go to the toilet to pass faeces more often than normal, shortness of breath, skin problems (such as hair thinning and itch), and menstrual changes (often periods become very light or infrequent). A swelling of the thyroid gland in the neck (goitre) may occur and eye problems (if the hyperthyroidism is caused by Graves' disease, see below.) (AACE Thyroid Task Force 2002, Cooper 2003, Weetman 2003).

Most people with hyperthyroidism do not have all these symptoms, but a combination of two or more is common (Clinical Knowledge Summaries 2008). Symptoms usually develop slowly over several weeks. All the symptoms can be caused by other problems, and so the diagnosis may not be obvious at first, particularly among older people and people with a learning disability (Reid and Wheeler 2005). Hyperthroidism may present with deterioration of pre-existing heart disease, depression, anorexia, weight loss or behavioural changes among people with a learning disability (AACE Thyroid Task Force 2002; Cooper 2003; BTA et al 2006). Symptoms may be mild to start with, but become worse as the level of thyroxine in the blood gradually rises.

Untreated

Left untreated, hyperthyroidism may lead to an increased risk of developing heart problems such as atrial fibrillation (an abnormal heart rhythm), cardiomyopathy (a weakened heart), angina, and heart failure. During pregnancy, there is an increased risk of developing some pregnancy complications, for example, miscarriage, eclampsia, premature labour, low birth weight, stillbirth, and possibly congenital abnormality. There is also an increased risk of developing osteoporosis, particularly in postmenopausal women, due to accelerated bone loss (AACE Thyroid Task Force 2002).

Prevalence

Hyperthyroidism is less common than hypothyroidism. About 2 in 100 women, and 2 in 1000 men, develop hyperthyroidism at some stage of their life (Clinical Knowledge Summaries 2008). It occurs mostly in people aged 30–60 years, especially when there is a family history of thyroid problems. Only 5% of patients are younger than 15 years (Scott 2012).

Causes

There are several causes of hyperthyroidism but Graves' disease is the commonest (Scott 2012). Graves' disease is an autoimmune disease. The immune system in the body normally makes antibodies to attack bacteria and viruses. However, in autoimmune disease, the immune system makes antibodies which are directed against certain tissues of the body. In Graves' disease, thyroid stimulating anti-bodies bind to and stimulate the TSH receptors of the thyroid gland to make high levels of thyroxine. The trigger for this autoimmune response is unclear; however, it is thought that genetic factors, immunological factors and the presence of other autoimmune endocrine abnormalities, such as type 1 diabetes mellitus, may play a role (Scott 2012).

In Graves' disease the thyroid gland usually enlarges, which causes a swelling in the neck (goitre). Thyroid eye disease occurs in up to half of people with Graves' disease (Cawood et al 2004, Cooper 2004, Reid and Wheeler 2005). If they are affected, the eyes are appear to be 'pushed' forward and look more prominent (proptosis). This can cause discomfort and watering of the eyes. Problems with eye muscles may also occur and lead to diplopia (double vision). It is not clear why eye symptoms occur in some people who have Graves' disease, however, the incidence of thyroid eye disease is four times more likely to occur in smokers or former smokers than in people who have never smoked (Nygaard 2007).

Thyroid nodules are a less common cause of hyperthyroidism. Thyroid nodules are lumps which can develop in the thyroid gland. It is not clear why they develop. They are usually benign but contain abnormal thyroid tissue. This abnormal thyroid tissue does not respond to the normal controlling system which ensures that the body makes the right amount of thyroxine and, as a result, the thyroid gland may make more than is needed.

There are several other rare causes of hyperthyroidism. For example, some people who take medication such as amiodarone and lithium develop hyperthyroidism. There are various other rare diseases that result in excess thyroxine being made.

Diagnosis

As with hypothyroidism, a thyroid function test (TFT) is used to identify suspected hyperthyroidism. The test measures levels of thyroid-stimulating hormone (TSH), thyroxine (T4) and T3.

* *Thyroid-stimulating hormone (TSH)*. This hormone stimulates the thyroid gland to make thyroxine. If the level of thyroxine in the blood is high, then the pituitary releases less TSH. Therefore, a low level of TSH means the thyroid gland is overactive and is making too much thyroxine.
* *Thyroxine (T4)*. A high level of T4 confirms hyperthyroidism.

Sometimes test results may be 'borderline'. For example, a normal T4 but a low TSH. Other tests are sometimes done to clarify the situation and the cause. For example, another blood test called T3 is sometimes undertaken. T3 tests are useful to diagnose hyperthyroidism or to determine its severity. Patients who are hyperthyroid will have an elevated T3 level.

An ultrasound scan of the thyroid may be performed in the presence of a nodular goitre. If tests are 'borderline', it may be necessary to repeat them a few weeks later, as sometimes borderline tests are due to another illness. Other tests may be done if a rare cause of hyperthyroidism is suspected.

Treatments

The main aim of treatment is to reduce the level of thyroxine to normal. Other problems such as a large goitre (thyroid swelling) or associated eye problems may also need treatment. Factors such as the underlying cause of the problem, patient's age, and the size of any goitre are taken into account. Treatment options include the following:

- *Antithyroid medicines*. Antithyroid medicines can reduce the amount of thyroxine made by the overactive thyroid gland. The most common medicine used in the UK is carbimazole (British National Formulary 2011). Carbimazole does not affect the amount of thyroxine that has already been made and stored but reduces further production. Therefore, it may take 4–8 weeks of treatment for the thyroxine level to come down to normal.

  The dose of carbimazole needed to keep the thyroxine level normal varies from person to person. Carbimazole is usually taken for 12–18 months at first. After this, in about half of cases, the condition will have settled down and the carbimazole can be stopped. If the condition flares up again in the future, a further course may be needed. In about half of all cases, carbimazole needs to be continued long-term to control symptoms. Carbimazole can, rarely, affect the white blood cells which fight infection. Development of a pyrexia, sore throat, mouth ulcers, or other symptoms of infection whilst taking carbimazole, requires the tablets to be stopped immediately and medical advice sought (British National Formulary 2011).
- *Radio-iodine treatment*. This involves taking a drink, or swallowing a capsule, which contains radioactive iodine. The main use of iodine in the body is to make thyroxine, therefore, radioactive iodine builds up in the thyroid gland. As the radioactivity is concentrated in the thyroid gland, it destroys some thyroid tissue which reduces the amount of thyroxine made. The dose of radioactivity to the rest of the body is very low and is not dangerous. In most people, hypermetabolic symptoms reduce within 6–8

weeks, however some people may require a second dose (Scott 2012).

It can be difficult for clinical staff to judge exactly the right dose of carbimazole or radio-iodine to give in each case. Too much treatment may make the thyroxine level to become too low; not enough treatment means the level remains higher than normal. Regular blood tests are needed to check on the thyroxine level.

- *Beta-blockers.* Some people are prescribed a beta-blocker medicine (for example, propranolol, atenolol, etc) for a few weeks whilst the level of thyroxine is reduced gradually by one of the above treatments. Beta-blockers can block some of the effects of a high level of thyroxine. In particular they help to reduce the symptoms of tremor, palpitations, sweating, agitation, and anxiety (British National Formulary 2011).

- *Surgery (partial thyroidectomy).* Partial thyroidectomy, which involves removing part of the thyroid gland, thereby decreasing its size and capacity for hormone production, is indicated for patients aged less than 40 years who have a large goitre (thyroid swelling) (Scott 2012). If too much thyroid is removed, the patient may need to take levothyroxine tablets after the surgery to keep the thyroxine level normal.

Continuing care

The prognosis following treatment for hyperthyroidism is good (Reid and Wheeler 2005). However, relapse may occur after cessation of therapy, and it is important, even after successful treatment, that annual blood tests are carried out to ensure that the hyperthyroidism has not returned. Equally, these blood tests will identify people who may develop an underactive thyroid in the future which needs to be treated with levothyroxine.

What do I need to know about diabetes mellitus?
Nikki Welyczko

Diabetes mellitus is one of the biggest healthcare challenges facing the NHS (Department of Health 2010a). It is a major cause of morbidity and mortality nationally and internationally, and has an increasing prevalence. There are now 2.2 million people with diabetes in England, and the number of people developing type 2 diabetes continues to rise (Department of Health 2010a). Estimates suggest that an additional 600 000 people may be unaware that they have the disease. The incidence increases with age, and it is the fifth leading cause of death in the UK (Scott 2012).

The National Service Framework for Diabetes (Department of Health 2002) recognises that significant inequalities exist in the risk of developing diabetes, in access to health services, the quality of those services, and in health outcomes, particularly with regard to people with type 2 diabetes. People who are overweight, physically inactive or have a family history of diabetes are at increased risk of developing the condition. People of South Asian, African, and African-Caribbean descent have a higher than average risk of developing type 2 diabetes, as do less affluent individuals and populations. Socially excluded people, including prisoners, refugees and asylum seekers, and people with learning difficulties or mental health problems may receive poorer quality care (Department of Health 2002).

There are nine million people with learning disabilities and it is estimated that 270 000 people in this group have type 2 diabetes (Diabetes UK 2009). People with learning disabilities are at a higher risk of developing diabetes than those without learning disabilities (Royal College of Nursing 2011). This may be attributed to increased levels of obesity, poor diet and inactive lifestyles. Common signs and symptoms associated with diabetes, such as an increase in incontinence (caused by polyuria), may be attributed to the person's learning disabilities rather than the disease itself. This is known as 'diagnostic overshadowing' (Royal College of Nursing 2011). Other issues, such as weight and communication difficulties, may also lead to delayed diagnosis with consequent complications. This section provides a brief overview of diabetes and a summary of the main complications and prevention strategies.

What is diabetes mellitus?

Diabetes is a disease of the pancreas, an organ situated behind the stomach that produces the hormone insulin. Insulin helps the body to store energy from food. When a person has diabetes, the pancreas either cannot produce enough insulin, the body uses the insulin incorrectly, or both. Insulin helps glucose in the bloodstream enter the body's cells to be stored or used. If the insulin is not functioning properly, glucose cannot enter the cells. This causes glucose levels in the blood to rise, creating a condition of high blood sugar or hyperglycaemia (Scott 2012), leaving the cells without fuel.

Types of diabetes

Diabetes mellitus occurs in two primary forms:

- *Type 1* (previously referred to as insulin-dependent diabetes mellitus) occurs because the insulin-producing beta cells of the pancreas are damaged. In type 1 diabetes, the pancreas makes little or no insulin, so glucose cannot get into the body's cells for use as energy. People with type 1 diabetes need to use insulin injections to control their blood glucose. The insulin must be injected via the subcutaneous route, since, taken orally, the drug would be destroyed by the acidic environment of the stomach. Type 1 is the most common form of diabetes in people aged under 20, but it can occur at any age. Ten percent of people with diabetes are diagnosed with type 1 (Department of Health 2002).
- *Type 2* (previously referred to as non-insulin dependent diabetes mellitus) is considerably more common and typically affects people over the age of 40 who are overweight (Department of Health 2002). However, the prevalence of type 2 diabetes is becoming increasingly common among children and younger age groups due to rising levels of obesity and other lifestyle factors (Department of Health 2010a) In type 2 diabetes, the pancreas makes insulin, but it either does not produce enough or the insulin does not work properly. Type 2 diabetes may sometimes be controlled with a combination of diet, weight management and exercise. However, treatment may also include oral glucose-lowering medications (oral hypoglycaemic drugs, such as glicazide and metformin) or insulin injections.

What causes diabetes mellitus?

The exact cause of diabetes is not known but causes are thought to be multi-factorial. The following factors may increase the risk of developing diabetes:

- Family history of diabetes or inherited tendency.
- South Asian, African or Caribbean ethnic background.
- Obesity (being 20% or more over desired body weight).
- Physical stress (such as surgery or illness).
- Use of certain medications.
- Injury to pancreas (such as infection, tumour, surgery or accident).
- Autoimmune disease.
- Hypertension.
- Abnormal blood cholesterol or triglyceride levels.
- Age (risk increases with age).
- Alcohol (risk increases with years of heavy alcohol use).

- Smoking.
- Pregnancy – gestational diabetes. (Pregnancy puts extra stress on a woman's body which causes some women to develop diabetes. Blood sugar levels often return to normal after childbirth. However, women who develop diabetes during pregnancy have an increased chance of developing diabetes later in life.)

How is diabetes diagnosed?

Diabetes is diagnosed by taking a fasting venous plasma glucose test (FBG). The FPG measures the blood glucose level after fasting for 10–12 hours (World Health Organization 2006). However, if diabetes is suspected as a concern, a simple urine dip (urinalysis) can be carried out to test for the presence of glucose (which is not normally present in urine). A capillary blood sample, carried out first thing in the morning, before breakfast, or over a 24 hour period, may also provide evidence that further testing for diabetes is required.

Common signs and symptoms

There are many common signs and symptoms that may alert individuals, carers or healthcare professionals to the presence of diabetes. These include:

- Exceptional thirst (polydipsia).
- Dry mouth.
- Frequent urination (polyuria).
- Loss of weight.
- Weakness or fatigue.
- Blurred vision.
- Cuts or sores that take a long time to heal.
- Itching skin or yeast infections (thrush).
- Leg pain.

Diabetes can have a major impact on the physical, psychological and social well-being of individuals and their families, and can lead to complications such as heart disease, stroke, renal failure, amputation and blindness. However, there is evidence (Department of Health 2002, 2010a) to show that:

- The onset of Type 2 diabetes can be delayed, or even prevented.

- Effective management of the condition increases life expectancy and reduces the risk of complications.
- Self/carer management is the cornerstone of effective diabetes care.

What are some of the long-term complications of diabetes?

Prolonged exposure to raised blood glucose levels damages tissues throughout the body by damaging the small blood vessels. The initial changes are reversible but, over time, prolonged raised blood glucose levels can lead to irreversible damage. Even a mildly raised glucose level that does not cause any symptoms can have damaging effects in the long term. These microvascular complications only occur in people with diabetes and include:

- *Diabetic retinopathy* (damage to the eyes), which can lead to visual impairment and blindness.
- *Diabetic nephropathy* (damage to the kidneys), which can lead to progressive renal failure.
- *Diabetic neuropathy* (damage to the nerves). Damage to the nerves supplying the lower limbs can lead to loss of sensation in the feet, thereby predisposing to the development of foot ulcers and lower limb amputation. Damage to other nerves can lead to a variety of symptoms, including postural hypotension (feeling faint on standing up), abnormal sweating, gastrointestinal problems (such as diarrhoea), difficulties with bladder emptying, and erectile dysfunction (impotence).

People with diabetes, particularly type 2 diabetes, are also at significantly increased risk of developing macrovascular disease. This results from damage to the walls of the large blood vessels, which can then become blocked. Cardiovascular disease includes:

- *Coronary heart disease*, which can lead to angina, acute myocardial infarction (heart attack) and heart failure.
- *Cerebrovascular disease*: Stroke and transient ischaemic attacks.
- *Peripheral vascular disease:* Blockage of the large blood vessels supplying the lower limbs resulting in poor circulation to the legs and feet, which can cause pain in the legs on walking and can also predispose to the development of foot ulcers and amputation.

A number of other conditions also occur more commonly in people with diabetes, including:

- *Cataracts*, which are twice as common in people with diabetes and occur about 10 years earlier than in people who do not have diabetes infections, particularly of the urinary tract and the skin.
- *Soft tissue conditions*, such as frozen shoulder and trigger finger.
- *Skin conditions*, some of which are specific to people with diabetes.
- *Mental health problems*, including depression and eating disorders.

What are the increased risks of complications with diabetes?

- *Obesity*. The National Audit Office (2001) suggests that 47% of type 2 diabetes cases in England could be directly attributed to obesity.
- *Heart disease*. Adults with diabetes have heart disease death rates about two to four times higher than adults without diabetes (YHPHO 2006).
- *Retinopathy*. Within 20 years of diagnosis nearly all patients with type 1 diabetes have a degree of retinopathy as opposed to approximately 60 per cent of individuals with type 2 diabetes (YHPHO 2006).
- *Blindness*. In 1995 diabetes was the single largest cause of blindness in the UK (Evans 1995).
- *A sedentary lifestyle*. A sedentary lifestyle increases the risk of developing diabetes (Department of Health 2002). The risk of developing type 2 diabetes is increased by 30-40% in sedentary people, compared with people who are regularly physically active (YHPHO 2006). Lifestyle interventions (such as exercise combined with dietary advice) have been found to reduce the incidence of diabetes by 58% (Diabetes Prevention Program Research Group 2002).
- *Stroke*. The risk of stroke is two to four times higher among people with diabetes (Folsom et al 1999).
- *Limb amputation*. Diabetes is the most common cause of non-traumatic lower limb amputation (Fox and Mackinnon 1999). Fifteen percent of people with diabetes develop foot ulcers and 5–15% of those need amputations (University of York NHS Centre for Reviews and Dissemination 1999). Every 30 seconds a leg is lost to diabetes somewhere in the world (International Diabetes Federation 2005).
- *Kidney disease*. Diabetes has become the single most common cause of end-stage renal disease (Ansell and Feest 1999). About 30% of patients with type 2 diabetes develop overt kidney disease (Viberti et al 1996).

Prevention

- *Lifestyle interventions.* Lifestyle interventions significantly reduce progression rates to diabetes in pre-diabetic individuals. Preventing diabetes is at the heart of the Diabetes National Service Framework (Department of Health 2002) and initiatives such as the NHS Health Check programme (Department of Health 2008a) and Change4Life are key to reducing the number of people at risk of developing diabetes. Evidence shows that sustained lifestyle changes in diet and physical activity can reduce the risk of developing type 2 diabetes (Department of Health 2010a).

  Diabetes UK (2009), with Speakup, a self-help advocacy charity for people with learning disabilities, has developed a DVD for people with type 2 diabetes who have learning disabilities. The DVD, which is called *Diabetes – Living a healthier Life*, will enable this audience to have access to the same information about the condition as people who do not have learning disabilities. It covers a range of topics including an explanation of what type 2 diabetes is, how to prevent it, how to manage and understand the condition, and the benefits of healthy eating and physical activity.

- *Weight loss.* For people who are obese, losing a fairly modest amount of weight (up to 10kg) has been shown to reduce diabetes-related mortality by 30–40% (UK Prospective Diabetes Study Group 1998). Helping a person to lose weight can significantly reduce their risk of developing type 2 diabetes (Department of Health 2010a). *Healthy weight, healthy lives* (Department of Health 2008b) and *One year on* (Department of Health 2009) set out the Government's strategy to reduce obesity and help people to maintain a healthy weight.

- *Early detection.* Early diagnosis and treatment can reduce the risk of complications (Department of Health 2010a). Half of all people with type 2 diabetes have complications on diagnosis, which could have been prevented if diabetes had been detected earlier (UK Prospective Diabetes Study Group 1998).

- *Eye screening and treatment* can reduce the risk of severe visual loss or blindness among people with diabetes to less than a half (University of York NHS Centre for Reviews and Dissemination 1999). Improvements in retinopathy screening is one of the targets of the National Service Framework (Department of Health 2002, 2010a).

- *Improved blood pressure control* reduces the risk of:

- Death from long-term complications of diabetes by a third.
- Strokes by more than a third.
- Serious deterioration of vision by more than a third (Clarke et al 2005).
- *Improved glycaemic (blood glucose) control* reduces the risk of:
  - Major diabetic eye disease by a quarter.
  - Early kidney damage by a third (Clarke et al 2005).
- *Improved self/carer care.* Structured patient education plays an important role in enabling people with diabetes to manage their diabetes on a day-to-day basis (Department of Health 2010a). The first recommendation in NICE (2009) is that every person with diabetes should be offered structured education. Ninety-five percent of diabetes management is self-care; therefore patient education is essential (Department of Health 2002). It is important that the diabetic person and carer also have knowledge about the effective management of hypoglycaemia and hyperglycaemia. The National Service Framework for diabetes (Department of Health 2002) highlights structured education programmes as a key part of systematic care. Various options exist, including:
  - Type 1: DAFNE (http://www.dafne.uk.com). DAFNE stands for Dose Adjustment For Normal Eating and aims to improve outcomes for people with type 1 diabetes through high quality structured education which is embedded in the Health Service.
  - Type 2: DESMOND (http://www.diabetes.co.uk/education/desmond.html). DESMOND is the acronym for Diabetes Education and Self-Management for Ongoing and Newly Diagnosed. DESMOND is an NHS organisation that helps to deliver high quality patient education to people with type 2 diabetes and those who are at risk of diabetes. DESMOND aims to educate people further about diabetes, acts as a resource for people to help manage diabetes-related changes, offers a range of education programmes for people with type 2 diabetes, and offers support to those with the disease.

The important role that personalised care planning has in the management of long-term conditions has been highlighted by several key policy drivers (Department of Health 2005, 2010b). Lord Darzi's NHS Next Stage Review (2008) set out the commitment that, by the end of 2010, everyone with a long-term condition should be offered a personalised care plan. Delivering health and well-being improvements for people with long-term conditions is challenging; delivering health and well-being improvements for people with long-term conditions and a learning disability presents even more of a challenge. This challenge is not just about treating illness, it is about delivering personalised, responsive, holistic care to improve the quality of people's lives. Planning care should fully involve the individuals, seeing them as equal partners in their health and well being, not passive recipients of care. This ethos supports the wider aims of personalisation and is the process of personalised care planning. The need for this is perhaps even more important for people with a learning disability for whom diabetes may be just one of many health and social challenges they face.

What do I need to know about cardiovascular disease?
Nikki Welyczko

In the UK, more than 1.4 million people suffer from some form of cardiovascular disorder (Duffy 2011). Cardiovascular disease is the primary cause of death worldwide (WHO 2005). In line with national and international statistics, cardiovascular disease is a leading cause of death amongst people with learning disabilities (14–20%) (Hollins et al 1998), with rates expected to rise due to increased longevity and lifestyle changes associated with community living (Wells et al 1995). In addition, people with moderate to profound learning disabilities are more likely than the general population to die from congenital abnormalities (Tyrer and McGrother 2009). Almost half of all people with Down's syndrome are affected by congenital heart defects (Brookes and Alberman 1996; Hermon et al 2001) and congenital heart disease is more prevalent among people with William's syndrome. However, the focus of this chapter is on the identification and prevention of cardiovascular disease and, as such, congenital heart problems are not addressed.

What is cardiovascular disease?

Cardiovascular diseases are diseases of the heart (cardiac muscle) or blood vessels (vasculature). In clinical practice, the term 'cardiovascular disease' usually refers to diseases of the heart or blood vessels that are caused by atheroma (atherosclerosis).

What is atheroma (atherosclerosis)?

Patches of atheroma can be described as small, fatty lumps that develop within the inside lining of arteries. Atheroma is also known as atherosclerosis and hardening of the arteries. Patches of atheroma are often called plaques of atheroma.

A patch of atheroma makes an artery narrower or stenosed and can reduce the blood flow through the artery. In time, patches of atheroma can become larger and thicker. Sometimes, a patch may develop a tiny crack on the inside surface of the blood vessel. This may trigger a blood clot (thrombosis) to form over the patch, which may completely block the blood flow. Depending on the artery affected, a blood clot that forms on a patch of atheroma can cause a heart attack, a stroke, or other serious problems.

Heart disease

The term heart disease, or coronary heart disease, is used for conditions caused by narrowing of one or more of the coronary (heart) arteries by atheroma. The problems this can cause include angina, myocardial infarction (heart attack) and heart failure. Heart disease is caused by a gradual build up of fatty deposits on the walls of the coronary arteries that deliver blood to the heart. This causes the artery to narrow (stenose) and makes it harder for it to supply the heart muscle with blood and oxygen. To function normally, the muscle tissue that constitutes most of the heart requires a constant supply of oxygen-containing blood. Blocking of the arteries leads to coronary heart disease, which may result in angina (heart-related chest pain) and eventually to sudden death from a heart attack. Heart attacks (myocardial infarctions) are the most common serious manifestation of coronary heart disease. They are generally triggered by a blood clot forming within a constricted coronary artery, obstructing blood flow and depriving a portion of the heart muscle of oxygen. As a result, the heart cannot pump properly and this can cause permanent disability or death, either immediately or through medical complications (Stocker and O'Halloran 2004).

Cerebrovascular disease - stroke and TIA

Cerebrovascular disease is disease of the arteries in the brain (cerebrum). The problems this can cause include a stroke and a transient ischaemic attack (TIA). In a stroke part of the brain is suddenly damaged. The common cause of a stroke is due to an artery in the brain becoming blocked by a blood clot (thrombus). The blood clot usually forms over a patch of atheroma. A TIA is a disorder caused by temporary lack of blood supply to a part of the brain and symptoms resolve within 24 hours.

Peripheral vascular disease

Peripheral vascular disease is narrowing (due to atheroma) of arteries other than arteries in the heart or brain. The arteries that take blood to the legs are most commonly affected. If the build up of atheroma in the arteries can be prevented, then the likelihood of developing peripheral vascular disease is significantly reduced.

Signs and symptoms of cardiovascular disease

As there are many conditions that fall under the umbrella of heart disease, the related symptoms are numerous but some key symptoms to be aware of are:

- Chest pain or chest discomfort.
- Heart palpitations. On occasion, palpitations can signal a more dangerous heart arrhythmia, such as ventricular tachycardia.
- Light-headedness or dizziness.
- Fatigue, lethargy or daytime sleepiness.
- Shortness of breath.

Risk factors for cardiovascular disease

Risk factors for cardiovascular disease can be divided into two categories: those that are modifiable and those that are non-modifiable.

Modifiable risk factors include:

- *Elevated serum lipid levels* – high cholesterol and high triglyceride (fat). In general, the higher the blood cholesterol level, the greater the risk of developing cardiovascular disease. The risk that a high cholesterol level poses is greater in the presence of other risk factors such as diabetes or high blood pressure (hypertension). As a general rule regardless of what an individual's cholesterol level is, lowering the level reduces risk. This is why people at high risk of developing cardiovascular disease are offered medication (statins) to lower their cholesterol level. A high blood level of triglyceride, another type of lipid (fat), also increases the health risk.
- *Hypertension* (high blood pressure). Over time, hypertension can damage arteries and put strain on the heart meaning the heart has to work harder to

keep the circulation going. This strain can clog or weaken the blood vessels which in turn can narrow the blood vessels further (Stroke Association 2010, World Heart Federation 2011). A systolic blood pressure greater than 140 mmHg or diastolic blood pressure greater than 95 mmHg (Scott 2012) is cause for concern. NICE (2010) has estimated that 40% of adults in England and Wales have hypertension, using the threshold of 140/90 mmHg, and this proportion increases with age. It has been estimated that a small reduction in systolic blood pressure of 2 mmHg in adults, would save more than 14000 UK lives per year (Information Centre 2008). Hypertension usually causes no symptoms, so unless it is checked it may go undetected, particularly in people with a learning disability. In some cases, high blood pressure can be lowered by losing weight, regular physical activity, and eating healthily. Medication may be required in the case of continuing hypertension.

- *Cigarette smoking*. Lifetime smoking approximately doubles the risk of developing heart disease (NICE 2010). The chemicals in tobacco get into the bloodstream from the lungs and damage the arteries and other parts of the body. The risk of stroke and developing other diseases, such as lung cancer, are also increased. Stopping smoking is often the single most effective thing that individuals can do to reduce their health risk. The increased risk drops dramatically within one year of cessation (Scott 2012).

- *Diabetes mellitus* (especially in women) *and renal disease*. The increased risk that these conditions pose to developing cardiovascular diseases can be modified. Good glycaemic control in people with diabetes reduces the risk as does maintaining blood pressure within normal parameters in people with diabetes and kidney disease.

- *Sedentary lifestyle*, inactivity. Regular physical activity can reduce the risk of coronary heart disease, stroke, type 2 diabetes mellitus, cancer, obesity, mental health problems and musculoskeletal problems. Even small increases in physical activity are associated with some protection against the development of many long-term conditions (Department of Health 2011).

- *Obesity*, particularly 'core central obesity'. There is a direct correlation between the size of the waist and cardiovascular risk. Cardiovascular risk is increased with a waist measurement greater than 102 cm in men and 88 cm in women (Scott 2012).

- *Diet*: Excessive intake of saturated fats, refined carbohydrates and salt. High levels of salt in the diet are linked to hypertension, which in turn can lead to coronary heart disease and stroke. NICE (2010) guidance reinforces the need to accelerate the reduction of salt intake among the general population. The maximum levels for adults are currently set at 6 g per day, however, the guidance calls for this to be reduced to 3 g per day by 2025 (NICE 2010). Reducing the consumption of saturated fats is central to the prevention of cardiovascular disease (NICE 2010).

- *Excess alcohol.* Long-term and heavy alcohol consumption is linked with weakness of the heart muscle, known as cardiomyopathy; a condition where the heart cannot pump blood efficiently. Heavy alcohol consumption, including binge drinking, increases the risk of developing coronary heart disease (Academy of Medical Sciences 2004). Conversely, there is a wealth of evidence suggesting that alcohol, particularly red wine, in moderation, may protect against cardiovascular disease (Hines and Rimm 2001) by preventing the narrowing of coronary arteries, allowing blood to flow more freely (Rubin 1999). There are studies that suggest alcohol may have a mild anti-coagulating effect by keeping platelets from clumping together to form clots (Hines and Rimm 2001). Despite the evidence, there is a dichotomy in that promoting moderate alcohol consumption may lead to alcohol abuse among certain 'at risk' individuals.
- *Lower socioeconomic status* is associated with a higher incidence of and mortality rate from cardiovascular disease (Lewis et al 2008). This may be due to this population being more likely to face major risk factors such as smoking and poor diet (ERPHO 2008).

Non-modifiable risk factors for cardiovascular disease include:

- *Age.* There is an increased risk over 40 years (Scott 2012).
- *Gender.* There is an increased risk for males.
- *Family history.*
- *Ethnicity.* People who are white or people who live in the UK with ancestry from India, Pakistan, Bangladesh, or Sri Lanka have an increased risk.
- *Learning disability.*
- *Early menopause.* This is due to reduction in 'cardio-protective' hormones.

Summary

Cardiovascular disease is one of the most significant single causes of death in the UK and worldwide and contributes to a substantial level of morbidity (Walsh and Crumbie 2007). As has been discussed, its origins are multifactorial and so it is impossible to advocate one single measure that will successfully prevent its occurrence. Therefore, a combination of health promotion measures and strategies are required if its incidence is to be reduced. Nurses from all fields of practice have an important role to play in preventing cardiovascular disease among their client groups. If nurses are to be effective within this role, increased knowledge and awareness of cardiovascular disease, latest research evidence and associated national standards and frameworks is essential. This is of particular importance for nurses working with people who have learning disabilities who may not always be able to make informed life choices for themselves.

What do I need to know about dementia?
Catherine Hart and Chris Knifton

The prevalence of dementia in people with learning disabilities remains unclear. Some research (e.g. Cooper 1997) suggests that people with learning disabilities are at greater risk of developing dementia compared to people without learning disabilities. However, other research has failed to support this finding (Janicki and Dalton, 2000).

Research has consistently found that individuals with Down's syndrome are at greater risk of developing dementia at a much earlier age than the general population. There is a wealth of neuropathological, neuropsychological and related evidence showing that people with Down's syndrome are at risk of developing Alzheimer's disease (see Oliver and Holland 1986, Janicki and Dalton 2000). Perhaps the biggest difficulty in terms of diagnosing dementia in people with a learning disability is the lack of reliable and standardised criteria and diagnostic procedures (Deb et al 2001), and a lack of appropriate baseline comparisons. Previously, general population neuropsychological assessments have been used, sometimes adapted, for people with learning disabilities. This has caused difficulties. Due to variability in degrees of learning disability it is impossible to apply normative data to these assessments and they are prone to floor effects. A poor performance on these types of tests, which would usually indicate dementia, may just be due to the assessment picking up the underlying disability.

Usual routine day-to-day activities in people with learning disabilities place very little demand on their cognitive abilities. This lack of change and challenge may make the early and often more subtle signs of dementia very difficult to detect. It also becomes difficult to collate baseline and background information on individuals if they live in care environments as the high turnover of staff means that the person's 'normal' levels of functioning and subtle changes to their behaviour may be missed.

There are many challenges when assessing patients with learning disabilities for dementia. However, one of the ways to overcome this difficulty is by carrying out prospective assessments, ideally before the onset of dementia, in early adulthood (30–35 years), in order to establish a baseline for future comparison and to help detect changes suggestive of dementia onset as early as possible (see for example Kalsy et al 2005, Jervis and Prinsloo 2007). The British Psychological Society (2009) advises that every adult with Down's syndrome should be assessed at the age of 30 to establish a baseline. However, early assessment would only be suggested in populations where there is research to suggest that the onset of dementia occurs at a younger age or where the prevalence is higher than average, since the NICE/SCIE (2006) dementia guidelines state that 'general population screening for dementia should not be undertaken'.

Best practice shows that assessment over time is essential and should incorporate both neuropsychological assessment of the person with learning disability (if appropriate) and information from other people who know the individual well. It also remains important for the individual to have a full health screen and further investigations so as to rule out any other physical conditions which may be impacting on cognitive functioning.

The difficulties with the assessment of dementia in adults with learning disabilities have been briefly outlined. Suggestions to overcome these difficulties whilst still providing accurate and useful clinical information would be:

- Adults with Down's syndrome over the age of 30 (as an at risk group) should have regular (yearly) screening for dementia using either the Dementia Questionnaire for People with Learning Disabilities (DLD) (Evenhuis et al 2007) or CAMDEX-DS (Ball et al 2006).
- Adults with learning difficulties other than Down's syndrome or other clinical syndrome that is known to increase the likelihood of developing early onset dementia, should not be routinely assessed for dementia unless there is qualitative evidence that there have been changes in their cognitive state which cannot be attributed to alterations in their mental state, until they reach the age of 50.
- Healthcare managers should ensure that all staff working with older adults with learning disabilities have access to dementia care training (skill development) that is consistent with their roles and responsibilities.

What do I need to know about epilepsy?

Kathleen McNicholas

Epilepsy is a common condition affecting up to 25% of the population with a learning disability (Gates and Barr 2009) and is caused by abnormal electrical activity in the brain. Seizures can be generalised (affecting both sides of the brain) or focal (affecting distinct focal points in the brain) and can present in many different ways. Types of seizures experienced by people with or without learning disabilities may include:

- Absence seizures
- Atonic seizures
- Atypical absence seizures
- Complex focal seizures
- Myoclonic seizures/jerks
- Simple focal seizures
- Tonic seizures
- Tonic-clonic seizures.

Sometimes the seizures are associated with other symptoms that may indicate an epilepsy syndrome, such as Dravet syndrome, Landau-Kleffner syndrome, Lennox-Gastaut syndrome or West's syndrome. The diagnosis of an epilepsy syndrome can be a key indicator in management.

The object of treatment in epilepsy is to prevent seizures, usually with anti-epileptic drugs. The dose frequency of the drug is determined by the 'plasma-drug half life'. Drugs with long half lives may be given once daily, whilst the shorter the half life, the more frequently the dose needs to be given. Large doses of drugs, however, may need to be given in divided doses thus requiring more frequent administration so as to avoid some adverse side effects associated with peak plasma-drug concentrations (British National Formulary 2011). Sometimes more than one anti-epileptic drug needs to be given, known as 'combination therapy', although this increases the risk of side effects.

When caring for individuals with epilepsy it is important to be familiar with how their seizures present (including seizure type, duration, frequency) and how they are treated. It is useful to keep a detailed diary of seizures; this helps to pinpoint triggers and patterns and track efficacy of treatment. When recording an episode, document the time it started, the duration, which limbs were involved, pupil deviation or dilation, incontinence, loss of consciousness, muscle tone, potential triggers, activity at the time, if there was any warning before the event and the recovery period. It is particularly difficult to diagnose epilepsy in people with learning disabilities as behaviour or movement disorders can be mistaken for seizure activity. Capturing the episodes on video (with carefully planned and documenneted permission/consent) can also be useful in forming a diagnosis. Anti-epileptic drugs are usually prescribed to prevent seizures. However, for people with difficult to treat (intractable) epilepsy other options may be considered, i.e. vagal nerve stimulation, surgery or a ketogenic diet.

Some people with epilepsy have prolonged seizures (status epilepticus) which require emergency treatment; nurses need to ensure that they are familiar with the patient's individualised protocol often provided by the paediatrician for children, or neurologist or specialist consultant as appropriate. The patient's treatment plan may recommend the administration of buccal midazolam, rectal diazepam or, more rarely, rectal paraldehyde. Status epilepticus needs to be recognised as a medical emergency due to risk of hypoxic-ischaemic insult, and nurses need to ensure that they are familiar with the patient's individual plan of care, including when to administer medication, if and how oxygen therapy needs to be administered and any first aid measures that may need to be acted on.

References

AACE Thyroid Task Force (2002) AACE medical guidelines for the evaluation and treatment of hyperthyroidism and hypothyroidism. American Association of Clinical Endocrinologists. Available from: www.aace.com

Academy of Medical Sciences (2004) Calling time: The nation's drink as a major health issue. London: Academy of Medical Sciences

Ansell D, Feest T (1999) The 2nd Annual Report of the UK Renal Registry. Bristol: UK Renal Registry

Ball SL, Holland AJ, Huppert FA, Treppner P, Dodd K (2006) CAMDEX-DS: The Cambridge Examination for Mental Disorders of Older People with Down's Syndrome and Others with Intellectual Disabilities. Cambridge: Cambridge University Press

Biondi B, Cooper DS (2008) The clinical significance of subclinical thyroid dysfunction. Endocrine Reviews 29(1): 76–131

British National Formulary (2011) BNF 62, September 2011. BMJ Group/Pharmaceutical Press, London

British Psychological Society and the Royal College of Psychiatrists (2009) Dementia and people with learning disabilities – Guidance on the assessment, diagnosis, treatment and support of people with learning disabilities who develop dementia. Leicester: British Psychological Society

Brookes ME, Alberman E (1996) Early mortality and morbidity in children with Down's syndrome diagnosed in two regional health authorities. Journal of Medical Screening 3: 7–11.

BTA, ACB and BTF (2006) UK guidelines for the use of thyroid function tests. British Thyroid Association, Association for Clinical Biochemistry, and British Thyroid Foundation. Available from: www.acb.org.uk

Cawood T, Moriarty P, O'Shea D (2004) Recent developments in thyroid eye disease. British Medical Journal 329(7462): 385–90.

Clarke PM, Gray AM, Briggs A, Stevens RJ, Matthews DR, Holman RR (2005) UK Prospective Study Group: United Kingdom Prospective Diabetes Study. Cost-utility analyses of intensive blood glucose and tight blood pressure control in type 2 diabetes (UKPDS 72). Diabetologia 48: 868–77

Clinical Knowledge Summaries (2008) Hyperthyroidism. Available from: www.cks.nhs.uk/hypertyroidism

Clinical Knowledge Summaries (2011) Hypothyroidism. Available from: www.cks.nhs.uk/hypothyroidism accessed

Cooper S-A (1997) High prevalence of dementia among people with learning disabilities not attributable to Down's syndrome. Psychological Medicine 27: 609–16

Cooper DS (2003) Hyperthyroidism. Lancet 362(9382): 459–68.

Cooper DS (2004) Subclinical thyroid disease: Consensus or conundrum? Clinical Endocrinology 60(4): 410–12.

Darzi, Lord (2008), High Quality Care for All: NHS Next Stage Review final report. www.dh.gov.uk/en/Publicationsandstatistics/Publications/PublicationsPolicyAndGuidance/DH_085825

Deb S, Mathews T, Holt G, Bouras N (2001) *Practice guidelines for the assessment and diagnosis of mental health problems in adults with intellectual disability.* Pavilion, Brighton

Department of Health (2002) The National Service Framework for Diabetes. Available from: http:// www.dh.gov.uk/en/Healthcare/NationalServiceFrameworks/Diabetes

Department of Health (2008a) Putting prevention first – vascular checks: Risk assessment and management. 'Next steps' guidance for Primary Care Trusts. Available from: www.dh.gov.uk/en/Publicationsandstatistics/Publications/PublicationsPolicyAndGuidance/DH_090277

Department of Health (2008b) Healthy weight, healthy lives: A cross-government strategy for England. Available from: www.dh.gov.uk/en/Publicationsandstatistics/Publications/PublicationsPolicyAnd Guidance/DH_082378

Department of Health (2009) Healthy weight, healthy lives: One year on. Available from: www.dh.gov.uk/en/ Publicationsandstatistics/Publications/PublicationsPolicyAndGuidance/DH_097523

Department of Health (2010a) Six years on: Delivering the Diabetes National Service Framework. Available from: http://www.dh.gov.uk/en/Publicationsandstatistics/

Publications/PublicationsPolicyAndGuidance/DH_112509

Department of Health (2010b) *Equity and excellence, Liberating the NHS.* Department of Health. The Stationary Office

Department of Health (2011) Start active, stay active. A report on physical activity for health from the four home countries. London: Department of Health

Diabetes Prevention Program Research Group (2002) Reduction in the incidence of type 2 diabetes with lifestyle intervention or metformin. New England Journal of Medicine 346: 393–403

Diabetes UK (2009) DVD to help people with learning disabilities. Available from: http://www.diabetes.org.uk/About_us/News_Landing_Page/Diabetes-UK-launches-DVD-to-help-people-with-learning-disabilities/

Duffy K (2011) Medical-surgical nursing made incredibly easy. London: Lippincott Williams and Wilkins

ERPHO (2008) Resource. Available from: http://www.erpho.org.uk/viewResource.aspx?id=13254

Evans J (1995) Causes of blindness and partial sight in England and Wales, 1990–91. London: Office of Population Censuses and Surveys, Studies on Medical and Population Subjects No. 57. HMSO

Evenhuis HM, Kengen MMF, Eurlings HAL (2007) Dementia questionnaire for people with learning disabilities (DLD). UK adaptation. San Antonio, TX: Harcourt Assessment

Folsom AR, Rasmussen ML, Chambless LE, Howard G, Cooper LS, Schmidt MI, Heiss G (1999) Prospective associations of fasting insulin, body fat distribution and diabetes with risk of ischemic stroke. Diabetes Care 22: 1077–83

Fox C, Mackinnon M (1999) Vital diabetes. London: Class Health

Frost L, Vestergaard P, Mosekilde L (2004) Hyperthyroidism and risk of atrial fibrillation or flutter: A population-based study. Archives of Internal Medicine 164(15): 1675–8.

Gates B, Barr O (2009) Oxford handbook of learning and intellectual disability nursing. Oxford: Oxford University Press

Gunzerath L, Faden V, Zakhari S, Warren K (2004) National Institute on Alcohol Abuse and Alcoholism report on moderate drinking. Alcoholism: Clinical and Experimental Research 28: 829–47

Hak AE, Pols HAP, Visser TJ et al. (2000) Subclinical hypothyroidism is an independent risk factor for atherosclerosis and myocardial infarction in elderly women: The Rotterdam Study. Annals of Internal Medicine 132(4): 270–8

Hermon C, Alberman E, Beral V, Swerdlow AJ (2001) Mortality and cancer incidence in persons with Down's syndrome, their parents and siblings. Annals of Human Genetics 65:167–76

Hines LM, Rimm EB (2001) Moderate alcohol consumption and coronary heart disease: A review. Postgraduate Medical Journal77: 747–52. doi:10.1136/pmj.77.914.747

Hollins S, Attard M, van Fraunhofer N, McGuigan SM, Sedgwick P (1998) Mortality in people with learning disability: Risks, causes, and death certification findings in London. Developmental Medicine and Child Neurology 40: 50–6.

Information Centre (2008) Cardiovascular disease and risk factors in adults. Health Survey for England 2006: 2008. Available at: http://www.ic.nhs.uk/webfiles/publications/HSE06/HSE%2006%20report%20VOL%201%20v2.pdf

International Diabetes Federation (2005) World Diabetes Day: Diabetes and Footcare. Brussels: International Diabetes Federation

Janicki MP, Dalton AJ (2000) Prevalence of dementia and impact on intellectual disability services. Mental Retardation 38: 276–88

Jervis N, Prinsloo L (2007) How we developed a multidisciplinary screening project for people with Down's syndrome given the increased prevalence of early inset dementia. *British Journal of Learning Disability* **36**: 13–21

Kalsy S, McQuillan S, Adams D, Basra T, Konstantinidi E, Broquard M, Peters S, Lloyd V, Oliver C (2005) A proactive psychological strategy for determining the presence of dementia in adults with Down syndrome: Preliminary description of service use and evaluation. Journal of Policy and practice in Intellectual Disabilities 2(2): 116–25

Lewis G, Sherringham J, Kalim K, Crayford T (2008) Mastering public health. London: Royal Society of Medicine Press

Mariotti S, Cambuli VM (2007) Cardiovascular risk in elderly hypothyroid patients. Thyroid 17(11): 1067–73.

National Audit Office (2001) Tackling obesity in England. London: HMSO

NICE (2010) Prevention of cardiovascular disease at population level. NICE public health guidance 25. Available from: htpp://www. nice.org.uk/guidance/PH25

NICE (2009) Type 2 diabetes: Newer agents for blood glucose control in type 2 diabetes (CG87). Available from: http://guidance.nice.org.uk/CG87/Guidance

NICE/SCIE (2006) *Clinical guidelines: Dementia. Supporting people with dementia and their carers in health and social care.* NICE/SCIE, London

Nygaard B (2007) Hyperthyroidism. Clinical evidence. London: BMJ Publishing Group Limited

Oliver C, Holland AJ (1986) Down's syndrome and Alzheimer's disease: A review. Psychological Medicine 16: 307–22

Razvi S, Shakoor A, Vanderpump M, et al. (2008) The influence of age on the relationship between subclinical hypothyroidism and ischemic heart disease: A meta-analysis. Journal of Clinical Endocrinology and Metabolism 93(8): 2998–3007

Reid JR, Wheeler SF (2005) Hyperthyroidism: Diagnosis and treatment. American Family Physician 72(4): 623–30.

Reid SM, Middleton P, Cossich MC, Crowther CA (2010) Interventions for clinical and subclinical hypothyroidism in pregnancy. Cochrane Review Issue 7

Rodondi N, den Elzen WP, Bauer DC, et al (2010) Subclinical hypothyroidism and the risk of coronary heart disease and mortality. Journal of the American Medical

Association 304(12):1365–74.

Royal College of Nursing (2011) Meeting the health needs of people with learning disabilities. RCN guidance for nursing staff. London: RCN

Rubin R (1999) Effect of ethanol on platelet function. Alcohol: Clinical and Experimental Research 23(6): 1114–18

Ruf J-C, Berger J-L, Renaud S (1995) Platelet rebound effect on alcohol withdrawal and wine drinking in rats: Relation to tannins and lipid peroxidation, Arteriosclerosis, Thrombosis and Vascular Biology 15(1):140–4

Scott WN (2012) Pathophysiology made incredibly easy. London: Lippincott Williams and Wilkins

Stocker R, O'Halloran R (2004) De-alcoholised red wine decreases atherosclerosis in apolipoprotein E gene-deficient mice independently of inhibition of lipid peroxidation in the artery wall, American Journal of Clinical Nutrition 79(1): 123–30

Stroke Association (2010) High blood pressure and stroke. Factsheet 6 2010. Available from: http://www.stroke.org.uk/campaigns/campaign_archive/weigh_up_your_risk_of_stroke/blood_pressure_check.html

Surks MI, Ortiz E, Daniels GH, et al (2004) Subclinical thyroid disease: Scientific review and guidelines for diagnosis and management. Journal of the American Medical Association 291(2): 228–38

Tyrer F, McGrother C (2009) Cause-specific mortality and death certificate reporting in adults with moderate to profound intellectual disabilities. Journal of Intellectual Disability Research 53(11): 898–904.

UK Prospective Diabetes Study Group (1998) Intensive blood-glucose control with sulphonylureas or insulin compared with conventional treatment and risk of complications in patients with type 2 diabetes (UKPDS 53). The Lancet 352: 837–53

University of York: NHS Centre for Reviews and Dissemination (1999) Complications of diabetes. Effective Health Care Bulletin 5: 1–12

Vaidya B, Pearce SHS (2008) Management of hypothyroidism in adults. British Medical Journal 337: 284–9

Viberti GC, Marshall S, Beech R, et al (1996) Report on renal disease in diabetes. Diabetic Medicine 13: S6–S12

Walsh M, Crumbie A (2007) Watson's clinical nursing and related sciences (7th edn). London: Balliere Tindall

Weetman AP (2003) The thyroid gland and disorders of thyroid function. In Warrell DA, Cox TM, Firth JD, Benz EJ Jr (eds) Oxford textbook of medicine (4th edn). Oxford: Oxford University Press

Wells MB, Turner S, Martin DM, Roy A (1995) Health gain through screening. Coronary heart disease and stroke: Developing primary health care services for people with intellectual disability. Journal of Intellectual & Developmental Disability 22: 251–63

World Health Organization and International Diabetes Federation (2006) Definition and diagnosis of diabetes mellitus and intermediate hyperglycaemia. Geneva: WHO.

Available from: url:http://www.who.int/diabetes/publications/Definition%20an%20 diagnosis%20of%20diabetes_new.pdf

World Health Organization (2005) Ten statistical highlights in global public health. Available from: http://www.who.int/healthinfo/statistics/en/ accessed 15/1/12

World Heart Federation (2011) Hypertension. Available from: http://www.world-heart-federation.org/cardiovascular-health/cardiovascular-disease-risk-factors/hypertension/

YHPHO (Yorkshire and Humber Public Health Observatory) National Diabetes Support Team (2006) Diabetes Key Facts htpp:// www.yhpho.org.uk/resource/item. aspx?RID=8872

NOTES

Chapter 6

Complex and challenging behaviours

Catherine Hart, Chris Knifton and Russell Woolgar

- What is common complex behaviour?
- What is challenging behaviour?
- How common is challenging behaviour?
- How do you assess challenging behaviour?
- What behavioural interventions are used in the management of challenging behaviour?
- Are any other non-pharmacological interventions used for the management of challenging behaviour?
- What medications are used to treat complex behaviour?
- What is ADHD and what medication is commonly used?
- Why is medication sometimes used in self-injury?
- Can medication be used for sexually inappropriate behaviour?
- What is the link between communication and behaviour?

What is common complex behaviour?

Russell Woolgar

Complex needs are defined as needs arising from both a learning disability and from other difficulties, such as physical and sensory impairment, mental health problems or behavioural difficulties (Scottish Executive 2000).

Complex behaviour is a term used when behaviours have a multi-factorial aetiology (causation), where other needs impact on the presentation of a behaviour. Causes of other such needs include epilepsy, genetic conditions/syndromes, profound and multiple learning disabilities, mental ill-health, dementia and autistic spectrum disorders.

When a person presents with challenging behaviour and a psychiatric disorder, the clinical picture is complex. This complexity can be highlighted by the possibility that changes in behaviour can result directly as a symptom of a mental illness, can present as a secondary feature of a mental illness, or can be an expression of previously established behavioural patterns or as an adverse effect of medication.

Diagnosis relies on the correct interpretation of symptoms. Individuals with a learning disability have difficulties in communicating how they feel, so it can be difficult to know whether a challenging behaviour is occurring because of a psychiatric disorder, or whether behaviours relate to something else, e.g. physical pain or over-stimulation. Anxiety disorders, depression and mania are all more prevalent in people with severe challenging behaviour. The joint presentation of mental health and learning disability is usually referred to as a 'dual diagnosis' (Menolascino 1970).

Common complex behaviour, as opposed to complex needs, is usually encompassed under the umbrella term 'challenging behaviour'.

What is challenging behaviour?
Catherine Hart and Russell Woolgar

According to Moss (2004) behaviours are described as 'challenging' primarily because they break fundamental social rules, i.e. that it is wrong to hurt others, hurt one's self, destroy property, or otherwise disrupt other people's lives. There are many reasons why someone might exhibit these kinds of behaviours including frustration, conflict with others, lack of significant relationships or a history of inappropriate learned behaviours.

When individuals present with 'aggressive behaviour' it has historically placed them at risk of institutionalisation, with resultant social isolation, over-reliance on physical restraint and over-use of medication. People who challenge services are at higher risk of exclusion from them, and of becoming victims of abuse. Aggression strains relationships between individuals and their caregivers, whether professionals or family members.

Physical aggression, self-injury and destructiveness towards the environment tend to be the most commonly reported specific forms of challenging behaviour. Naylor and Clifton (1993) state that:

Non-specific use of the term [challenging behaviour] is accompanied by indiscriminate use... by front line care staff when referring to behavioural disorders across the spectrum.

In practice it is necessary to state specifically what behaviours are challenging, how they occur, to what degree (Slevin 1995), and in what situation. The topography, frequency, intensity and duration are the key measures.

The term challenging behaviour refers to many different types of behaviours which services, or the community in which someone is living, may find difficult to cope with. Challenging behaviour is a socially constructed idea and is a product of an interaction between the individual and his or her environment. Assessment and intervention must therefore address the person, the environment and the interaction between the two. Behaviour can be described as challenging when it is of such an intensity, frequency or duration as to threaten the quality of life and/ or the physical safety of the individual or others and is likely to lead to responses that are restrictive, aversive or result in exclusion. This may include:

- Physically aggressive behaviour to the self or others, such as self-injurious behaviour, hitting, head butting, biting, screaming, spitting, kicking.
- Inappropriate sexualised behaviour, such as public masturbation, making sexualised comments or groping.
- Behaviour directed at property, such as throwing objects or stealing.
- Stereotyped behaviours, such as repetitive rocking, whistling, echolalia or elective incontinence.

In defining the term severe challenging behaviour, Emerson's (1995) classic description is often adopted:

Severely challenging behaviour refers to culturally abnormal behaviour(s) of such an intensity, frequency or duration that the physical safety of the person or others is likely to be placed in serious jeopardy, or behaviour that is likely to seriously limit use of, or result in the person being denied access to ordinary community facilities.

An alternative definition of challenging behaviour is behaviour that causes problems for people around the person, making them feel powerless. Here the focus is on those caring for the individual. Carers may require support and need to change to a low arousal approach (Elven 2010).

How common is challenging behaviour?
Russell Woolgar

Prevalence rates of challenging behaviour in the learning disabled population vary markedly between studies. Zarkowska and Clements (1988), for example, suggest that up to 60% of people with a learning disability display some type of challenging behaviour. The Mental Health Foundation (1996) suggests that 10% of people registered with a learning disability in Great Britain exhibit challenging behaviour, and the Mansell Report (Department of Health 1993) states that only 20 people per 100000 (less than 0.5%) present 'severe' challenging behaviours.

How do you assess challenging behaviour?
Catherine Hart and Russell Woolgar

It is important to remember that challenging behaviour may be due to a number of different causes. Individuals with learning disabilities may be expressing unhappiness in their current environment through their behaviour, and clinicians may be expected to provide interventions in environments that are inadequate to meet the person's needs. It is also important to recognise that the behaviour exhibited will usually serve a purpose for the individual, e.g. as a means of communicating these needs to others. They may be communicating:

- *Biological/physiological needs*: pain, medication, the need for sensory stimulation.
- *Psychological needs*: feeling excluded, lonely, devalued, labelled, disempowered, living up to people's negative expectations.
- *Social needs*: boredom, seeking social interaction, the need for an element of control, lack of knowledge of community norms, insensitivity of staff and services to their wishes and needs.
- *Environmental needs*: Physical aspects such as noise and lighting, or gaining access to preferred objects or activities.

Challenging behaviour is socially constructed and is a product of an interaction between the individual and his or her environment. Assessment and intervention must therefore address the person, the environment and the interaction between the two (Lowe and Felce 1995).

The purpose of assessment is to collect enough information to lead to a coherent formulation or diagnosis. Complex behaviour (for some the preferred term for challenging behaviour) clearly implies complexity. A thorough and detailed assessment is required to fully understand the constituent parts of this complexity and the origin of the behaviour. A comprehensive assessment needs to address three factors:

- The individual and any underlying medical and organic factors, e.g. psychological/psychiatric factors and communication.
- Social/environmental factors.
- The interaction or 'fit' between the individual and the environment.

Assessment of the individual should include:

- Physical factors: discomfort, pain, illness and any physiological imbalance, e.g. thyroid disorder and treatment/medication.
- Mental illness: mood disorders including depression and mania, psychosis and anxiety-related disorders as well as the effects of any treatment/ medication (e.g. side effects).
- Neuropsychiatric disorders including epilepsy, ADHD and dementia.
- Pervasive developmental disorders, the main one being autism.
- Phenotype-related behaviours related to specific syndromes: Smith–Magenis syndrome, Lesch–Nyhan syndrome and fragile X syndrome as examples.
- Psychological trauma: reaction to abuse or loss.
- Communication difficulties: hearing loss, unclear communication, insufficient vocabulary or means of expression, difficulties understanding communication of others.
- Degree and nature of the learning disability, including sensory and motor disabilities.
- History of relationships and experiences.
- Result of previous interventions used and their effectiveness.

Environmental factors may include the characteristics of the organisation/ service, and include:

- Number of staff.
- Training and experience of staff.
- Consistency of staff provision.
- Working relationship with the client.
- Working relationships between staff.
- Quality of the material environment.
- Opportunities and the ability of the service to understand and respond to unique needs of the individual.

A poor fit between the individual's needs and their environment may result in:

- Limited opportunities to gain social attention.
- Escape from or avoidance of excessive demands.
- Attempts to gain access to preferred activities or objects.
- Attempts to gain alternative forms of sensory feedback.
- Attempts to reduce arousal and anxiety by other means.
- Exertion of choice or control over the environment.

All these should provide clues as to why the behaviour occurs, why it has changed and ultimately what function (use and importance) it is to the individual.

A functional assessment or functional analysis is a specific behaviour-analytical procedure, where structured observation and other methods of assessment (e.g. interviewing people who are in frequent contact with the person, or the use of standardised questionnaires) are employed to generate:

- Hypotheses about the challenging behaviour.
- Antecedents that might be acting as stimuli for the behaviour.
- Consequences which may be reinforcing the behaviour.

The aim of a comprehensive assessment of 'complex behaviour' is as in the tradition of the nursing process, to lead to an intervention plan which fits the person and his or her environment and results in an improvement in quality of life, and to establish a baseline that enables subsequent evaluation of effectiveness. The focus of the assessment should be determined by the impact of the behaviour on the individual and those around him or her, including the degree of physical harm to the person and others, the risk of loss of access to opportunities for development and community participation, the levels of distress being experienced by the person and others, and the capacity and motivation for change in the person and in his or her environment. Assessments need to highlight the level of risks to the person and others and inform risk management strategies as part of the intervention plan.

An assessment of capacity to consent to current and potential interventions will help determine and shape how to proceed with regard to patient/client involvement and inclusion. Interventions should be delivered in a person-centred context and within a framework of positive behavioural support. It is important that all interventions are routinely evaluated for their effectiveness.

To improve services for people who present with complex or challenging behaviour and to enable them to remain in their own homes and communities requires the creation and support of 'capable environments'. These environments exist where services for people with learning disabilities have the capacity to support people who present with behaviour that challenges. As a learning disability nurse, awareness of the contextual and service factors that influence and maintain behaviours is an important aspect that has an impact on the effectiveness of interventions.

What behavioural interventions are used in the management of challenging behaviour?
Catherine Hart

A comprehensive assessment should initially be carried out in order to establish the function of the behaviour to be targeted. The assessment should cover a functional assessment of behaviour, underlying medical and organic factors, psychological/ psychiatric factors, communication, and social/environmental factors. Carrying out a detailed functional analysis is a fundamental part of assessment of challenging behaviour and should help to develop a clear formulation of the presenting problem. Once there is a clear idea about the function of a behaviour then interventions can be designed to increase adaptive behaviours and decrease maladaptive ones.

Many forms of behavioural interventions are based on the principles of operant conditioning. Operant conditioning suggests that a 'reinforcer' is a consequence that increases or maintains the frequency of a behaviour. What is reinforcing is defined by what happens to the frequency of the behaviour. It has nothing to do with whether the individual finds the reinforcer 'pleasant' or not. For example, if a child gets slapped whenever he/she says a 'naughty' word but the frequency of naughty words increases, the slap is a positive reinforcer. Here, the positive reinforcer increases or maintains the frequency of a behaviour. It is not punishment. The terms 'reinforcement' and 'punishment' are thus often misused. Additionally, consequences are not universally reinforcing. For example, happy face stickers may be effective reinforcers for some children; other children may find them silly.

Table 6.1 shows the relationships between positive/negative reinforcements and increasing/decreasing required behaviour. Distinguishing 'positive' from 'negative' can be difficult, especially when there are many consequences. Some reinforcement can be simultaneously positive and negative, such as a drug addict taking drugs for the euphoric effects while at the same time eliminating withdrawal symptoms.

Table 6.1. Reinforcers and behaviours		
	Decreases likelihood of behaviour	*Increases likelihood of behaviour*
Presented	Positive punishment	Positive reinforcement
Taken away	Negative punishment	Negative reinforcement

Once a clear formulation of the challenging behaviours has been drawn up, then interventions should be delivered in a person-centred context within a framework of positive behavioural support. Interventions may include:

• Psychotherapy
• Communication
• Positive programming
• Physical and/or medical treatment
• Psychopharmacological treatment.

It is important that all interventions are routinely evaluated for their effectiveness. Communication and feedback between professionals, carers and service users, and the timely sharing of information is an essential component at all stages of care.

Once a behavioural management plan is in place and being used consistently, it is common to see an increase in the targeted behaviour. This is known as 'extinction burst' and occurs soon after a behavioural management plan is introduced. An extinction burst consists of a sudden and temporary increase in the response's frequency, followed by the eventual decline and extinction of the behaviour. It is important that staff working with the individual are aware of the behavioural management plan and implement it consistently, otherwise the increase in the behaviour may unknowingly be reinforced and may actually increase.

Are any other non-pharmacological interventions used for the management of challenging behaviour?
Chris Knifton

Before medication or pharmacological interventions are considered, all practical steps need to be taken to consider non-pharmacological approaches. These are numerous, and some require additional qualifications or training. Some can be carried out by a learning disability nurse with appropriate experience and qualification, and others by a qualified alternative therapy professional. It is important to remember that people react differently to interventions, and there is no one size fits all formula. Effective interventions need to be based on a carefully considered holistic assessment, need, and appropriate goal selection.

Examples of possible interventions may include:

• Anger management

- Animal assisted therapy
- Art therapy
- Behavioural interventions
- Cognitive analytical therapy and cognitive behavioural therapy
- Complementary therapies – including aromatherapy, reflexology, massage, etc
- Counselling
- Creative therapy/approaches
- Doll therapy
- Drama
- Family therapy
- Gentle teaching
- Horticultural therapy
- Multisensory stimulation
- Music therapy
- Psychosocial interventions
- Psychotherapy
- Rational emotive therapy
- Relaxation techniques
- Social skills training
- Total communication – includes augmentative and alternative communication.

It is important to check what therapeutic interventions are currently offered by your organisation. You may want to look at these in further detail to acquaint yourself not only with their use but also with their limitations. Many learning disability nurses undertake post-registration qualification courses in some of the above interventions.

What medications are used to treat complex behaviours?
Russell Woolgar

Many people with a learning disability take medication for epilepsy and mental and physical health symptoms. Historically people with a learning disability have also received medication to 'treat and manage' the presentation of challenging behaviour.

The primary aim should be to discover the underlying cause of the behaviour. It is this underlying cause that should become the focus for management strategies and interventions rather than the behaviour itself.

Medication should only be prescribed following a proper biopsychosocial assessment and where there is a clear reason for a particular medication to be used. There is a long history of excessive and inappropriate use of medication (usually those that have a tranquilising side effect) in the care of vulnerable people. Gardner (in Thomas 1994) found that an 'excessive' number of patients in institutional settings received pharmacotherapy as their major form of treatment for psychological symptoms. Psychotropic medication is used more frequently in adults with a learning disability, 20–45% of whom are prescribed psychotropic medication, in 14–30% of cases to control 'behaviour disorder' (Deb and Fraser 1994).

Antipsychotics

Antipsychotics (also referred to as neuroleptics and, historically, major tranquilisers) include common 'typical' antipsychotics and the relatively newer 'atypical' antipsychotics. The research evidence for the efficacy of antipsychotics in the treatment of complex behaviours is variable. Although there is extensive documentation, particularly single case studies showing some positive treatment effects, there is currently not enough evidence available to recommend specific medication for specific behaviour problems (Deb et al 2007). Brylewski and Duggan (2004) could find no definitive evidence that antipsychotic medication helps or harms adults with learning disability and challenging behaviour. However, antipsychotics may be prescribed where the symptoms of psychosis are felt to be the cause of the behaviour.

What are the commonly used typical antipsychotics?

The antipsychotics commonly used include chlorpromazine, thioridazine, levomepromazine, trifluoperazine, haloperidol, droperidol and zuclopenthixol. Typical antipsychotics were first developed in the 1950s and used to treat psychosis. They were often given to people in care to quieten or tranquilise them. They are primarily used to manage the symptoms of psychosis, i.e. delusions, hallucinations, and disordered thought, particularly in schizophrenia and bi-polar disorder. In the learning disabled population their use to manage behaviours has long been controversial because their action can also impair function as a direct result of sedation and as a result of debilitating side effects.

What are the side effects?

Atypical antipsychotics are part of a group of drugs referred to as phenothiazines, due to their chemical make-up, and have a range of similar side effects. It is important to be aware of what the common side effects are, due to the difficulties people with a learning disability may have in describing how they feel. Common side effects include dry mouth, muscle stiffness and cramps, tremors and weight-gain. Extra-pyramidal side effects are a cluster of symptoms consisting of akathisia (restlessness), parkinsonism (tremor, hypokinesia – reduced bodily movement), rigidity, postural instability and dystonias (muscle contractions with twisting and repetitive movements or abnormal postures).

Longer-term use can lead to more serious side effects such as tardive dyskinesia, which is characterised by repetitive, involuntary, purposeless muscular movements, and which is extremely difficult to treat and is sometimes irreversible. Neuroleptic malignant syndrome is a rare, but potentially fatal side effect of antipsychotic treatment. It is characterised by fever, muscle rigidity, autonomic dysfunction, and an altered mental state. These side effects, as well as their overly prominent action of tranquilisation (which gave rise to their use in behavioural management), has led to the quest for medication with fewer side effects. As prescribers have increasingly moved towards newer atypical antipsychotics, these side effects have become less evident in the learning disabled population.

What are the commonly used atypical antipsychotics?

These include risperidone, olanzapine, quetiapine, amisulpiride, sulpiride, and aripiprazole. Clozapine (Clozaril) is usually used as a last resort in patients who have not responded to other antipsychotic treatments, due to the risks of agranulocytosis, as well as the costs of continually having to have blood tests during treatment. However, it has been used in single case studies to treat symptoms related to personality disorder (Biswas et al 2006).

Atypical antipsychotics, specifically risperidone, have been used to reduce behaviour associated with autism, such as stereotypy and aggression, but benefits may be limited and a number of studies have been with children and not adults (Aman et al 2005). They are used to treat the symptoms of anxiety and associated behaviours and may also be efficacious for hyperactivity and stereotyped behaviour (Posey et al 2008).

What are the side effects?

Atypical antipsychotics on the whole have fewer side effects than typical antipsychotics. However, they have a number of specific effects that alter an individual's metabolism. This metabolic syndrome is a combination of medical disorders that, when occurring together, increase the risk of developing cardiovascular disease and diabetes. Appetite stimulation with associated weight gain, is potentially a major risk to an individual's physical health.

Antidepressants

As with antipsychotics, medication used to treat depression is divided into the old and new; the older tricyclics and newer selective serotonin re-uptake inhibitors (SSRIs). Antidepressants may be used when the cause of the challenging behaviour is linked to affective disorders, such as depression or bi-polar disorder. Their role in the treatment of complex behaviours relates to how these disorders present in the learning disabled population, e.g. they may be used to help lift mood and increase motivation to engage in activities of daily living. In some circumstances, antidepressants may also be prescribed for anxiety and sometimes even for pain relief. Both of these symptoms may be antecedents for challenging behaviour. In addition SSRIs are also used to treat perseverative and repetitive behaviours, including those seen in people with autistic spectrum disorder, preoccupations in Asperger's syndrome, and to treat self-injurious behaviour (Einfeld 2001).

What are the commonly used tricyclic antidepressants?

These include amitriptyline, clomipramine, dosulepin/dothiepin, doxepin, imipramine and lofepramine. They are used primarily to treat major depressive disorder and bi-polar disorder. They are also used in the treatment of generalised anxiety disorder, social phobia and obsessive-compulsive disorder (OCD). Antidepressants can take up to four weeks before they reach a therapeutic level. Standard antidepressant treatments seem to be effective in individuals with Down's syndrome and depression (Walker et al 2011).

What are the side effects?

Common side effects are related to their anti-muscarinic effects on certain neurotransmitters in the brain. These side effects are relatively common and may include dry mouth, dry nose, blurred vision, lowered gastrointestinal motility or constipation, urinary retention, and cognitive and/or memory impairment. Due to the nature of these side effects and dangers relating to risk of death in overdose, SSRIs are more commonly prescribed.

What are the commonly used SSRI antidepressants?

These include citalopram, fluoxetine, paroxetine and sertraline. As for tricyclic antidepressants, SSRIs are used to treat clinical depression, and are frequently prescribed for anxiety disorders, such as social anxiety, panic disorders, and OCD. They may also be used for post-traumatic stress disorder (PTSD) and social phobia (Cooray and Bakala 2005).

What are the side effects?

SSRIs are better tolerated and present with fewer serious side effects than tricyclics (Bhaumik et al 1995). Side effects however can include agitation, nausea, sexual dysfunction, dizziness, loss of appetite, insomnia and in some cases increased rumination (thoughts) about suicide. There are also important withdrawal concerns that the nurse needs to be aware of when the medication is being discontinued.

Mood stabilisers

Mood stabilisers fall into a number of medication groups: those given solely to treat bi-polar mood disorder (manic-depression), those that are used principally to treat epilepsy but have efficacy in the treatment of mood disorder, and those used to treat the symptoms of psychosis and/or depression. Current evidence supports the use of mood stabilisers (such as lithium carbonate and some anticonvulsants) for the management of behaviour problems in adults with a learning disability (Deb et al 2008).

What are the commonly used mood stabilisers?

These include lithium carbonate, sodium valproate, carbamazepine, and lamotrigine. Mood stabilisers are used to help stabilise the ups and downs experienced as part of bi-polar disorder. A person with a learning disability may have times when they are withdrawn, and then become over-active or 'manic'. In the learning disabled population there is some evidence of an increased incidence of rapid-cycling mood disorder (Olubokun and Menon 2004). Some mood stabilising medication may be familiar as anticonvulsants (e.g. carbamazepine, sodium valproate and lamotrigine).

What are the side effects?

For lithium the most common side effects include thirst and increased appetite. Thyroid and renal functioning can also be affected. When taking lithium, individuals need to have regular blood tests (at least once every three months) to ensure that their levels of lithium are not too high or too low. If the dose is incorrect, it may cause side effects, such as diarrhoea and vomiting. In serious cases (lithium toxicity), there can be a risk of more serious effects including coma.

For sodium valproate, carbamazepine and lamotrigine, common side effects include drowsiness, headaches and migraines, aggression, impaired motor co-ordination, tremor, ataxia, and gastro-intestinal disturbances, including diarrhoea, nausea, vomiting or abdominal pain, increased appetite and weight gain. There are additional specific side effects dependent on the medication, but with lamotrigine there is a chance of patients reacting with Stevens–Johnson syndrome, a rare and potentially fatal skin condition.

Anxiolytics

Anxiolytics or minor tranquilisers are drugs used principally to alleviate the symptoms of anxiety and anxiety disorders. In some circumstances, beta-blockers, used to treat heart conditions, have also been found to be beneficial in treating the somatic symptoms of anxiety. Anxiolytics are used to treat both the psychological and physical symptoms of anxiety. They are used in the learning disabled population to aid the reduction of anxiety-related symptoms and help calm individuals. As such they can be used as a 'pre-med' before medical investigations and as prn (as required) medication, using their sedative properties. Benefits have also been observed in people with an autistic spectrum disorder, where individuals may be highly anxious (Cooray and Bakala 2005).

What are the commonly used anxiolytics?

These include clonazepam, diazepam, and lorazepam and are known as benzodiazepines. SSRIs listed under antidepressants are also used to treat anxiety as are some beta-blockers such as propranolol.

What are the side effects?

Common side effects include sedation, impairment of attention, impaired psychomotor performance, and memory difficulties. Continuous use of benzodiazepines over two weeks can increase the risk of the development of withdrawal and rebound difficulties. Tolerance and dependence may occur if treatment continues longer-term.

Anticonvulsants

Medication used to treat epilepsy has also been shown to directly affect behavioural presentation in people with a learning disability. Typical anticonvulsants used successfully as pharmacological behavioural interventions have included sodium valproate, carbamazepine and lamotrigine.

What are the side effects?

Anticonvulsant medication can cause dose-related or unusual individual behavioural side effects. These can be linked to the way a particular medication's side effects impact on cognitive functioning, to adverse physical effects and/or to adverse mental health effects. Aggressive behaviour can also result either during or after a complex-partial seizure, or result from post-ictal (an altered state of consciousness) confusion following a seizure. Treatment of epilepsy may result in a reduction in 'challenging behaviour' but in some cases specific medication can lead to an increase (Brodtkorb et al 2004).

What is ADHD and what medication is commonly used?
Russell Woolgar

Attention deficit hyperactivity disorder (ADHD) is a group of behavioural symptoms that include inattentiveness, hyperactivity and impulsiveness. It is a diagnosis usually made in children or young people, although it can persist into adulthood. There is increasing evidence that ADHD is a valid diagnosis in the learning disabled population (Maltezos et al 2008). Since these symptoms can overlap with symptoms present in individuals with a learning disability, it is important to ensure that a detailed assessment and diagnosis is made first.

The medications recommended to treat ADHD are methylphenidate and dexamfetamine (stimulants), and atomoxetine (selective norepinephrine reuptake inhibitor) (NICE 2008). Side effects can include weight loss or not reaching an expected height in children and young people, an increase in heart rate or blood pressure, anxiety, changes in mental state (hallucinations), seizures, and the appearance of tics. Methylphenidate or atomoxetine should normally be used if the person also has tics, Tourette's syndrome or anxiety, or if he or she is misusing stimulants (NICE 2008). If an individual has a diagnosed mental illness or a conduct disorder, methylphenidate should not normally be offered as a treatment.

Why is medication sometimes used in self-injury?
Russell Woolgar

The treatment of self-injury needs to adhere to guidance that seeks to identify the underlying cause of the behaviour. It has been documented that in a number of cases medication has precipitated a reduction in self-injurious behaviours. Both opioid antagonists (naloxone and naltrexone) (Jones et al 2007) and serotonergic antidepressants (Xenitidis et al 2001) have been used for the reduction of self-injurious behaviour within the learning disabled population. There are few noted side effects to opiate antagonist administration. The most serious potential side effect associated with naltrexone, however, is a temporary increase in liver enzymes, which can indicate liver malfunction and damage (Symons et al 2004).

Can medication be used for sexually inappropriate behaviour?

Russell Woolgar and Chris Knifton

Psychosocial therapeutic approaches are generally effective for sexually inappropriate behaviours. However, as a last resort where individuals are classed as 'a danger and pose a severe and ongoing risk to others', antilibidinal drugs such as cyproterone acetate, and neuroleptic drugs, such as benperidol, may be considered. Side effects include liver toxicity, adrenal suppression, hyperkalaemia (excess potassium), depression, gynaecomastia (breast growth), galactorrhoea (milk outflow), and erectile dysfunction.

It is important, however, as with all reported 'challenging behaviour', to fully assess the perceived problem before formulating a diagnosis. What is seen as sexually inappropriate behaviour may actually be attempts to eliminate (e.g. exposing genitals in public might actually be an attempt to micturate), or to adjust uncomfortable clothing.

What is the link between communication and behaviour?

Russell Woolgar

All people will at some point in their life experience communication problems: this may be an inability to hear a conversation in a night club with loud music, receiving only part of a story, or becoming angry with someone you think has not done what they said they would do. People with learning disabilities will experiences difficulties above and beyond this, be it due to sensory loss, poor impulse control or altered/damaged brain structure causing an absence of speech. *Table 6.2* outlines the potential impact of communication difficulties on functioning. Up to 80% of people with a learning disability have communication difficulties, with 50% having significant difficulties (Royal College of Speech and Language Therapists 2009).

The result of this will be difficulties understanding what other people say (receptive communication) and/or difficulties in making themselves understood (expressive communication). Improving communication as part of a positive

Table 6.2. The potential impact of communication difficulties on functioning
Impaired communication, cognition and function can cause: • Difficulty understanding language and expressing ideas • Limited attention span and memory span • Limited vocabulary • Dysfluency and difficulty controlling speech musculature for sound production • Limitations in understanding or showing appropriate communicative intent • Limitations in understanding social use of language • Difficulties with feeding and drinking
Performance ability and behaviours can involve the following difficulties: • Ability to use language to communicate and speak intelligibly • Follow instructions or learn through verbal teaching • Express needs, choices and opinions • Use appropriate behaviour in social situations • Take appropriate nutrition and hydration • Consider options and come to informed decisions
Communication and intellectual difficulties can limit ability to: • Function appropriately in social settings • Access education and work opportunities • Be autonomous in life, possibly needing life-long support • Interact socially with peers and in wider society • Socialise in other than 'safe' environments
Inability to express needs effectively can lead to: • Anger and frustration • Depression, low self-esteem, low self-confidence • Challenging behaviour

skills-building approach will be helpful in reducing or preventing challenging behaviour. This works by addressing these difficulties and the subsequent frustration that people experience when they cannot express their needs or understand those of others. It should be remembered that challenging behaviour is 'an attempt to communicate or understand what is going on' (Sense 2008). Someone who has a severe learning disability is more likely to have increased difficulties in communicating. Someone with fewer communication skills may have more frequent challenging behaviour.

There is a clear link between learning disability, challenging behaviour and communication difficulties. Challenging behaviours have been found to increase in frequency, intensity and/or duration when individuals are assessed as having increased communication difficulties. Chamberlain et al (1993) found a correlation between communication level and 'behavioural problems', and Bott et al (1997) found that people with good understanding but no speech have significantly more behaviour problems than those with good speech. In a further study, only 32% of service users whose behaviour was severely challenging were assessed as able to communicate most or all of their wants and desires (Desrochers et al 1997).

Assessment of communication needs should occur in the context of the individual with a learning disability, the people who support and care for that person, and the interactions between the two, i.e. within a partnership model.

Money (1997) talks about assessment and intervention needing to focus on three key areas:

- *The means of communication*: To support/teach people *how* to communicate.
- *The reason to communicate*: To give people the choice and autonomy to influence motivation as to *why* to communicate.
- *The opportunity to communicate*: To give people the right environment, where people will respond and act as 'communicative partners'. *Where* to communicate.

Bartlett and Bunning, (1997) found major differences between the communication skills used by support staff and the comprehension levels of the participants with learning disabilities.

What are the possible reasons for communication difficulties?

These may be classified as either 'receptive' or 'expressive'.
Receptive difficulties include:

- People overestimating individuals' ability to understand what is said to them. As a result an individual can be given too much language to process and only pick up on and understand key words. 'Not going to the shops until after today' can be picked up as 'going to the shops'.
- An individual having an unrecognised hearing loss.
- People using abstract language (talking about things that cannot be seen or touched). Examples include time and negatives, as in the above example.
- Difficulties in attending to and remembering what has been said.

- Literal interpretation of language, particularly in those with an autistic spectrum disorder, e.g. 'It's raining cats and dogs'.

Expressive difficulties include:

- Individuals having physical difficulties in articulating speech or forming clear signs.
- Individuals using the right words but in the wrong order.
- Individuals lacking the appropriate supporting body language.
- Individuals having a limited vocabulary.
- Psychological trauma.

How can we support communication to reduce individual negative emotions and frustration?

Challenging behaviour may be more likely to occur in situations where people either do not understand what is expected of them or are unable to use communication to control their environment or influence others.

If we know someone well we can avoid misunderstanding by:

- Communicating in a way that the person understands, for example using simple, short sentences.
- Communicating what will be happening next/throughout the day (being able to anticipate events is important).
- Using an 'easier' form of communication with an individual, by supplementing spoken language with signed communication, and/or using pictures, symbols or objects.
- Facilitating this with 'communication partners' so individuals have a two-way and meaningful interaction.
- Responding consistently to what the person is trying to communicate.
- Providing individuals with opportunities to use communication in a meaningful way, where they can exercise choice and control.
- Promoting 'good' listening environments with reduced distractions and background noise. This needs to be in all situations, not just where challenging behaviour may occur.
- Remembering that communication skills vary according to the situation. If an individual is anxious, in pain or highly emotional, move the communication level down. As a 'rule of thumb' follow the hierarchy of

communication complexity, moving from the written word, the spoken word, and signed language, to signs, symbols, photos and, finally, to 'objects of reference'. Someone using symbols may benefit from photos or objects when emotionally aroused.
- Arranging for specialised assessment by a speech and language therapist.

What is functional communication training?

The key to understanding challenging behaviour is not to think that all challenges are the same or have the same 'attention seeking' cause. Wanting or seeking attention is an individual showing a desire to communicate, to have a basic need met.

As clinicians we need to support people to communicate in a manner that gets the same outcome for them as the challenging behaviour, but in a manner more acceptable for those around them. Teaching an individual to replace 'hitting out' behaviour with a Makaton sign for 'break', gives that person a positive communication choice, and enables increased options for community inclusion. Such interventions have been widely shown to reduce the level of behaviours that are challenging, e.g. Carr et al (1994).

People with an autistic spectrum disorder have difficulties with social communication. These difficulties are often key features as to why they express challenges, because people 'tend not to listen to people with a learning disability unless they do something really interesting' (Osgood 2004). Osgood describes challenging behaviour as a form of 'exotic communication'.

An example of a communication system designed to be used with individuals with a learning disability and/or autistic spectrum disorder is the Picture Exchange Communication System (PECS). PECS is recommended as an evidence-based intervention for enhancing functional communication skills of individuals with autistic spectrum disorder. It introduces the idea of exchanging pictures representative of an object, for that object.

Functional communication training, as part of skills building in the context of positive behavioural support, uses a four-pronged approach to develop strategies that:

- Identify, work with and modify motivating factors and setting events.
- Identify, work with and modify antecedent events.
- Develop interventions to teach replacement skills (functional communication training as one example).
- Identify, work with and modify consequence strategies.

References

Aman G, Arnold LE, Lindsay R, Nash R (2005) Risperidone treatment of autistic disorder: Longer-term benefits and blinded discontinuation after 6 months. *American Journal of Psychiatry* **162**: 1361–9

Bartlett C, Bunning K (1997) The importance of communication partnerships: A study to investigate the communicative exchanges between staff and adults with learning disabilities. *British Journal of Learning Disabilities* **25**: 148–53

Bhaumik S, Collacott RA, Gandhi D, Duggirala C, Wildgust HJ (1995) A naturalistic study in the use of antidepressants in adults with learning disabilities and affective disorders. *Human Psychopharmacology: Clinical and Experimental* **10**: 283–8

Biswas A, Gibbon S, Gangadharan S (2006) Clozapine in borderline personality disorder and intellectual disability: A case report of four-year outcome. *Mental Health Aspects of Developmental Disabilities* **9**: 13–17

Bott C, Farmer R, Rohde J (1997) Behaviour problems associated with lack of speech in people with learning disabilities. *Journal of Intellectual Disability Research* **41**: 3–7

Brodtkorb E, Klees TM, Nakken KO et al (2004) Levetiracetam in adult patients with and without learning disability: Focus on behavioral adverse effects. *Epilepsy and Behaviour* **5**(2): 231–5

Brylewski J, Duggan L (2004) Antipsychotic medication for challenging behaviour in people with learning disability. *Cochrane Database of Systematic Reviews*, Issue 3. Art. No.: CD000377. DOI: 10.1002/14651858.CD000377.pub2

Carr EG, Levin L, McConnachie G, Carlson JI, Kemp DC, Smith CE (1994) *Communication-based intervention for problem behavior: A user's guide for producing positive change.* Baltimore: PH Brookes Publishing Company

Chamberlain L, Cheung Chung M, Jenner L (1993) Preliminary findings on communication and challenging behaviour in learning difficulty. *British Journal of Developmental Difficulties* **VXXXIX**(2): 77

Cooray E, Bakala A (2005). Anxiety disorders in people with learning disabilities. *Advances in Psychiatric Treatment* **11**: 355–61

Deb S, Chaplin R, Sohanpal S et al (2008) The effectiveness of mood stabilizers and antiepileptic medication for the management of behaviour problems in adults with intellectual disability: A systematic review. *Journal of Intellect Disabilities Research* **52**(2):107–13

Deb S, Clarke D, Unwin G (2006) *Using medication to manage behaviour problems among adults with a learning disability. Quick reference guide (QRG)* University of Birmingham Available from: www.LD-Medication.bham.ac.uk

Deb S, Fraser W (1994). The use of psychotropic medication in people with learning disability: Towards rational prescribing. *Human Psychopharmacology* **9**: 259–72

Deb S, Sohanpal SK, Soni R et al (2007) The effectiveness of antipsychotic medication in the management of behaviour problems in adults with intellectual disabilities.

Journal of Intellectual Disability Research **51**: 766–77

Department of Health (1993) *Services for people with learning disabilities and challenging behaviour or mental health needs.* London: Department of Health

Desrochers MN, Hile MG, Williams-Moseley TL (1997) Surveys of functional assessment procedures used with individuals who display mental retardation and severe problem behaviours. *American Journal of Mental Retardation* **101**: 535–46

Einfeld SL (2001) Systematic management approach to pharmacotherapy for people with learning disabilities. *Advances in Psychiatric Treatment* **7**: 43–9

Elven BH (2010). *No fighting, no biting, no screaming: How to make behaving positively possible for people with autism and other developmental disabilities.* London: Jessica Kingsley Publishers

Emerson E (1995) *Challenging behaviour: Analysis and intervention with people with learning difficulties.* Cambridge: Cambridge University Press

Glick M, Zigler E (1995) Developmental differences in the symptomatology of psychiatric inpatients with and without mild mental retardation. *American Journal on Mental Retardation* **99**(4): 407–17

Jones E, Allen D, Moore K et al (2007) Restraint and self-injury in people with intellectual disabilities: A review. *Journal of Intellectual Disabilities* **11**(1): 105–18

Lowe K, Felce D (1995) How do carers assess the severity of challenging behaviour? A total population study. *Journal Intellectual Disabilities Research* **39**(2): 117

Maltezos S, Bramham J, Paliokosta E, Rose E, Xenitidis K (2008) The clinical presentation of ADHD in adults with learning disability: Experience from a national specialist adult ADHD clinic. *Annals of General Psychiatry* **7**(Suppl 1): S213

Mansell J (1993) *Services for people with learning disabilities and challenging behaviour or mental health needs: Report of a Project Group.* London: Department of Health

Menolascino FJ (1970) *Psychiatric approaches to mental retardation.* New York: Basic Books

Mental Health Foundation (1996) *Don't forget us: Services for children with a learning disability and challenging behaviour.* London: Mental Health Foundation

Money D (1997) A comparison of three approaches to delivering a speech and language therapy service to people with learning disabilities. *European Journal of Disorders of Communication* **32**: 449

Moss S (2004) *Information Sheet. Psychiatric disorders in people with learning disability.* Chatham, Kent: Challenging Behaviour Association. Available from: http://www.thecbf.org.uk/12pscyh.pdf

Moss S, Prosser H, Costello H, Simpson N, Patel P, Rowe S, Turner S, Hatton C (1998) Reliability and validity of the PAS-ADD checklist for detecting disorders in adults with intellectual disability. *Journal of Intellectual Disability Research* **42**(2) 173–83

Naylor V, Clifton M (1993) People with learning disabilities: Meeting complex needs. *Health and Social Care in the Community* **1**(6): 343–53

NICE (2008) *Clinical guideline 72. Attention deficit hyperactivity disorder.* Available from: http://www.nice.org.uk/nicemedia/pdf/CG72UNG.pdf

Olubokun J, Menon K (2004) Rapid cycling affective disorder presenting as challenging behaviour in a service user with mild learning disability. *British Journal of Developmental Disabilities* **50**(2): 99–108

Osgood T (2004) *'Suit you, sir': Challenging behaviour in learning disability services.* Available from: http://www.paradigm-uk.org

Posey DJ, Stigler KA, Erickson CA, McDougle CJ (2008). Antipsychotics in the treatment of autism. *Journal of Clinical Investigation* **118**: 6–14

Qureshi H, Alborz A (1992) Epidemiology of challenging behaviour. *Mental Handicap Research* **5**: 130–45

Royal College of Speech and Language Therapists (2009) *Resource manual for commissioning and planning services for SLCN, learning disability.* Available from: http://www.rcslt.org/speech_and_language_therapy/commissioning/learning_disability

Scottish Executive (2000) *The same as you? A review of services for people with learning disabilities.* Available from: http://www.scotland.gov.uk/Resource/Doc/159140/0043285.pdf

Sense (2008) *Factsheet 13. Challenging behaviour in adults.* Available from: http://www.sense.org.uk/Resources/Sense/Publications/Publications%20by%20topic/Factsheets/challenging_behaviour_in_adults.pdf

Slevin E (1995) A concept analysis of, and proposed new term for, challenging behaviour. *Journal of Advanced Nursing* **21**: 928–34

Symons FJ, Thompson A, Rodriguez MC (2004) Self-injurious behaviour and the efficacy of naltrexone treatment: A quantitative synthesis. *Mental Retardation and Developmental Disabilities Research Reviews* **10**: 193–200

Thomas JR (1994) Quality care for individuals with dual diagnosis: The legal and ethical imperative to provide qualified staff. *Mental Retardation* **32**(5): 356–61

Walker J, Dosen A, Buitelaar JK, Janzing JGE (2011) Depression in Down syndrome: A review of the literature. *Research in Developmental Disabilities* **32**(5): 1432–40

Xenitidis K, Russell A, Murphy DGM (2001) Management of people with challenging behaviour. *Advances in Psychiatric Treatment* **7**: 109–16

Zarkowska E, Clements J (1988) *Problem behaviour in people with severe learning disabilities: A practical guide to a constructional approach.* London: Croom Helm

NOTES

Chapter 7

Management dilemmas and mentoring learners

Dave Dalby and Kevin Power

- How do I deal with complaints?
- What is involved in incident reporting?
- What is a mentor?
- How are learners assessed in practice?
- What can mentors do to promote positive placements for learners?
- What may happen when learners have a poor placement experience?

How do I deal with complaints?

Kevin Power

In the report for 2007–2008, the Parliamentary and Health Service Ombudsman stated that complaints about care are often aggravated by the way they are dealt with. 'Poor complaint handling by NHS bodies and individuals was a recurrent theme across our health investigations in 2007–08' (Parliamentary and Health Service Ombudsman 2009: 36). The problem with some complaints is that they may begin as minor issues, but, if not dealt with properly, can become a major confrontation. The way a nurse deals with a complaint at the beginning can thus have an effect on the whole process of the complaint.

The simplest way to deal with complaints is to prevent them occurring in the first place. Be on the lookout for signs that a patient or relative is getting irritated; do not wait for the complaint, ask whether there is a problem. I remember sitting completing a duty rota and overhearing a father sounding cross on the telephone outside the ward office. It was clear that something was wrong. When I went to investigate, it seemed that no-one had told him what was going on with his young daughter who had been admitted as an emergency, and he had an important business meeting to attend. When I asked the staff caring for the child to explain what the delay was and the likely timeframe for her admission, he was able to make some arrangements with his work and became much calmer.

If this situation had been ignored it is highly likely that a formal complaint would have been lodged. However, it is unlikely that the health service is going to please all of the people all of the time, no matter how high your personal standards of care or how good your communication skills. Patients and relatives may be in pain or anxious and certainly in a strange environment. Additionally, as staff are under pressure because of high workloads and staff shortages, there are always likely to be complaints of some kind or another.

Most NHS trusts actively seek feedback from patients and service users as part of clinical governance (Robotham 2001). This may enable trusts to forestall complaints through improvements to the service. It may also encourage more people to complain. Each trust will have protocols and policies in place for dealing with formal complaints and you should be familiar with these. Let us focus for the purposes of this section on those situations where a relative or patient makes a complaint to you. Think of a time when you had complained about something:

- What was the cause of the complaint?
- Who did you complain to?
- How was the complaint dealt with?
- How did this make you feel?

Most complaints are fairly mundane, but no matter how trivial to the member of staff, all are important to the complainant. When thinking about times when I have complained, the response of the person I have complained to has had a great impact on how far I wanted to take the complaint and the level of redress I expected. So how do you, as the nurse receiving a verbal complaint, respond? The Wilson Report (Department of Health 1994) identified several lessons from the private sector:

- *Complainants want an apology*, even if the organisation was not at fault: This does not mean accepting responsibility for the problem. Just saying sorry that the person feels there is a problem may at least show that you are acknowledging their concerns.
- *Complainants want a speedy response*: Show that you are willing to take action immediately, even if it is just to make the time to listen to the complaint. This is difficult when you are busy, but making the complainant wait or passing them on to a more senior member of staff can escalate the situation (see also Robotham 2001; Parliamentary and Health Service Ombudsman 2009).
- *Complainants want reassurance* that the organisation is taking the matter seriously and will try and prevent a recurrence: Do inform complainants what you intend to do about their complaint and how the trust will respond.
- *Complainants do not want to be told*:

- That rules were being followed, so the organisation was right all along.
- That they made a mistake, so it is their own fault.
- Detailed explanations of why a problem arose, which come across as an excuse for poor services.

- It should be an objective to resolve as many complaints as possible at the first point of contact: It is important that when a person complains, you try to handle it yourself in the first instance. Find out whether your employer provides training on complaints handling and ask to attend any training on offer. This can mean that you are better prepared to deal with complaints as they arise. However, if, after listening carefully, it becomes clear that you cannot resolve the issue or that it is a serious matter, you should inform the complainant about how to take the matter further.

If this is the first time that you have had to deal with a complaint, make sure you seek support from your senior nurse or duty manager. You will not be expected to deal with a complaint by yourself, and more senior staff will expect to be involved. Also, no matter how competently you deal with a complaint, some people will not be satisfied until they have spoken to someone 'in authority'. If your situation seems to be heading this way, do not see it as a failure – swallow your pride and call in a suitable member of staff.

Finally do not forget to record the complaint and the action you took. Even if you feel that the complaint was dealt with immediately, the complainant may want to take things further at a later date. Clear records of the complaint, times and dates and the outcome will be vital if a formal investigation takes place.

What is involved in incident reporting?

Kevin Power

According to the Government's Chief Medical Officer, one in 10 hospital patients suffers some accidental harm (*British Journal of Nursing* 2002). Your immediate response to the incident is important. Clearly the priority is to ensure that anyone who is actually hurt receives prompt attention for their injuries. Green (2001) notes some confusion regarding how to respond when an incident occurs. Where an incident occurs that may lead to a claim against a nurse, the Royal College of Nursing (RCN) (2009) advises:

> *Remember that you should never admit liability for an incident or submit any written statement about it until you have taken advice from the RCN.*

It is likely that other professional indemnity schemes will contain similar advice. This advice is contrary to the stated aims for the management of clinical risk in the NHS (Green 2001). One of these aims is for staff to be able to listen, apologise and learn from their mistakes.

So what do you do when faced with an incident? Do you apologise or seek union advice? Green (2001) advises that a nurse should not rush to apologise for an incident, but should record the facts, ensure that the line manager is made aware of the incident promptly, and cooperate with the complaints procedure. Green goes on to suggest that completion of the investigation may be an appropriate point at which to apologise without compromising any indemnity insurance you may have.

It is clear that all incidents leading to harm, whether minor or major, must be reported (Department of Health 2001). Any incidents that nearly lead to harm (near misses) must also be reported. Each employer will have a local system for reporting incidents and near misses, and you should be familiar with the system in operation in your area.

There are minimal requirements for the recording of incidents:

- The fact that an examination was carried out.
- Whether any injury was apparent.
- Any advice given to the injured person.

When writing the record it is important to note clear and unambiguous facts, i.e. what you saw or what others say they saw, not what you or they think happened. For example, if a patient falls, do not write, 'Mrs Smith seemed to have fallen out of bed.' Instead write, 'Mrs Smith was found lying on the floor next to her bed.' You can record what someone says, for example, 'Mrs Smith stated that she fell out of bed.'

Where you do record what someone says, it is important to make it clear that it is someone else's words by enclosing the statement in quotation marks. You should also write down the events in chronological order as this can help to clarify precisely what happened. Any witnesses to the event should make a statement, and if the witness is another patient, a relative or a junior member of staff, they may need advice on how to write what happened to ensure that they also report facts rather than what they think happened.

If any person was injured or there is a suspicion of injury as a result of the incident, a doctor should examine the person. You should ensure that the doctor carrying out such an examination records:

- What happened (event or near miss description, severity of actual or potential harm, people and equipment involved).
- Where it happened (location/specialty).
- When it happened (date and time).
- How it happened (immediate or proximate cause/causes).
- Why it happened (underlying or root cause/causes).
- What action was taken or proposed (immediate and longer term).
- What impact the event had (harm to the organisation, the patient, others).
- What factors did, or could have, minimised the impact of the event.

(Department of Health 2001)

What is a mentor?
Dave Dalby

You will need to be involved with the mentoring of learners very soon after you qualify as a learning disability nurse. As a senior student nurse you may well be involved in the mentoring of junior learners as part of a buddying system (Eaton et al 2007).

There are many different definitions of mentoring and they often relate to the profession and type of learner being mentored. The following are a few definitions from nursing practice.

- The term mentor is used to denote the role of the nurse, midwife or health visitor who facilitates learning and supervises and assesses students (English National Board and Department of Health 2001a).
- A 'registrant who, following successful completion of a Nursing and Midwifery Council approved mentor preparation programme, has achieved all the knowledge, skills and competence required to meet the defined outcomes' (Nursing and Midwifery Council 2006).
- A good mentoring relationship is a dialogue between two people committed to improvement (Neary 1994 cited in Dix and Hughes 2004).

It is worth elaborating on the three definitions to demonstrate how mentorship has been perceived and changed over the last 10 years or so. The first definition identifies the three aspects of mentoring: teaching, supervision and assessment. It is fair to say that at one time mentorship was not seen as an integral part of the nurse's role. One could attend a half day session on mentoring and be deemed suitably prepared to take on the role of mentor.

The second definition is somewhat more formal and prescriptive as it identifies that the nurse has to successfully complete a Nursing and Midwifery Council approved course and meet the required outcomes. These outcomes can be seen in the Nursing and Midwifery Council (2008a) document, *Standards to support learning and assessment in practice*. Your local university will be able to give you details of mentorship courses and I would strongly recommend you attend such a course.

Although the final definition may be considered 'old', for me it encapsulates what mentorship is all about. Two or more people (you may have more than one mentor) working together with the goal of improving practice and consequently care of people with learning disabilities and their significant others. What is the purpose of mentorship if care is not improved?

What are the characteristics of an effective mentor?

Think of a mentor you have worked with whilst on placement who you felt was effective in some way or other. What were the characteristics that made him or her that bit special?

Like definitions of mentorship there are different descriptors of the qualities of an effective mentor. Price (2004) suggests that effective mentorship encompasses the functions outlined in *Table 7.1*. Whilst 'role model' in the table includes the mention of skills, I think this is worthy of a category in its own right. The role of the learning disability nurse is increasingly using 'hands on' skills such as those mentioned in *Chapter 4* on physical health. The learning disability nurse also needs to demonstrate competence in other skills, such as counselling, teaching and facilitation; in working with others in the care of people with a learning disability; working with families; and intervention strategies, just to name a few.

Whilst all the above functions are important, it is worth considering the advantages of encouraging learners to work with and experience a range of skills, knowledge and attitudes that colleagues in other disciplines within the learning disability community have to offer. Students should be encouraged to arrange 'experiences' with speech and language therapists, occupational therapists, psychologists, physiotherapists and other nurses who offer different 'specialisms'. It is also worth considering the career pathway senior learners wish to take and encouraging experiences that will be of benefit to them, whether this be in the NHS, voluntary or private sector.

Table 7.1. Functions of a mentor (adapted from Price 2004)	
Function	*Example from practice*
Advisor or coach	Helping the learner to decide upon an appropriate way to assess some aspect of practice that the learner will have to demonstrate competence in
Networker	Putting the learner in contact with knowledgeable colleagues who the learner will spend time with and benefit from their experiences
Sponsor or advocate	Informing other mentors and colleagues who the learner will be working with, about their abilities, efforts or circumstances
Resource consultant	Directing the learner to useful resources, such as articles, websites, policies and people
Role model	Demonstrating best practice to the learner, this will include 'hands on' skills and other skills such as communication, empathy and multi-disciplinary working
Assessor or monitor	Judging objectively the learner's progress whilst on placement and giving feedback to the learner and significant others
Facilitator of critical thought and reflection	Helping the learner to use and reflect upon past experiences and to learn from them, and planning future experiences and anticipating outcomes

How are learners assessed in practice?
Dave Dalby

An integral part of mentoring learners is assessing their competence in practice. The education of student nurses requires half their time in theory and half in practice. The assessment of practice is therefore extremely important and onerous and should be conducted transparently and fairly but with rigour. The assessment of learners in practice can also be very rewarding.

What is assessment?

According to Price (2005) there are two types of assessment:

- *Formative assessment.* This is where the mentor acts as an advisor and informs the learner of the progress he or she is making towards certain goals and competencies.
- *Summative assessment.* This is different in that the mentor acts as an examiner. It is designed to judge the competency of the learner's practice as measured against stated benchmarks such as the Nursing and Midwifery Council's competency statements. Summative assessment is a hurdle learners must overcome if they are to continue with their studies.

The following definitions of assessment describe what assessment entails.

A process by which a learner's level of competence, achievement or performance is judged. Assessment is also undertaken to identify learning needs.
(Vaughan in Hinchliff 2008)

Assessment is about talking, doing and writing.
(English National Board and OU 2001)

These two definitions impart what mentors have to do if they are to provide learners with appropriate assessment processes and procedures. The first definition highlights that it is not just about assessing competence but also about the learning needs of mentees. The second definition is very practical in that it tells mentors to talk with their learners and do 'hands on' care with them. It also highlights the importance of writing with learners such things as care plans, health action plans, etc, and also action plans that will help learners achieve competence.

I would like to make a couple of additions to this process of assessment that can be used to inform interactions with learners:

Talking + Doing + Writing = Planning and Action

What process can I use when assessing learners?

The process outlined in *Table 7.2* may be useful.

How should I complete practice placement records?

- Detail what skills, knowledge and attitudes need to be developed during placement with you and on future placements. Recording this on the

Table 7.2. Process for assessing learners in practice	
1	Discuss with learners how you are going to be making decisions about their competence
2	Decide what assistance the learners are going to require and who is to provide this
3	Inform the learners of what criteria they are being assessed against
4	Discuss with the learners what opportunities they are going to have to check on their progress throughout the placement. Arrange meeting times and dates
5	What records of progress are you going to keep and who is going to keep them? It may be better that you both keep them; this will help you to compare and use them as a basis for discussion
6	Who will decide when summative assessment is to take place? Again the records identified in step 5 above will help in deciding this
7	Ensure plenty of formative assessment has taken place before summative judgements are made
8	Meet with your learners regularly so that they are kept informed and are aware of their progress

student's on-going achievement record that is carried with the student from placement to placement will be useful.

- Identify skills, knowledge and attitudes where progress is slower, and work on these with your student.
- Specify what the strengths of your student are and how these can be developed to help improve areas of practice that are not as well developed.
- Specify any areas of weakness and develop action plans or learning contracts to combat these.

How can I give my learner timely and constructive feedback?

Allocate regular and sufficient time to give your learner feedback. I would suggest you aim for one hour per week spread across the week. Whenever possible provide private space to give feedback. Involve other colleagues in the feedback process either directly or by you discussing with them their assessment of the learner's progress. Mentorship is not about you and the learner in isolation, involve others. Provide opportunities for discussion of decisions made but when they are based on summative assessment these should not be changed.

Table 7.3. Feedback process	
Psychomotor	Give the learner feedback on their 'hands on' ability
Cognitive	Does the learner have the underpinning knowledge and understand why psychomotor skills are performed in the way they are?
Inter-personal or affective	Is the learner able to communicate effectively with service users and significant others. Does the learner demonstrate sensitivity and empathy?

What areas could be useful when giving my learner feedback?

The areas identified in *Table 7.3* can be useful when deciding upon and developing feedback to learners. It is important to give feedback regularly.

What can I do to reduce subjectivity in assessment?

Subjectivity of assessment is an area of concern throughout professions where assessment of competence is required. Involving others and gaining a comprehensive 'picture' of your learner will help you make decisions that are as objective as possible.

You may want to consider all or some of the following:

- Involve other learning disability nurses, whether qualified or not.
- Involve service users and significant others.
- Involve the wider multi-disciplinary and multi-agency team.
- Does the learner adopt a holistic approach to care?
- Is the learner person-centred?
- Is the learner's care evidence based?

How can I schedule assessments throughout the learner's placement?

Table 7.4 is based on a learner on a 10-week allocation. Timings can be altered to suit shorter or longer placements.

What do I do if a learner is in danger of failing a placement?

This is never an easy situation to manage and it is usually very time consuming and can be emotionally draining. The strategies outlined below may be of help and

Table 7.4. Assessment schedule (adapted from Price 2007)	
Assessment week and focus	*Notes*
Week 1	
Induction and training in key essentials. Close supervision to avoid unsafe practice. Performances are selected that are appropriate for the module learning outcomes and which are likely to be available during the placement	Students are able to estimate the challenge ahead. Mentors are able to establish assessments that are realistic given the nature of clinical situations available
Weeks 2–3	
One or more performances are targeted during this week and assessed formatively. The mentor provides verbal feedback to the student on achievements, and plans for adjusted practice are noted in the student's practice document	Students perceive forthcoming assessments as fair following the evaluation of skills performed and guidance from mentor
Weeks 4–6	
Two or three performances are now completed for the purposes of competency assessment. Each performance is likely to last long enough to show how care is arranged and sequenced, and to provide an opportunity to demonstrate reasoning	Because summative assessments have taken place, stress levels have reduced for the student. The first competencies assessed will help to develop the student's confidence
Weeks 7–8	
More complex performances might be used, depending on placement objectives and student seniority. These are discussed and rehearsed, while the mentor rehearses aloud his or her own performance, that is, describes the reasoning for care decisions and actions demonstrated	The mentor acts as guide and advisor. Feedback is on distinctive areas of practice and the student gains incremental information on his or her performance. The focus on areas of learning enables the student to concentrate and improve his or her practice
	Table cont/

Weeks 9–10	
More complex performances are assessed for competency. Achievements, strengths and limitations are discussed. Placement ends with a review of all performances, identification of learning left to do and results shared on whether placement objectives or learning outcomes have been met	There are no final interview surprises about achievement

are developed from the work of several authors including Quinn (2007), Hinchliff (2008), Gopee (2011), and personal experience.

Consideration of the following is not intended to arouse anxiety but rather to increase awareness and encourage disciplined and professional practice in the assessment of learners. This will enhance accuracy in assessment decisions and safeguard you as the mentor.

Accountability, legal and ethical issues

- You are accountable or answerable for the assessment decisions you make and you may need to be able to justify them.
- Professional registration is a legal procedure and assessment decisions contribute to the eligibility of a learner to register at the completion of training.
- Registration assumes competence and if not demonstrated could lead to questions being asked about the accuracy of assessments.
- There could be legal challenges to assessment decisions, particularly by those who have failed.

Dealing with assessment-related problems

Poor performance:

- Try to identify cause (personal problems, new country/culture, poor career choice, homesickness, real or assumed discrimination, etc).
- Check learners' insight into their standard of performance. Are they aware of underperformance? A lack of insight is more of a challenge than when insight is present.
- Discuss and negotiate with learners a realistic plan of action, I would

suggest you involve others at this stage particularly your manager and relevant personnel from the university.

- If learners have shared confidential information with you this should not be disclosed without their permission. It is worth encouraging learners to inform other appropriate people about information that is relevant to their underperformance.
- Carefully document all the actions you have taken to address the situation.
- Avoid undue delay in addressing underperformance and bringing it to the attention of appropriate individuals. The longer you leave it the harder it will be for you and your learners.
- Utilise advice given by appropriate individuals and provide learners with regular feedback on performance.
- If a successful outcome was not achieved, failure should not come as a complete surprise to the student.

Challenge of assessment decision by a learner who has failed

- Always provide the learner with detailed and specific reasons for a fail decision. Feedback to the learner should be balanced, identifying strengths as well as the areas of concern which contributed to the fail decision. Many learners, although disappointed, will accept the decision. Challenges are very infrequent.
- Always carefully document your reasons for failing a learner while incidents are fresh in your mind.
- Notes should be specific and precise.
- Explain again to the learner your reasons for failing him or her. Do not allow yourself to be intimidated by the learner even if threats are made of taking it further or accusations are made about discrimination.
- Be prepared to participate in any investigation/appeal that may follow (your records will be indispensable at this time).
- If you have carried out the assessment fairly, have followed the correct procedures and can justify your decision, do not change it even if you are pressurised to do so.

It has been identified by Duffy (2003) that some mentors failed to fail learners, for some of the following reasons.

- Learners were early on in their training.
- Many felt uncomfortable 'putting pen to paper' either because they found

181

the clinical assessment document full of jargon and difficult to put into practice or they were worried about repercussions from the university.
- Some mentors saw failing learners as uncaring.
- The learners were close to completion of their course and the mentor did not want to jeopardise the learners' future.
- Learners had personal problems.

It is important to recognise that some learners need to fail. Passing learners in the hope that they will improve later has consequences for service users, carers and significant others.

What can mentors do to promote positive placements for learners?
Dave Dalby

Get off to a good start

First impressions count so it is important that we make a good first impression. Getting off to a good start will help us to achieve this. It is worth considering what mentors can do prior to a learner starting his or her placement, during the first few days of the placement, and during the rest of the placement. *Table 7.5* identifies what can be done.

Prior to placement

If an orientation/induction pack is to be used then it may contain all or some of the following;

- Shift patterns usually worked.
- Contact names and numbers.
- Information about the placement and service users.
- Information about the lead mentor and associate mentor.
- Directions to the placement including a map and bus/train services (if appropriate).
- Commonly used terms and abbreviations.
- Article/s pertaining to the service user group, e.g. epilepsy, autism, enteral feeding, etc.
- SWOT (strengths, weaknesses, opportunities, threats) analysis.

Table 7.5. Mentor support		
Prior to placement	*First few days*	*Rest of placement*
• Send the learner a welcome letter • Encourage the learner to 'get in touch' • Arrange a pre-placement visit • Send the learner an orientation/induction pack • Include learner on the off-duty and give information about the first few shifts	• Introduce to service users and significant others (including other members of staff) • Try to establish the learner's personal situation and needs • Conduct the initial/first interview within the first seven days • Make sure the 'lead mentor' is on duty for the learner's first shift • If at all possible try to arrange it so the 'lead mentor' is supernumery for the learner's first shift • Establish the learner's previous learning and experiences • If not already done, give the learner an orientation/induction package • Familiarise the learner with paperwork he or she will come into contact with and have to complete	• Ensure whenever possible the learner is working with the 'lead mentor' • Maintain regular one-to-one meetings – try for once a week • Keep a close eye on whether learning objectives/outcomes are being achieved • Are the learners getting the experience they need? • Involve the learners in any training – in house or out of house • Arrange visits to other professionals and departments • Arrange de-briefing sessions when appropriate • Last, but not least, invite to any social events

It is important to keep any orientation/induction package succinct and to the point. Too long or too complicated and they will put learners off. If using articles I would advise against using long and arduous ones. Something from *Learning Disability Practice* or journals of a similar vein will be suitable.

A SWOT analysis is useful in getting learners to think about their strengths and weaknesses, the opportunities that they are looking forward to when on placement and any perceived threats they may feel anxious about. A simple sheet of A4 presented as in *Table 7.6* can be included in the orientation/induction pack.

Table 7.6. SWOT analysis	
Strengths You may want to consider here your previous placements and academic studies	*Weaknesses* You may again want to consider here your previous placements and academic studies
Opportunities What are you looking forward to? You may want to think about the service users and placement speciality	*Threats* What anxieties do you have about the placement? Again you may want to think about the service users and placement speciality

First few days

When establishing learners' personal situations and needs, it is worth considering issues such as do they do bank work, do they have children, are there any cultural or religious needs, etc?

It is recommended by the Nursing and Midwifery Council and the Royal College of Nursing that the first/initial interview should be completed within the first seven days of placement. If a SWOT analysis was included in the orientation/induction pack then this can be used for the basis of a discussion. If not, ask the learner to complete one prior to your meeting.

When deciding upon who is going to be mentoring learners, consider the availability of individual mentors. If a member of staff is going to be unavailable for the first week or two of a placement for whatever reason is that person the most appropriate mentor or should another be considered?

If your placement area is usually very busy at a particular time and that time coincides with the student's first arrival, consider asking the student to start at a time later in the day when it is less busy and you are able to give him or her more of your time and attention.

Rest of placement

As a mentor you should endeavour to spend at least 40% of your time working with your learner either directly or indirectly. If you let other staff members take responsibility for your learner then you must:

- Establish that anyone you delegate to is able to carry out your instructions.
- Confirm that the outcome of any delegated task meets the required standard.

- Ensure that everyone you are responsible for is supervised and supported
  (Nursing and Midwifery Council 2008b)

What may happen when learners have a poor placement experience?

Dave Dalby

From the above it is obvious that the mentor plays a crucial role in providing a positive and rewarding practice placement experience. Without such positive experiences it is more likely that learners will feel devalued and they may even leave their courses before completion of their studies (Pearcey and Elliott 2004).

A good mentoring relationship is one that is committed to improvement for the student, service users, carers and significant others alike, but it is a two-way street with responsibility for that relationship not just resting with the mentor but also with the learner.

Mentors can expect learners to take some responsibility for their own learning, to act professionally, to communicate with their mentors and others effectively and to have the interests of service users, carers and significant others at the forefront of what they do. Starting off well makes the learner feel welcome and reduces anxiety. Providing a quality placement will help to reduce the number of learners who consider dropping out of their course (Beskine 2009).

An extremely valuable document, *Guidelines for mentors of nursing students and midwives*, is available from the Royal College of Nursing (2007).

References

Beskine D (2009) Mentoring students: Establishing effective working relationships. *Nursing Standard* **23**(30): 35–40

British Journal of Nursing (2002) One in ten hospital patients suffer some form of harm. *British Journal of Nursing* **11**(12): 796

Department of Health (1994) *Being heard: The report of a review committee on NHS complaints procedures* (Wilson Report). London: HMSO

Department of Health (2001) *Building a safer NHS for patients: Implementing an organisation with a memory*. London: Department of Health

Dix G, Hughes S (2004) Strategies to help students learn effectively. *Nursing Standard* **18**(32): 39–42

Duffy K (2003) *Failing students: A qualitative study of factors that influence the decisions regarding assessment of students' competence in practice*. Glasgow: Caledonian University

Eaton E, Henderson A, Winch S (2007) Enhancing nurses' capacity to facilitate learning in nursing students: Effective dissemination and uptake of best practice guidelines. *International Journal of Nursing Practice* **13**(5): 316–20

English National Board and Department of Health (2001a) *Placements in focus*. London: English National Board and Department of Health

English National Board and Department of Health (2001b) *Assessing practice in nursing and midwifery*. London: English National Board and Department of Health

English National Board and Open University (2001) *Assessing practice in nursing and midwifery*. Open University Press, Milton Keynes

Gopee N (2011) *Mentoring and supervision in healthcare* (2nd edn). London: Sage

Green C (2001) Benefiting from the end of blame culture. *Professional Nurse* **16**(7 Suppl): S3–4

Hinchliff S (2008) *Nursing practice and healthcare* (5th edn). London: Hodder Arnold

Nursing and Midwifery Council (2006) *Standards to support learning and assessment in practice*. London: Nursing and Midwifery Council

Nursing and Midwifery Council (2008a) *Standards to support learning and assessment in practice*. London: Nursing and Midwifery Council

Nursing and Midwifery Council (2008b) *The Code: Standards of conduct, performance and ethics for nurses and midwives*. London: Nursing and Midwifery Council

Parliamentary and Health Service Ombudsman (2009) *Annual Report 2007-08*. London: The Stationary Office

Pearcey P, Elliott B (2004) Students' impressions of clinical nursing. *Nurse Education Today* **24**(5): 382–7

Price B (2004) Becoming a good mentor. *Nursing Standard* **19**: 13

Price B (2005) Assessing a learner's progress. *Nursing Standard* **19**(48): 73–4

Price B (2007) Practice-based assessment: Strategies for mentors. *Nursing Standard* 21(36): 49–56

Quinn F (2007) *Principles and practice of nurse education*. Cheltenham: Nelson Thornes

Royal College of Nursing (2007) *Guidelines for mentors of nursing students and midwives*. London: Royal College of Nursing

Royal College of Nursing (2009) *Legal help*. Available from: http://www.rcn.org.uk/support/legal

Robotham M (2001) How to handle complaints. *Nursing Times* **97**(30): 25–8

NOTES

Chapter 8

Dealing with emergencies

Chris Knifton, Cormac Norton, David Parker and Judi Thorley

- What types of emergencies might I face?
- What are my responsibilities and how should I respond if I suspect abuse, or if abuse is disclosed to me?
- What should I do if there is a sudden or unexpected death?
- What are the essential first aid procedures I need to know when working with people with learning disabilities?
- What do I need to consider if sending someone with learning disabilities to A&E?

What types of emergencies might I face?
Chris Knifton

As a nurse working with people with learning disabilities and their carers, it is likely that you will come across a number of emergency situations. It is difficult to know what to do in each event as the possibilities are numerous, and requirements may change depending on setting and organisation. Your organisation will help you prepare for this in a number of ways, including immediate access to policy and procedure, clinical supervision, and training days/courses. It is your responsibility to ensure you attend training days as requested and that you keep yourself up-to-date with changes in local policy and procedural practice.

Most policy and procedure folders are large, and it is not always easy to know which you need to read first. Because emergencies cannot be foreseen, and might occur at any time, I would suggest that you read through policies dealing with emergencies first, and then seek guidance from your line manager for anything you do not fully understand. Your line manager can help you identify areas felt to be emergency situations in your clinical area, as this may vary between services and the people you come into contact with. Examples of possible emergency situations, however, may include:

- Absconding
- Anaphylaxis
- Cardiac arrest
- Choking

- Disclosure/suspected abuse
- Fire or bomb reports
- Infection outbreaks
- Medication errors
- Seizures (particularly status epilepticus)
- Some examples of complex behaviour requiring restraint (physical or chemical)
- Sudden or unexpected death
- Trauma/injury (including bleeding, burns and poisoning).

Discuss this list with your line manager. There may be other areas your line manager thinks are important, depending on the type of organisation you work in. Next refer to your organisation's own policy and procedure for each, making a list of any questions you may have so you can seek clarification. Given the diversity between organisations and services it would be impractical to write a response to each in this book, although some examples are provided in this chapter to give you an idea.

What are my responsibilities and how should I respond if I suspect abuse, or if abuse is disclosed to me?
Judi Thorley

We all have a responsibility for the safety and wellbeing of patients and colleagues. Our responsibilities to our patients/clients are to ensure that they are always treated with dignity and respect. Living a life that is free from harm and abuse is a fundamental human right of every person. *Safeguarding adults is about ensuring the safety and well-being of all patients, but those least able to protect themselves from harm or abuse may need to be provided with additional measures.* If you suspect abuse, or if abuse is disclosed to you, there are a number of things you must consider.

Stay calm, reassure the person and ensure he or she is safe. Make sure that both your verbal and non-verbal communication demonstrates that you are taking disclosure seriously (consider use of communication aids/language line if required). If patients disclose to you, it is important you let them know they have done the right thing in disclosure.

You will need to inform patients that other people may need to talk to them but do this in a sensitive and supportive way, as this may lead to anxiety. If you consider the adult is vulnerable as defined under the Department of Health's

(2000) *No secrets*, document, you will need to raise a safeguarding concern within you own organisation/agency following local policy and procedures. You have a responsibility to read and understand the local policy and procedures for safeguarding adults within each practice area.

Your initial assessment should be holistic and thorough and should consider the patient's emotional, social, psychological and physical presentation as well as the identified clinical need. You need to be alert to:

- Inconsistencies in the history or explanation.
- Skin integrity.
- Hydration.
- Personal presentation, e.g. is the person unkempt?
- Delays or evidence of obstacles in seeking or receiving treatment.
- Evidence of frequent attendances to health services or repeated failures to attend.
- Environmental factors, e.g. signs of neglect, the reactions and responses of other people with the adult.
- Does the adult have capacity for the decision required?
- Is the adult able to give informed consent or is action needed in his or her best interests?
- Are there others at risk, e.g. children or other vulnerable adults?
- Is immediate protection required?
- Has a crime been committed and should the police be informed?
- Preserve any evidence, e.g. discourage any attempt to remove what may be evidence (such as bathing if sexual abuse is suspected).
- Is any action that is being considered proportionate to the risk identified?
- What are the individual's views/wishes?
- Are there any relevant cultural or religious beliefs?
- Are there valid reasons to act even without the individual's consent, e.g. where others are at risk.
- Does a service failure that may affect others need to be addressed?

No attempt should be made to ask possibly leading questions or enquire too deeply. Be open and honest and do not promise to keep a secret. Seek consent to share information if the individual has capacity and if it is in the public interest in order to prevent crime or protect others from harm. It is important to carefully document what has been said, or what you have observed. Ensure what you record is legible, factual, timely and an accurate account of what you did and why, to demonstrate transparent, defensible decision making. Do not delay unnecessarily. Seek advice if you have any doubt, it is important you follow the guidance under the Department of Health's *No secrets* and your own organisation's policy and procedures. Remember you are accountable for what you do or choose not to do.

Safeguarding adults is a fundamental part of patient safety. The following summarises your responsibilities when you have safeguarding concerns:

- Assess the situation, i.e. are emergency services required?
- Ensure the safety and wellbeing of the individual.
- Establish what are the individual's views and wishes.
- Maintain any evidence.
- Follow internal procedures for reporting incidents/risks.
- Remain calm and try not to show any shock or disbelief.
- Listen carefully and demonstrate understanding by acknowledging regret and concern that this has happened.
- Inform the person that you are required to share the information, explaining what information will be shared and why.
- Make a written record of what the person has told you, using the person's own words or what you have seen, and record your actions.

(NHS Midlands and East 2011)

What should I do if there is a sudden or unexpected death?

Chris Knifton

An unexpected death is one that is not expected at that moment as a result of the person's current health. This even applies to people with a terminal illness where death is not expected to be imminent. A sudden death is any violent or unnatural death or one where the death is unanticipated. Different policies and procedures however may have slightly different definitions. Be sure you know how your organisation defines each.

If you come across a client who has collapsed and there are no signs of life, it is important that you start basic life support (cardiopulmonary resuscitation) and call the emergency services (999 or 112). However, there may be times as a registered nurse where there is no reasonable doubt that the person has died and that resuscitation would be futile. It is in these circumstances that the sudden and unexpected death policy must be followed.

Some nurses are trained in verification of death. However in cases of unexpected or sudden death, nurses cannot verify death. You must contact the GP or the on-call medical practitioner, depending on your working environment, to confirm the death. If the death is sudden or suspicious, the scene must not be disturbed and the police must be contacted. If the deceased has any equipment (i.e. catheters, cannulas, PEG feeds, etc.) these must *not* be removed until consent is given by a coroner (in event of unexpected death) or the police (in sudden death). Inform your line manager or person on call if out of hours. Do not forget to complete an incident form and make thorough notes in the nursing records. You may wish to seek advice on contacting relatives if you have not done this before (see *Chapter 2* on breaking bad news). Policies and procedures may vary slightly between areas so it is crucial to read through your own organisation's policy at your earliest convenience.

Remember you are not alone and that the on-call manager is there to support you. It is not unusual for nurses to experience anxiety when dealing with a sudden or unexpected death, particularly if this is their first experience of death or when they are liaising with the police. If you are the nurse in charge, remember that you may need to arrange support for other members of staff on duty as well as being responsible for other clients.

This is a basic guide, and different organisations/services may have differing ways of responding. Ensure you take personal responsibility for reading your own policy/procedure on sudden and unexpected death.

What are the essential first aid procedures I need to know when working with people with learning disabilities?
David Parker and Chris Knifton

No matter where you work, understanding basic first aid is more than useful – it could save a life! It is advisable to obtain a recognised first aid qualification, and there should be a trained first aider on every shift. As nurses working with people with learning disabilities, in emergency situations you may come across a range of injuries, trauma or ailments that require first aid intervention. Consider how prepared you would be if there was a first aid emergency while you were on duty. The Health and Safety (First Aid) Regulations 1981 place a duty on all employers to ensure first aid provision is made available. Guidance is available at www. hse.gov.uk/firstaid/. It is important you know where to get the best up-to-date information on first aid, since first aid procedures may change between courses.

The *First aid manual (9th edn, revised)* (St John Ambulance et al 2011) is the current manual used by first aid organisations. The main changes to the manual since the publication of the 9th edition in 2009 concern the treatment for choking and resuscitation, including the depth and speed of compressions; additional instructions if a casualty starts breathing during cardiopulmonary resuscitation (CPR); and a changed emphasis on compression-only CPR for untrained members of the public. There are also some minor changes in other areas. To make sure you get the latest version, look for the word Revised above the 9th edition and the BMA Medical Award Winner symbol on the cover. The new first aid instructions are based on the updated guidelines from the UK Resuscitation Council which regularly updates protocols where evidence shows an improved chance of survival. I would strongly recommend you obtain the latest version of this manual.

Some examples of injuries and the recommended first aid measures that you may encounter are shown below. However, reading this is no substitute for attending a first aid course.

Choking

This occurs when a foreign object, such as food or an inedible object gets stuck at the back of the throat, causing a blockage and sometimes muscular spasm. The risk of this occurring in people with a learning disability is high, and may be particularly relevant when feeding people with profound and multiple learning disability, or in cases of challenging/complex behaviour including self-injury or those displaying signs of pica. It can be mild or severe.

Mild obstruction

In mild obstruction people are unable to speak, cry, cough or breathe. They may be panicking, particularly if they cannot understand what is happening. It is important, particularly for people with profound and multiple learning disability, that you remain vigilant for signs of mild obstruction during feeding. Although people will usually be able to clear blockages themselves, depending on cough reflex, positioning, muscle tone or other congenital and physical abnormalities, this may not always be the case. Therefore, in some groups, a mild obstruction may quickly become a severe obstruction.

Severe obstruction

In a severe obstruction people will be unable to speak, cry, cough or breathe. Without assistance they will eventually become unconscious and collapse (St John Ambulance et al 2011).

Treatment

The aim of treatment for adults (treatment for infants is different and not the subject of this chapter) is to remove the obstruction if possible, or to arrange urgent admission to hospital if necessary (St John Ambulance et al 2011).

- If the obstruction is mild:
  - Encourage the patient to continue coughing
  - Remove any obvious obstruction from the mouth.
- If the obstruction is severe:
  - Give up to five back blows
  - Check the mouth and remove any obvious obstruction.
- If the obstruction is still present:
  - Give up to five abdominal thrusts
  - Check the mouth and remove any obvious obstruction.
- If the obstruction does not clear after three cycles of back blows and abdominal thrusts:
  - Dial 999 (or 112) for an ambulance
  - Continue until help arrives.

(St John Ambulance et al 2011)

You need to attend a first aid course to be shown how to perform back blows and abdominal thrusts safely, and to practise on models. It is important to consider the possibility of soft tissue injuries or abdominal injuries when you have carried out back blows and abdominal thrusts. Clearing the obstruction through the above techniques, however, is your first priority. Medical examination may be needed following back blows and abdominal thrusts on any person.

Severe bleeding

Severe bleeding can be caused by accident, assault or through self-injury. In rare circumstances, severe bleeding may also be the result of attempted suicide, although this is rare in learning disability. When arteries are ruptured, bleeding is always severe and will often 'spurt' out in time with the heartbeat. Bleeding from veins tends to result in darker coloured blood, which may gush from wounds. Examples of wounds include contusions (bruises), lacerations (tears such as from claws or barbed wire, often associated with contamination), incisions (clean cuts by sharp objects such as glass, which may involve damage to nerves and tendons), puncture wounds (nails or needles, again with increased risk of contamination), stab wounds (by knives, with added risk of internal organ damage if occurring on the trunk of the body), and, rarely, gunshot wounds (often involving a small entry wound and a large exit wound). In the presence of severe bleeding:

- Ensure that it is safe to approach the person. This is important because where there is severe bleeding, you need to be mindful of the cause and that you do not put yourself into danger. Be on the lookout for the object that caused the wound.
- If possible, wash your hands using soap and water to minimise the risk of cross-infection; however, if the bleeding is severe, do not waste time as the wound may be life threatening.
- If they are available, put on gloves, being mindful of any allergies the person may have to gloves you are wearing.
- Carefully remove any clothing that is covering the casualty's wound to expose the area.
- If an object is embedded in the wound, do not remove it.
- Place a sterile dressing pad over the wound. If this is not available, improvise by using a clean piece of non-fluffy material to cover the wound (St John Ambulance et al 2011).
- Apply firm pressure to the pad using the fingers or palm of the hand. In some situations, it may be reasonable and practical to ask the person to maintain this pressure. Ensure no pressure is applied to an embedded object (St John Ambulance et al 2011). It is important that the person is able to comply with these instructions, and concerns about mental capacity and best interests may need to be considered in people with learning disabilities.
- Handle the injured part as carefully as possible as there may be an associated injury such as a limb fracture.
- If appropriate, raise the injured limb so it is higher than the level of the heart. Gravity will help to reduce the flow of blood to the wound. If you suspect a facture (broken bone), do not move the limb as moving broken bones could cause further injury. A good tip is to ask patients if they can move the area/limb independently, if they can, it is usually safe to elevate the area (but examine first); broken bones tend to cause an inability to move the affected area.
- Encourage the casualty to lie down; this will reduce blood flow to the wound and help to minimise the effects of shock (St John Ambulance et al 2011). Recheck the bleeding, if it is coming through the dressing, apply another one on top. If it comes through the second dressing, remove both

and reapply a fresh dressing large enough to cover the whole of the wound, ensuring pressure is applied at the point of bleeding (St John Ambulance et al 2011). Check circulation beyond the bandage every 10 minutes, loosening the bandage and reapplying if necessary (St John Ambulance et al 2011).

- Ensure that the emergency services have been alerted (St John Ambulance et al, 2011).
- Reassure the casualty and stay with him or her until expert help arrives.
- Keep the patient warm, for example by using a blanket or coat.
- If you are able to do so, regularly monitor the casualty's vital signs including respiratory rate, pulse rate and level of consciousness.
- If the casualty's level of consciousness deteriorates, place him or her in the recovery position and continue to monitor vital signs. If the casualty stops breathing, send someone to alert the emergency services again and start resuscitation.
- Where wounds are extensive, effective haemorrhage control may only be achieved by applying indirect pressure over a proximal artery, such as the femoral or brachial artery (Greaves and Porter 2007) for which you need additional training.

Standard precautions

Blood is the single most important source of HIV and hepatitis B viruses, as well as other potential bacteraemia (bacteria infecting the bloodstream) infections. Although possibly difficult in a first-aid setting, great care should be taken to minimise the risk of cross-infection. Person-to-person spread of infection through direct contact can be prevented with good hand hygiene and use of personal protective equipment such as gloves and aprons (Dougherty and Lister 2011). Using gloves is one of the most important ways this can be achieved. Effective hand washing should also be undertaken after all first aid measures in line with local policy.

Head injuries

Falls are one of the more common problems requiring first aid which you may encounter. Additional concerns however will arise when the fall includes a knock to the head. The risk of head injury following a fall is high and as a registered nurse you need to act quickly and decisively. Due to the increased risk of epilepsy in people with a learning disability, head injury following a seizure is often a cause for concern. Some people, following a detailed risk assessment, may wear protective head wear to reduce injury. All head injuries are potentially serious and require careful assessment because they can result in impaired consciousness, and may be often associated with damage to the brain or blood vessels, or with a skull fracture (St John Ambulance et al 2011).

A head injury may produce concussion, which is a brief period of unconsciousness followed by complete recovery. Some head injuries may produce compression of the brain (cerebral compression), which is life-threatening (St John Ambulance 2011). It is therefore important to be able to recognise possible signs of cerebral compression, in particular, a deteriorating level of response. Alterations in levels of consciousness may vary from slight to severe and indicate the degree of potential brain injury (Aucken and Crawford 1998). The Glasgow Coma Scale (GCS) is used to rate the severity of a coma.

A head wound should alert you to the risk of deeper, underlying damage, such as a skull fracture, which may be serious. Bleeding inside the skull may occur and lead to compression. Clear fluid or watery blood leaking from the ear or nose are signs of serious injury. Any casualty with an injury to the head should be assumed to have a neck (spinal) injury as well and be treated accordingly (St John Ambulance 2011). The only safe procedure with a head injury is to refer the casualty to hospital or call for medical attention, depending on your organisation. If the person is conscious, assist him or her to sit, supported in a comfortable position. Where appropriate, apply a cold compress to hold against the head/ bump. It is important you look out for *one or more* of the following signs which indicate that immediate medical attention is required:

- Drowsiness
- Worsening or intense headache
- Vomiting
- Confusion, disorientation or irritability
- Visual problems
- Seizures
- Unequal pupil size
- Noisy breathing
- Paralysis
- Bruising around the eye (black eye) development
- Clear fluid or blood from the ear or nose.

If the person becomes unconscious, the airway must be opened using the 'jaw thrust method' (St John Ambulance et al 2011). If you do not know how to open an airway using this method, it is important you ask about relevant training. This technique should be taught on good first aid courses.

If the person is not breathing, or if breathing stops, then immediately give 30 compressions at a rate of 120 per minute to a depth of 5–6cm in the average sized adult. Ensure the emergency services have been contacted without delay. Consult your organisation's own policy and guidance for giving CPR with or without respirations. If the person is in the late stages of pregnancy, ensure the *right* hip is tilted to the left with rolled up clothing, a pillow or a blanket, when giving chest compressions (St John Ambulance 2011).

Scalp and head wounds are common after a fall, and may occur without skull or brain injury. These types of wound bleed profusely due to the large amount of blood vessels at the skin surface, so it is easy to panic. Head/scalp wounds must be covered with a sterile dressing, and careful examination of the person for possible head injury should be carried out.

Fractures

There are approximately 206 bones in the average human skeleton. During falls, or following an accident, seizure or assault, a fracture may occur to any one of these bones. A fracture is a complete or partial break in a bone due to excessive force applied either directly or indirectly. Fractures may be a particular concern for some people with a learning disability who have brittle or weakened bones or for older people. Older people (with or without a learning disability) are particularly at risk of hip (femur) fractures following a fall. Fractures may also occur after an epileptic seizure, either during the fall as the patient loses consciousness and/or during tonic/clonic movements if a limb strikes a hard surface.

The patient should be examined for:

- Swelling
- Unnatural range of movement
- Immobility
- Grating noise or feeling
- Deformity
- Loss of strength
- Shock
- Twisting
- Shortening or bending of a limb (St John Ambulance et al 2011).

Treatment for fracture consists of:

- Support for the injured limb using bandages, clothing or blankets depending on the area.
- Immobilisation of the affected part using bandages where appropriate.

Triangular bandages are usually used as slings to support and immobilise shoulder, collar bone, rib, arm, wrist, hand or finger fractures. Broad bandages can be used, for example, for bringing legs together to support and immobilise hip, thigh, pelvis, and leg fractures. Sometimes an 'open fracture' may occur. This happens when the bone breaks and protrudes through the skin. It is extremely important not to move the injury as this would move the bone and cause more tissue damage. The wound should be covered with a sterile dressing, then padding placed and built up around and over the bone. The area should then be bandaged (St John Ambulance et al 2011) and immobilised, and the patient can then be sent to hospital.

Sunburn

Sunburn is a common problem that can affect people with a learning disability. It can be caused by over-exposure to the sun or a sun lamp. At high altitudes sunburn can occur even on an overcast day in summer.

People with learning disabilities may be prescribed antipsychotic or anti-epileptic drugs, and a common side effect of these is photosensitivity. Nurses need to be particularly aware of this. Most sunburn is superficial, although in severe cases, the skin is a lobster red in colour and blistered. Nurses have a professional responsibility to recognise the risk of sunburn in the people under their care, and take appropriate action to prevent this from occurring. This can be done by recommending the wearing of appropriate clothing and use of sunscreen.

Sunburn is recognised by:

- Reddened skin.
- Pain in the area of the burn.
- Later, blistering to the affected skin (St John Ambulance 2011).

Treatment

When dealing with somebody with sunburn the aim should be to move the casualty out of the sun or away from the source of the sunburn and to relieve any discomfort and pain. However, if there is extensive blistering or any other skin damage you need to seek medical advice.

- With minor sunburn, cover the casualty's skin with light clothing or a towel.
- Move the casualty into the shade or preferably indoors.
- Cool the skin by sponging it with cool water or by soaking the affected area in a cold bath or a cool shower for 10 minutes.
- Encourage the casualty to have frequent sips of cold water.
- If the burns are mild, calamine lotion or an after-sun preparation may be soothing (St John Ambulance et al 2011).
- For severe sunburn obtain medical aid.

Summary

The above subjects are covered in most first aid courses. The current certification given by St John Ambulance for Health and Safety Executive related courses remains valid for only three years. Volunteers with St John Ambulance carry out more rigorous training at a variety of levels from First Aider through Advanced First Aider to Emergency Ambulance Attendant. As a registered nurse you may wish to consider attending a basic first aid course. Typical training courses for first aid at work cover the following topic areas:

- Acting safely, promptly and effectively in an emergency.
- Preventing cross-infection, recording incidents and actions and using available equipment.
- Cardiopulmonary resuscitation.
- Care of an unconscious casualty (including seizure).
- Choking.
- Wounds and bleeding.
- Shock.
- Minor injuries.
- Muscular-skeletal injuries including fractures, sprains and strains.
- Spinal injuries.
- Chest injuries.
- Severe burns and scalds.
- Eye injuries.
- Poisoning.
- Anaphylaxis.

- Heart attack.
- Stroke.
- Asthma.
- Epilepsy.
- Diabetes.

Consider how essential, or useful, it is for you to know first aid procedures. Look around your workplace: is there a clear notice stating who is the first aider, how they can be contacted, and where the first aid box is? You may want to ask your line manager if you can attend the next first aid course to update your skills.

How often should I update my first aid?

Following successful completion of a first aid course, you will receive a certificate, which will be valid for three years. Please note, the Health and Safety Executive also strongly recommends undergoing a half-day skills update course each year between your full certificate renewals, to avoid 'skills fade'.

What do I need to consider if sending someone with learning disabilities to A&E?
Cormac Norton

The emergency care environment is fast paced and can be distressing for clients with learning disabilities. Such environments include emergency departments (formerly accident and emergency departments), walk in centres, medical/surgical admission units and high dependency units. Nursing care in these environments should be based on as much information as is available on the client.

Carers/nurses of those clients who are to be admitted to emergency care should consider the following when planning for that admission:

- Patient demographics, i.e. date of birth, address, contact details of next of kin or legal guardian, etc.
- History of the present problem. If this is an injury, when did it occur, what was the mechanism of the injury, how has the client been since the injury? If this is an illness, when did the symptoms start, what makes the condition worse/better, how has the client's behaviour changed since the onset of symptoms?
- Past medical history including any operations, procedures, or illness

requiring hospitalisation.
- Any allergies to medicine, food, latex, etc.
- Ongoing medical problems, e.g. diabetes mellitus, congenital heart problems.
- Current or recent medication (this should be brought with the client) and a record of when this was last administered.
- Any record of tetanus immunisation.
- Social history, where do clients normally live, who normally cares for them? What are clients' normal functional abilities like, e.g. can they normally walk independently, which hand do they normally write with?
- How does the client usually communicate? Has provision been made for that communication in the emergency care area, e.g. is there a member of staff who can use Makaton? Are there specific methods that help comfort clients should they become distressed?
- What are the client's preferences/requirements with regard to food and drink?

From the emergency practitioner's perspective such information is invaluable. Not only can the client's physical complaint be treated, but plans can be made to ensure specific emotional/psychological needs can be met in as individual a manner as possible. Carers may find it useful to develop a template in which the information above can be recorded prior to transfer to the emergency care area.

References

Aucken S, Crawford B (1998) Neurological observations. In Guerrero D (ed) Neuro-oncology for nurses (pp 29–65). London: Whurr

Department of Health (2000) No secrets: Guidance on developing and implementing multi-agency policies and procedures to protect vulnerable adults from abuse. London: Department of Health

Dougherty L, Lister S (2011) The Royal Marsden Hospital Manual of Clinical Nursing Procedures (8th edn). Oxford: Blackwell Publishing Ltd

Greaves I, Porter K (2007) Oxford handbook of pre-hospital care. Buckingham: OU Press

NHS Midlands and East (2011) *Safeguarding adults*. NHS Midlands East, East Midlands Office

St John Ambulance, St Andrew's Association and British Red Cross (2011) First aid manual (9th edn revised). London: Dorling Kinsley

NOTES

Glossary and abbreviations

The following list serves as an aid to understanding terminology used in learning disability services. Only a brief definition is provided. For some abbreviations, please be aware that alternatives may be used in other services.

A

ABA	applied behavioural analysis
abasia	inability to walk due to poor co-ordination
ABCDE	airway, breathing, circulation, disability and exposure
abduct	to move away from the body
ABS	Adaptive Behavioural Scales
a.c.	*ante cibum* (before food)
acataphasia	inability to connect thoughts in an orderly manner
acrocephaly	skull deformity, being tall and pointed
acromegaly	excessive bone growth, especially jaw, hands and feet
ADD	attention deficit disorder
ADHD	attention deficit hyperactivity disorder
adduct	to draw towards the body
ADL	activities of daily living
ADR	adverse drug reaction
akathisia	constant movement or restlessness, sometimes a side effect of antipsychotic drugs
agnosia	difficulty in recognising names of objects
AMHP	Approved Mental Health Professional under the Mental Health Act 1983
amimia	lack of facial expression
amisulpride	an antipsychotic drug
Angelman syndrome	also know as happy puppet syndrome, signs include uncoordinated arm movements and bouts of laughter
AOT	assertive outreach team
APA	American Psychiatric Association
Apert syndrome	also known as acrocephalosyndactyly. An autosomal dominant inherited condition, sometimes causing learning disability
aphagia	inability to swallow

arachnodactyly	abnormally long and thin fingers
ASD	autism spectrum disorders
ASW	approved social worker
ataxia	nervous system disorder resulting in gait problems and lack of control over movements
ataxia telangiectasia syndrome	also known as Louis-Bar syndrome. Autosomal inherited disorder leading to learning disability

B

bacteraemia	bacteria infecting the bloodstream
b.d.	*bis die* (twice daily)
BILD	British Institute of Learning Disabilities
Binet-Simon Test	intelligence test to estimate IQ and mental age
BLS	basic life support
BMI	body mass index
BNF	*British National Formulary*
BP	Either blood pressure, or British Pharmacopeia
BPS	British Psychological Society
bradycardia	pulse rate slower than 60 beats per minute in adults

C

CAB	Citizens Advice Bureau
cachexia	severe debility
CAMHS	Child and Adolescent Mental Health Services
carbamazepine	antiepileptic drug, sometimes also used in mood disorders
CAT	cognitive analytical therapy or computerised axial tomography
CBT	cognitive-behavioural therapy
CD	controlled drug
cerebral palsy	umbrella term for a range of nervous system disorders causing impaired movement and co-ordination; may be slight or severe affecting the whole body
Ch	Charriére
chlorpromazine hydrochloride	an antipsychotic drug
citalopram	an *SSRI* antidepressant
CLDT	community learning disability team

clobazam	a benzodiazepine used to treat epilepsy or anxiety
clonazepam	a benzodiazepine used to treat epilepsy, including status epilepticus
clozapine	an antipsychotic drug
CMHT	Community Mental Health Team, in the past this abbreviation used to refer to community mental handicap team
CMV	cytomegalovirus
CNMH	community nurses mental health
Coffin-Lowry syndrome	Possibly X-linked inherited disorder causing learning disability
Community Treatment Order	a legal order allowing a patient to be discharged from formal detention to supervised community treatment under the Mental Health Act 1983
Cornelia de Lange Syndrome	sometimes referred to as Amsterdam dwarfism, causing learning disability
COSHH	Control of Substances Hazardous to Health
CPA	care programme approach
CPS	Crown Prosecution Service
CRB	Criminal Records Bureau
Cri-du-chat syndrome	Partial deletion of the short arm chromosome 5 (5p) leading to learning disability
cryptophthalmos syndrome	also known as Fraser syndrome. Usually skin fold covering one or both eyes (cryptophthalmos means hidden eye). Disorder causing learning disability.
CTO	Community Treatment Order
cytomegalovirus	organism which may cause infection during pregnancy leading to learning disability

D

DASH	Diagnostic Assessment for the Severely Handicapped
De Grouchy syndrome	deletion of short arm chromosome 18 (18p) causing learning disability
DC-LD	diagnostic criteria – learning disabilities
diazepam	a benzodiazepine used to manage anxiety and status epilepticus
DisDaT	Disability Distress Assessment Tool
DLA	Disability Living Allowance

DNAR	do not attempt resucitation
DoLS	Deprivation of Liberty Safeguards
donepezil hydrochloride	drug used in the treatment of mild to moderate Alzheimer's disease
Down's syndrome	trisomy of chromosome 21 (21+) causing learning disability
DSA	Down's Syndrome Association
DSM-IV	Diagnostic Statistical Manual, 4th Edition
dysphagia	difficulty in swallowing
dysphasia	difficulty in speaking
dysphonia	difficulty in controlling voice production
dyspnoea	difficulty in breathing
dystonia	impaired muscle tension, including abnormal face and body movements, sometimes a side effect of antipsychotic drugs

E

EAMHMR	European Association of Mental Health in Mental Retardation
echolalia	repetition of words spoken to person
echopraxia	repetition of actions observed by the person
ECT	electroconvulsive therapy
Edward's syndrome	trisomy of chromosome 18 (18+) causing learning disability
epicanthic fold	small fold of skin on the inner angle of the eye, sometimes noted in Down's syndrome
epilepsy, Jacksonian	form of epilepsy where jerking spasms may occur in one part of the body, often spreading to other areas, without loss of consciousness
epiloia	*see* tuberous sclerosis
ethosuximide	antiepileptic drug, particularly for treatment of absence seizures
EWS	Early Warning Scores
extrapyramidal symptoms	these include parkinsonian symptoms, *dystonia, dyskinesia, akathisia* and *tardive dyskinesia*

F

Farber lipogranulomatosis lipid metabolism disorder causing learning disability

foetal acohol syndrome	foetus damage, possibly leading to learning disability, caused by high alcohol intake in pregnancy
fluoxetine	an *SSRI* antidepressant
FPLD	Foundation for People with Learning Disabilities
fragile X syndrome	also known as Gillian Turner-Type X-linked mental deficiency syndrome/Martin-Bell syndrome. Sometimes causing learning disability, but not always. X linked chromosome inheritance.
Fraser syndrome	see *cryptophthalmos syndrome*

G

gabapentin	antiepileptic drug
GAD	generalised anxiety disorder
galactorrhoea	milk production
galantamine	drug used in the treatment of mild to moderate dementia in Alzheimer's disease
GCS	Glasgow Coma Scale used to assess a person's level of consciousness
Gillian Turner-Type X-linked	see *fragile X syndrome*
GORD	gastro-oesophageal reflux disorder
GT	gentle teaching
Guthrie test	detection test for *phenylketonuria* in infants
gynaecomastia	abnormal breast growth in males

H

haloperidol	antipsychotic drug
HAP	Health Action Plan
happy puppet syndrome	see *Angelman syndrome*
Hartnup disease	autosomal recessive inherited disorder, causing problems with amino acid metabolism leading to learning disability in some cases
HF	health facilitator
HPC	Health Professions Council
hydrocephalus	poor distribution of cerebrospinal fluid causing fluid accumulation to the head leading to pressure on the brain.

hyperglycaemia	raised blood sugar
hyperkalaemia	excess potassium
hyperkinesia	overactive restlessness
hyperphagia	overeating
hypertelorism	increased distance between two structures of the body, usually associated with abnormal wideness between the eyes
hypotonia	lack of muscle tone or floppiness
hypotrichosis	hair sparseness

I

ICD-10	International Classification of Disorders, 10th edition
IMCA	Independent Mental Capacity Advocate
INR	International Normalised Rate (such as that used in warfarin)

K

kernicterus	rhesus incompatability sometimes leading to learning disability
ketogenic diet	diet containing excessive amounts of fat causing excretion of acetone and ketones in the urine. May be used in some cases of epilepsy
ketonuria	ketones (substance produced when fats are not properly metabolised) in the urine
Klinefelters syndrome	also known as XXY syndrome, where an extra X chromosome is present in males. Importantly, does not always lead to a learning disability
KSF	Knowledge and Skills Framework
kyphosis	outward spine curvature

L

lamotrigine	antiepileptic drug, sometimes also used in bipolar disorder to prevent depressive episodes
lansoprazole	a proton pump inhibitor drug used in the treatment of benign gastric ulcers, duodenal ulcers, gastro-oesophageal reflux disease, acid related dyspepsia and Zollinger-Ellison syndrome

Laurence-Moon-Beidl syndrome	autosomal recessive inherited disorder leading to learning disability
Lesch-Nyan syndrome	autosomal recessive inherited disorder causing problems with uric acid metabolism, leading to learning disability. Self-injurious behaviour has been linked to this syndrome.
lithium carbonate	an antimanic drug used in the treatment of mania, bipolar disorder, recurrent depression, aggression and self-mutilating behaviour
lofepramine	a tricyclic antidepressant drug
lorazepam	a benzodiazepine used to treat anxiety and status epilepticus
Louis-Bar syndrome	see *ataxia telangiectasia syndrome*
LUNSERS	Liverpool University Neuroleptic Side Effect Rating Scale

M

Makaton	form of sign language used as a communication system by some people with a learning disability who cannot speak
MAOI	monoamine oxidase inhibitor
Martin-Bell syndrome	see *fragile X syndrome*
MCA	Mental Capacity Act 2005
memantine hydrochloride	drug used in the treatment of moderate to severe dementia in Alzheimer's disease
MEWS	Modified Early Warning Score
MHA	Mental Health Act
MHC	Mental Health Commission
MHT	Mental Health Tribunal or Mental Health Team
microcephaly	abnormally small cranium
midazolam	used in the treatment of status epilepticus
mirtazapine	an antidepressant drug
MMSE	Mini-Mental State Examination
motor skills	usually divided into gross motor skills (whole body/ large limb movements) and fine motor skills (such as hands/fingers)

N

neuroleptic malignant syndrome (NMS)	A rare but potentially fatal side-effect of antipsychotic drugs
NICE	National Institute of Health and Clinical Excellence
NMC	Nursing and Midwifery Council
NNLDN	National Learning Disability Nurses Network
NPSA	National Patient Safety Agency
NSAID	non-steroidal anti-inflammatory drug
NSF	National Service Frameworks

O

OCD	obsessive compulsive disorder
OSA	obstructive sleep apnoea
omeprazole	a proton pump inhibitor drug used in the treatment of benign gastric and duodenal ulcers, NSAID-associated ulcers, Zollinger-Ellison syndrome, acid reflux disease, gastro-oesophageal reflux disease
olanzapine	an antipsychotic drug

P

Parkinsonian symptoms	extrapyramidal symptoms including tremor, a side effect of antipsychotic drugs
Patau syndrome	trisomy of chromosome 13 (13+) causing learning disability
PALS	Patient Advice and Liaison Service
paroxetine	an *SSRI* antidepressant
PAS-ADD	Psychiatric Assessment Schedules for Adults with Developmental Disabilities
PECS	Picture Exchange Communication System
PEG	percutaneous endoscopic gastronomy
phenylketonuria	autosomal recessive disorder of amino acid metabolism leading to the accumulation of phenylalanine, causing learning disability
phenytoin	anti-epileptic drug, also used in status epilepticus
PGD	Patient Group Direction
PIMRA	Psychopathology Instrument for Mentally Retarded Adults

PKU	see *phenylketonuria*
PMLD	profound and multiple learning disabilities
PN	parenteral nutrition
POVA	Protection of Vulnerable Adults
Prader-Willi syndrome	possible chromosome 15 deletion abnormality. Key features include excessive demands for food and insatiable appetite
procyclidine hydrochloride	an antimuscarinic drug used to treat drug-induced extrapyramidal symptoms
promazine hydrochloride	an antipsychotic drug
PTSD	post-traumatic stress disorder

Q

quadriplegia	paralysis of all four limbs
quetiapine	an antipsychotic drug

R

RCN	Royal College of Nursing
RCT	randomised controlled trial
RCSLT	Royal College of Speech and Language Therapists
RCP	Royal College of Psychiatrists
rigor	sudden rise in body temperature, usually denoted by episodes of shivering and sweating
risperidone	an antipsychotic drug
rivastigmine	drug used in the treatment of dementia in Alzheimer's disease or Parkinson's disease
RNLD	Registered Nurse Learning Disability
RNMH	Registered Nurse Mental Handicap, now referred to as *RNLD*, also sometimes used to refer to a Registered Nurse Mental Health
RNLD	Registered Nurse Learning Disability

S

Sanfilippo syndrome	an autosomal recessive inherited disorder causing mucopolysaccaridosis III (defective enzyme activity in the breakdown of complex sugars), leading to learning disability
sertraline	an *SSRI* antidepressant

SIB	self-injurious behaviour
SLT	speech and language therapist
SNRI	serotonin-norepinephrine reuptake inhibitor
sodium valproate	anti-epileptic drug, sometimes used in mood disorders
SSRI	selective serotonin reuptake inhibitor
sulpiride	antipsychotic drug
supervised community treatment	arrangement where a patient discharged from detention under the Mental Health Act 1983 is required to comply with conditions set out in a *Community Treatment Order*

T

tardive dyskinesia	rhythmic, involuntary movements of the tongue, face and jaw, sometimes a side effect of antipsychotic drugs
Tay-Sachs disease	autosomal recessive inherited lipid metabolism disorder leading to learning disability
TCA	tricyclic antidepressant
temazepam	a hypnotic drug used for insomnia
tetraplegia	paralysis of all four limbs
topiramate	antiepileptic drug
trazodone hydrochloride	tricyclic-related antidepressant drug
tuberous sclerosis	also known as *epiloia*. Disorder of autosomal dominant inheritance, can lead to learning disability
Turner syndrome	XO syndrome. Chromosome abnormality affecting females. Sometimes leading to learning disability in a few cases

V

venlafaxine	drug used in depression and generalised anxiety disorder
vigabatrin	anti-epileptic drug

W

Wechsler Intelligence Test	test for learning, memory and reasoning
WHO	World Health Organization

| Wilson's disease | also known as progressive hepatolenticular degeneration. Disorder of copper metabolism. Caused by autosomal recessive inheritance and if untreated may cause learning disabilities. |

X

XO syndrome	*see* Turner syndrome
XXX syndrome	Extra X chromosomes in females, XXXXX syndrome is also known as penta-X syndrome. Often leading to learning disability
XXY syndrome	*see* Klinefelter's syndrome

Z

| zopiclone | a hypnotic drug used in insomnia |
| zuclopenthixol | an antipsychotic drug |

Resources

British Institute of Learning Disabilities
www.bild.org.uk

Down's Syndrome Association
www.downs-syndrome.org.uk

Epilepsy Action
http://www.epilepsy.org.uk/

Epilepsy Society
http://www.epilepsysociety.org.uk/

Estia Centre
The Mental Health in Learning Disability Forum, based at the Estia Centre
www.estiacentre.org/mhildnetwork.html

Foundation for People with Learning Disabilities
www.learningdisabilities.org.uk/

Improving Health and Lives: Learning Disability Observatory
www.improvinghealthandlives.org.uk

Mencap
www.mencap.org.uk/

National Autistic Society
www.nas.org.uk/

National Development Team for Inclusion
www.ndti.org.uk

National Learning Disabilities Nurses Network (NNLDN)
www.nnldn.org.uk

Appendix 2

National Network for the Palliative Care of People with Learning Disabilities
www.helpthehospices.org.uk

Profound and Multiple Learning Disability Network
www.pmldnetwork.org

Index